CHOOSING
OUR
KING

CHOOSING OUR KING

POWERFUL SYMBOLS
IN PRESIDENTIAL POLITICS

MICHAEL NOVAK

MACMILLAN PUBLISHING CO., INC.
New York

Library of Congress Cataloging in Publication Data

Novak, Michael.
    Choosing our king.

    1. Presidents—United States—Election—1972.
    2. Presidents—United States. 3. Symbolism.
    4. National characteristics, American. I. Title.
    JK526 1972.N68   353.03'2   73-11835
    ISBN 0-02-590720-4

Macmillan Publishing Co., Inc.
866 Third Avenue, New York, N.Y. 10022
Collier-Macmillan Canada Ltd.

FIRST PRINTING 1974

Printed in the United States of America

For journalists and politicians

OF THE

congressional campaign of 1970

AND THE

presidential campaign of 1972

ACKNOWLEDGMENTS

The author is grateful to several publishers for permission to quote from the following works:

James David Barber, *The Presidential Character: Predicting Performance in the White House*, Prentice-Hall, Inc., Englewood Cliffs, N.J., 1972.

Robert N. Bellah, "Civil Religion in America" which first appeared in *Daedalus*, Journal of the American Academy of Arts and Sciences, Boston, Winter 1967, *Religion in America*.

H. L. Mencken, *A Mencken Chrestomathy*, Alfred A. Knopf, Inc., New York, 1949.

Gunnar Myrdal, *An American Dilemma*, Vol. I, Harper & Row, New York, 1962.

Ray Price, memorandum of November 28, 1967. Subject: "Recommendations for General Strategy from Now through Wisconsin."

Woodrow Wilson, *Constitutional Government in the United States*, Columbia University Press, New York, 1908.

Bob Dylan, "The Times They Are A-Changin'," © 1963 M. Witmark & Sons. All rights reserved. Used by permission of Warner Bros. Music.

John Lennon, "Imagine," © 1971 Northern Songs Ltd. All rights for the United States of America, Canada, Mexico and The Philippines controlled by Maclen Music, Inc. c/o ATV Music Group. All rights reserved. Used by permission. International copyright secured.

Peter Yarrow, "Weave Me the Sunshine," © 1972 Mary Beth Music, 75 East 55th Street, New York, N.Y. 10022. All rights reserved. Used by permission.

CONTENTS

Preface: THE GOD-KING

PART ONE

PRIEST, PROPHET, KING

PART FIVE

A NEW AND DARK FAITH

PREFACE

The God-King

"The American people have created almost a God-King in the office of the presidency."
—Senator Edward R. Brooke (R.-Mass.)

This book was conceived in the fall of 1970, long before activities symbolized by Watergate had come to light like insect canals beneath a rock. I was working as a writer for Sargent Shriver, supporting Democratic candidates for the Congress in some 37 states.

The audiences I then observed—and had to write for—lived "worlds apart" from one another: law students in a hall at Yale, and Polish working men in a living room in Baltimore; ranch hands in Wyoming and Spanish-surname crowds in Albuquerque; a union breakfast in Pittsburgh, and cocktail parties at elegant clubs in Kansas City, Palm Beach, and Santa Barbara; a room full of rebellious Vista volunteers in Washington, and a politically besieged black crowd in Oakland. Nothing in my education had quite prepared me for how different Americans are from one another.

A sentence from George Reedy's lucid book, *The Twilight of the Presidency,* stuck in my memory: "The most important, and least examined, problem of the presidency is that of maintaining contact with reality." I felt exhilarated that fall, alive with the staggering variety of the nation's life. President Nixon's "law and order" campaign seemed to me out of touch with many people's real feelings; it was too simplistic and too mean-spirited, and it failed. Reedy wrote about the world "inside" the White House. I wanted to write about "outside" reality, the presidency as it actually operates among and is perceived in the different worlds in which Americans live.

I began with two convictions: that the presidency is the nation's most central religious symbol, and that American civilization is best understood as a set of secular religious systems. The drama of the last six months has lent my thesis public demonstration I did not expect.

"The hopeful view of Watergate," writes Anthony Lewis of *The New York Times,* "is that it represents only a personal aberration in a still sound political structure. The fault, then, would lie with Richard Nixon, not in the presidential institution." His own view is different: "The danger goes back long before the present crisis of confidence. It lies in confiding too many of our hopes and fears in the President. . . . We shall not cure the deeper disease of Watergate until we get over the cult of personality and return to the American system of law and constitutional order."

But our problem is not the cult of personality. It will not be solved by a return to law and constitutional order. (Moralists of the Left only yesterday denounced the inadequacies of the American system; now they outdo one another in conservative constitutional sentiment. For a decade they demanded a strong presidency; now some desire a weak one. Should one think the Left unprincipled—or teachable?) Closer to the heart of our problem is the cult of moralism: on the Right, the cult of America;

on the Left, the cult of "change." Americans treat America as a religion. Hatred for political opponents waxes theological. Like separate islands, the political religions of the land are connected through a single office. The president is the one pontiff bridging all. Such an office imposes on him more than mere pragmatic functions. The Constitution pays the symbolic functions of the president too little heed. Against his symbolic power, it provides too little countervailing balance.

Many Americans wish the presidency were businesslike: flat and literal and unmysterious. Such is the preference of a practical people. But the presidency conveys immense symbolic powers over "rational" people which they may be loathe to admit. These powers cannot be eliminated. They can, at best, be redistributed. To talk about the presidency with realism, we must explore symbolic worlds we ordinarily skirt. We come, necessarily, to the edges of theological reflection.

1. What symbolic values of the American people allow us to speak of "saving the presidency," of "confidence" and "faith" in the presidential office, of the "sacredness" of that office, and of "trust" in it? These words seem appropriate to religion, not to a secular state.

2. How deeply does the personality of a president shape our personal response to national life and our own inner life?

3. How does one distinguish morality in the president from moralism? To what extent must our king have "dirty hands"? How does one distinguish genuine symbols from "image-making"?

4. Should the nation prepare itself for a fundamental revision of the Constitution of the United States in order to protect itself from the presidency? It may be idle to approach our problems as though they are administrative problems, subject to the adjustment of a few procedural techniques. Basic symbols—an approach to life—may have to be altered.

This book explores the symbolic geography of national politics. Its focal point is the presidency. Its illustrative materials come mainly from the presidential campaign of 1972. From a practical point of view, it may be useful for political leaders who seek symbols powerful among the people.

From a theoretical point of view, this book may encourage greater attention to symbol-making in politics. It may help to balance the merely pragmatic tendency of American thought. It may also suggest a fresh and potent point of view for the discussion of ethical questions. Specifically, it may help to clarify the nature of "civil religion." A few words may illustrate how inextricably these themes are intertwined.

Many practical persons felt betrayed by Watergate. They were dismayed by not being able to trust the president, to have confidence in his words, to rely on his self-restraint. That we must learn to become cynical about the presidency and ring it round with restrictions has raised the specter of heavy costs. Only when the symbols of trust, decency, and restraint have broken down do we realize how practical and inexpensive they had been.

"Symbolic realities" are structures of human consciousness effective in human perception and action. These structures may be institutionalized in offices, performances, or rituals. They shape the psyches of persons. A courtroom, for example, institutionalizes acts of testimony, assessment of evidence, and approximate justice. If witnesses lie, the institution can be frustrated. If persons adhere to key symbols, "improper" conduct is ruled out. If they do not, other constraints must be supplied. When you can rely on people not to steal library books, you do not have to pay the salary of a guard. When you can rely on presidents to tell the truth to the public, you do not have to spend weeks, months, and years tracking down evidence to unmask their lies.

Those symbolic realities that constitute moral ty increase the frequency of acts of honesty, courage, freedom, justice, and community. Such realities have only a fragile hold upon our psyches. Thus, practical men frequently discount them. Often we are obliged to live as though we cannot depend upon the honesty, loyalty, understanding, and cooperation of others. "We must learn not to trust people," we tell ourselves. "If you want a job done, do it yourself." We tailor our expectations to the level of human practice. For this reason, thinking that follows moral symbols and thinking that follows practical experience are often at odds. Men *should* act like brothers, *should* trust one another and co-operate, *should* try to be reasonable. But in fact, frequencies of self-serving conduct are rather high. "Morality" is based on humans as they are in fact; "moralism" is based on humans as they would be "if only. . . ." In the United States, moralism has a long history. Americans of all persuasions preach incessantly. Moral exhortation is a national style. Even our hedonists itch to convert our puritans. (*Playboy* is presented as "liberation.") Moralism promises excessive benefits for private pieties. Yet alongside this tradition, and even in the depths of it, a strong moral tradition calls humans, despite their faults, to simple, plain speech and straightforward honesty. On this latter and rather high standard for human behavior part of the American way of life—as distinct, say, from that of Mexico, or France, or Italy, or Indonesia, or other lands—is built. Perhaps naïvely so.

We expect a degree of honesty from our leaders that people in some other lands seemingly do not. They tolerate a wider range of authoritative cover-up, administrative evasion, and even "official truth" than we do—not that we *have* less cover-up, simply that we keep watch on our leaders in this respect. Foreign commentators on Watergate frequently remarked upon this difference in national character. Americans overseas had to explain that the public reaction to Watergate was not simply a manifestation of a rather narrow puritanism.

Our national life *is* built upon a kind of moralism—a dubious blessing; but a blessing nonetheless. For within the excesses and ambiguities of moralism lie moral possibilities. Learning how to disengage morality from moralism—how to avoid the corruptions of the latter and how to deepen the realism of the former —is one of the tasks of our maturity.

Americans have high symbolic expectations of the presidency. Violation of these expectations brings retribution. After barely a week of revelations in early 1973, Richard Nixon fell from the height of presidential power to the threat of impeachment. His physical and material power did not change; but symbolically he was discredited.

We are, we like to think, "the last, best hope of mankind." We are, we once thought, entrusted with this planet's fairest dream: a new world, a new Eden. The twentieth would be the "American century," during which an almost chosen people would lead mankind to unprecedented moral heights. Our self-understanding has been more than only factual. We have entertained extraordinary hopes.

Surely we may hold that the United States is at the threshold of a new maturity, that the nation can, if it wishes, admit into consciousness a sense of its own capacity for evil, an awareness of the tragic quality of life, a respect for limits. These are, I believe, the sole hope for a truly radical and liberal assault on such social progress as is open to us on this planet.

At various times, five persons helped me to gather a vast set of files on the election of 1972 and accumulated texts on the presidency: Virginia Perrell, Eileen Zanar, Kathleen Kennedy, Mildred Gorman, and Jacqueline Slater. Judy Lally and Dori Walther typed most of the manuscript—again and again. Martin Marty, David Tracy, Peter H. Wood, Robert McAfee Brown, Peter Bellerman, and Richard Fox read parts of this manuscript in earlier drafts and saved me from many errors.

One important symbol of modern politics is "commitment"—commitment to exhausting work. Such commitment has real effects upon one's family. Because of the campaign of 1972, during which I worked the month of November (1971) for Edmund Muskie, throughout the primaries as a journalist, and from August onward on the staff of George McGovern and Sargent Shriver, our newborn daughter, Jana Marya, came into the home of an absentee father. Compared to her, politics and its symbols seem unreal. Yet the shadowy world of politics is our reality, too, and so taking politics seriously is, in some poor way, also an act of love for her.

Bayville, New York
August 5, 1973

Part One

PRIEST, PROPHET, KING

We, too, the enlightened Americans, feel the need of myth and mystery in national life—of magic parchments like the Declaration of Independence, of shrines like Plymouth and the Alamo, of slogans . . . of hymns . . . of heroics . . . of heroes. . . . And who fashioned the myth? Who are the most satisfying of our folk heroes? With whom is associated a wonderful web of slogans and shrines and heroics? The answer, plainly, is the six Presidents I have pointed to most proudly. Each is an authentic folk hero, each a symbol of some virtue or dream especially dear to Americans. Together they make up almost half of the company of American giants, for who except Christopher Columbus, Benjamin Franklin, Daniel Boone, Robert E. Lee, and Thomas A. Edison in real life, Deerslayer and Ragged Dick in fiction, and Paul Bunyan and the Lonesome Cowboy in myth can challenge them for immortality?   —Clinton Rossiter

The American Presidency

1

Symbolic Realism

Every four years, Americans elect a king—but not only a king, also a high priest and a prophet. It does not matter that we are a practical and sophisticated people, no longer (we think) influenced by symbols, myths, or rituals. To what our president represents, we react with passion.

The president of the United States is no mere manager of an insurance firm. The way he lives affects our image of ourselves. His style and his tastes weigh upon our spirits. Eisenhower encouraged a "silent" generation, Kennedy an "activist" decade. Nixon at first made some feel solid and appreciative and others, even in the beginning, heavy and ashamed. Intimate and personal feelings are affected by our experience of various presidents.

The symbolic power of the president is real. Ten million police officers, heads of boards of education, lawyers, judges, realtors, union leaders, and local officials calibrate their daily decisions according to the support or the resistance they expect from the White House. What will the Justice Department do, or fail to do? The president is able to make his own views felt in every town and village of the nation, by compulsion and enforcement, by imitation and antipathy. On the local level, if ultimately one expects support far up the line, great risks can be taken. If one is left to one's own resources merely, one must confront the local balance of powers.

Some speak of the "moral leadership" of the presidency as though what we need is a moral man out in front, like a cavalry officer lowering his saber. Yet moral leadership in the presidency is not something habitually "out in front" of us, but something that infiltrates our imaginations and our hearts. The president, whoever he is, affects our *internal* images of authority, legitimacy, leadership, concern. By his actions, he establishes a limit to national realism. What he *is* drives us away from America and makes us feel like exiles—or attracts our cooperation. Cumulatively, the presidents under whom we happen to live influence our innermost attitudes.

For this reason, the election of a president is an almost religious task; it intimately affects the life of the spirit, our identity. Who the man is determines in real measure who we are. Thus, the swirling, otherwise inexplicable passions of many presidential elections. Not only power or money are at stake, important as these are, but our own inner life. The presence of one man rather than another, the ascendance of Nixon (say) rather than the ascendance of McGovern, has great power to depress or to elate, to liberate energies or to shrink them.

Eugene McCarthy said we must "depersonalize" the presidency, "demystify" the office. Without separating kingship from administration, that can scarcely be accomplished. Today the symbolic role inheres in the office. It is enhanced by the nation's bigness, diversity, and tightening networks of power.

Dostoevsky once wrote that an invisible filament of humble charity covers the entire earth. An act at any one point on the earth, he imagined, reverberates until it touches every other person. In our day, on television, a single act simultaneously inhabits the fantasy of millions of humans everywhere, *becomes* them, obliges them to accept or to reject, enters immediately into the structures of their psyche. We do not know what the truth is, but if on television the president says our ships were attacked in the Gulf of Tonkin, then that attack (even if it did not occur) occupies our attention and demands that we refute it or accept it or dismiss it. Whatever we do, there stands the president's assertion, solid until painstakingly disproved. This power over our attention, over our power to structure issues, is so enormous that it dwarfs all others.

The president of the United States is one of the great symbolic powers known to human history. His actions seep irrepressibly into our hearts. He dwells in us. We cannot keep him out. That is why we wrestle against him, rise up in hatred often, wish to retch—or, alternatively, feel good, feel proud, as though his achievements were ours, his wit the unleashing of powers of our own.

Hands are stretched toward him over wire fences at airports like hands extended toward medieval sovereigns or ancient prophets. One wonders what mystic participation our presidents convey, what witness from what other world, what form of cure or heightened life. The president arouses waves of "power," "being," "superior reality," as if where he is is history. It is true that the president's hand is on the button of destruction. Life and death are in his hands; honor and dishonor too. What he does affects the daily life of each of us in ways witch doctors could scarcely even dream. His office is, in quite modern and sophisticated form, a religion in a secular state. It evokes responses familiar in all the ancient religions of the world. It fills a perennial vacuum at the heart of human expectations.

Lest these perceptions seem unsettling, we might well consult familiar guides.

2

What Are Symbols?

What James David Barber says of the presidency in *The Presidential Character* is to the point:

> The Presidency is much more than an institution. It is a focus of feelings. . . . The Presidency is the focus for the most intense and persistent emotions in the American polity. The President is a symbolic leader, the one figure who draws together the people's hopes and fears for the political future. On top of all his routine duties, he has to carry that off—or fail.

The president himself—the man, his character, his personality —becomes the best-known figure in the Republic. Compared with him, other politicians are secondary figures. He is the main symbol of government. He gives an intelligible, symbolic stamp to an entire era: The Age of Jackson, The Roosevelt Years. By reference to him, citizens interpret political developments. These expectations are excessive, of course. They bring to bear on the president, Barber writes, "intense moral, sentimental, and quasi-religious pressures which can, if he lets them, distort his own thinking and feeling." Still, these expectations are facts about our system and ourselves. They are altogether real.

Barber interprets the personality of individual presidents by the way they balance three psychological qualities in their lives: world view, style, and character. By *world view* he means the president's way of *seeing,* the conceptions of reality he has developed over a lifetime—how things work in politics, what people are like, what are the main purposes and the central moral conflicts of the time. The president's world view includes what he pays attention to; a great deal of the president's job consists of paying attention and, in turn, directing the attention of the public.

By *style* Barber means how the president goes about doing what the office requires him to do. The president speaks to audiences, large and small; he deals with politicians and other influential persons or groups; he scans, reads, studies, and organizes an endless flow of detail. The distribution of energy and the personal signature he gives each of these three unavoidable types of activity are his style.

By *character* Barber means the way the President orients himself toward life—not for the moment, but enduringly. "Character is the person's stance as he confronts experience." Wisely, Barber draws attention to two central aspects of character: a person's fundamental self-esteem and the criteria by which he judges himself. Some men feel inadequate to the job; some measure themselves by the affection in which they are held; some, by their achievements.

Professor Barber uses these conceptions to study the personality structure of presidents. Our route is different. We will use them to study the constituencies that try to identify with the presidents.

An action by a president is always and in every case symbolic, but what it symbolizes to each group depends upon the system of interpretation in that group. (A visit to the United Nations is greeted enthusiastically by parts of the population, with hostility or contempt by other parts, with relative indifference by others.) A president's actions are always symbolic because he is not only an executive officer but a carrier of meaning. From the beginning to the end of his term in office, his every action is a means by which citizens interpret life in the United States. It would be much easier for the president if he were a prime minister, called simply to manage the affairs of government in as practical and unadorned a way as possible. Yet, in American politics what critics refer to as "the cult of personality" arises. It arises not because it is willed either by the citizenry or by the presidents themselves, but because of the nature and the limits of the human imagination.

Causes, institutions, and administrative processes must be personified before humans can passionately engage them. Humans are flesh and blood, and they understand best what is flesh and blood. Thus, Martin Luther King made black civil rights a cause that it has ceased to be since his death. Thus, Eugene Mc-Carthy in 1968 observed that antiwar sentiment in the United States needed to be personified in order to be a political force, and he agreed to step forward as the person. McCarthy's deed was a great one and it catalyzed a great new force in American politics, the new politics of the "new class." Yet, great as that force is in American life, it is no stronger than its ability to personify itself in a leader able to command the dedication of a wide range of people. Leaderless, it is ineffective.

Thus, the general law of politics: political movements depend for their general acceptance on the greatness of their leaders. Not an absolute law, it nearly always holds. In a similar way and for similar reasons, the American people place huge symbolic demands on the character of their presidents.

What are the symbols through which the president or a candidate for the presidency communicates to the people? Words, looks, actions, visits to special places, interventions, the acceptance of awards from others, the patterns of a previous career —these and other signals provide a president or a candidate ways of expressing what he stands for, with whom he identifies, what is important to him. But what makes each of these signals *symbolic?* A cluster of memories and associations inheres in them, although inhering differently for different audiences. Words like "patriotism" or "Americanism," a visit to the bedside of a fasting Cesar Chavez, a speech to honor George Wallace in Birmingham, a telephone call to Martin Luther King's wife, a tour with the mayor of Chicago, a capacity to identify the moral struggle of the times in terms drawing on earlier American understandings of the nation's destiny—these sometimes hackneyed, sometimes passion-arousing signals establish a president's relation to the complicated layers of the American experience. They give a candidate, or a president, symbolic definition.

What exactly are symbols? Symbols are more than mere signs. Signs attempt to be ostensive, economical, unambiguous. Highway engineers have discovered how hard it is to create unambiguous signs at freeway entrances and exits, instantaneously warning motorists away from possible errors. Still, the art of the sign-maker is the art of excising ambiguity: "No parking." Signs at the border of Canada and the United States indicate simply, "Welcome to the United States" and "Welcome to Canada." But the American and Canadian flags near these signs are not merely geographical markers. The flags are symbols. Each suggests the deeds and events of a particular history, each represents loyalties and aspirations, each signals distinctive attitudes and ways of life. Signs aim at clarity and directness; symbols aim at suggestion and comprehensiveness. Signs aim at rather abstract conceptions (stop, slow, danger, this way, navigable channel); symbols aim at the complex texture of experience. Signs are directed at our information-seeking, abstractive intelligence; symbols are aimed at our passional intelligence, concerned with how we should shape our lives. Signs exist in a nonhistorical dimension, the dimension of the timeless present; symbols relate the future to a past, offering to individuals and groups an identity through time.

In a sense, the actions of every person are always symbolic as well as practical. Each act of ours is part of our personal story, a revelation of our personality. A president's acts are symbolic in a larger sense. His actions convey not only his own personality; they convey a personality that has become a source of meaning for the people. It might be thought that only naïve, simple people relate to the president as a source of meaning.

But, in fact, journals like *The New York Review of Books,
The New Republic, The New York Times* (Sunday) *Magazine,*
and others reveal a profound fixation on the character, associations, style, and views of the presidents. The character of the
president in office sets the terms in which intellectual debate about
the state of the nation is established. It is not necessary to accept the symbols generated by a president's words and actions;
to tear them to shreds bit by bit is sufficient evidence of engagement.

Thus, talk about "doing away with the cult of personality"
or "demythologizing the presidency" must be taken as gestures
toward an unrealistic rationalism. The president dominates not
only the news, but also the language of policy, the shape and
pace of legislation, and the spirit of appointments to the federal
courts. His idiosyncrasies, ambitions, and failures dominate more
conversations than those of any other citizen—as truly if he is
unpopular as if he is popular. Let us be as skeptical as may be,
we are living in a symbolic world over which the president has
unparalleled power. To cease believing in his power will not
make it go away. To say we must not vest our hopes or fears
in him runs counter to the plain fact that he has nuclear power
at his fingertips, more police power than any sovereign in history, more power to dominate the organs of public opinion than
any other human, more power in defining who are the nation's
enemies, more power over the military and the making (if not
the declaring) of war than any citizen or group of citizens.

Thus, the president is rather more like a shaman than we
might wish. Our lives *do* depend on him. A person with power
over life and death is raised above a merely pragmatic level.
He is surrounded, as it were, with a nimbus of magic. He
necessarily lives on a level that must seem to him "above" that
of other humans. The fact that he *is* human gives a sort of
reassurance about which we endlessly read—that he eats breakfast food, prefers mysteries, listens to Bach or Lawrence Welk.
But our survival is linked to his deeds. Our lives participate in
his. His nerves, his wisdom, his panic, his steadiness make us
vulnerable. Even if we have contempt for him, he has power
over the shape and direction of our lives. If he decides that the

great moral conflict of our time is permissiveness or the need for individual selfishness, not only must those who disagree fight against the ordinary tides of evil, they must also fight against the respectability the president gives their opponents. If he symbolizes an America we despise, he divides our own hearts against themselves.

The president also affects the cultural tone of the entire nation. It makes a difference if he prefers Bach to Welk or John Wayne to Dustin Hoffman or enjoys the company of Pablo Casals rather than Bob Hope and Billy Graham. Such choices on his part send out a signal either that discrimination is worth an effort, or else that it is well to glory in what happens to be popular.

Thus, the president enters into the innermost symbols by which we identify ourselves. We do not think about him all the time; on many days we give him not a thought. It is the property of basic symbolic forms to influence us even when we are not conscious of them. When the president acts as president, he acts in our name. He is us. If he goes by a way we do not approve, he uses us against ourselves. This alone is a remarkable power.

3

Who Are We?

Most peoples of the world, past and present, do not share Western experience. We tend to mean by "religion" drab institutions and rigid forms; we identify religion with theism and rather narrow definitions of "God." A more accurate, transcultural meaning would point to the secret springs of the imagination, the secret loves and longings of the heart, the hidden capacity for making X real and letting Y be ignored as if Y had no existence or significance whatever. It is these things that constitute a religion: what a people takes to be real, gives significance to, permits to dominate its imagination. In the broadest, most useful sense, a religion is a sense of reality, a way of structuring consciousness. (There are, for example, atheistic religions.) Her instinct for these matters makes Frances FitzGerald's study of the Vietnamese and the Americans in Vietnam, *Fire in the Lake,* so powerful. American and Vietnamese, she shows, live in almost wholly different symbolic worlds. The nation of Vietnam nourishes one set of self-understandings; America, another. The difference is not the difference between Buddhism and Christianity, but between the Vietnamese experience and the American experience.

We must train our eyes to see the signals in behavior that reveal the discrete senses of reality within which people live. Within America, as well as in the world at large, there are separate symbolic worlds. Why is it that in our midst "amnesty" stirs one audience, while "Watergate" for so long left it cold? Why did Muskie's tears in New Hampshire repel one group while attracting another? Why did some go after the President because of Watergate—*Newsweek* on a blood-red cover showed the White House doors—with all the zeal of an offended "Protestant" nation that still believes authority should be pure, while others felt the king should be protected by the press no matter what the scandal, and while still others felt that "politics is politics!" and that "*of course,* they spy and cheat!"

Symbols operate within limited worlds. Physically, a political leader can shake hands with every person in an audience. Yet any one issue will arouse quite different responses in different sections of the hall. Encased in their sense of reality, people in the same room live in different symbolic worlds. Across the many great regions of the United States, there are many universes of feeling and understanding. It is something of an education to try to move audiences—not merely to address them but to move them—in every section of our country, in their diversity of region, worship, class, occupation, education, and cultural background.

For example, we speak of "the Protestant work ethic." But there are several quite different Protestant traditions in America, and six or seven major symbolic attitudes toward work.

We speak of "white racism." But in different ethnic cultures, experiences with persons of other races vary quite widely, and traditions of racial antagonism arise around significantly different symbols. No known peoples on the earth are indifferent to race. But Puerto Ricans in the Bronx, for example, have conflicts with blacks different from those of silk-stocking Anglo-Saxons in Manhattan or Chicanos in Texas. German-Americans near Janesville, Wisconsin, have a different attitude toward blacks than do Italian-Americans in Milwaukee or Anglo-Saxon Americans in Wauwautosa. In one group, a historical store of available symbols provides resources—and biases—that are lacking in another. There is more than one kind of racism, and there are more kinds of conflict between cultural groups than conflict based upon color: conflicts over scarce housing, jobs, scholarships, etc.

Yet, although there are many different self-understandings flourishing among us, there is in a sense an overarching *American* canopy. Every group, in its own way, wishes to emphasize that it is as American as any other. Attachment to the American idea—or rather, to *some* idea or other of America—is fierce in its intensity.

The fundamental creed can be accented either way. *E pluribus unum* may mean *While many, one* or *While one, many*.

For a person who would become the symbolic representative of all the people, accepted as the leader by all, the political challenge is to find the openings through which to penetrate *every* symbolic world, while respecting the unique contours of each. A difficult task, for the symbolic worlds of others do not parallel one's own, are baffling, tangential, remote, angular. No maps exist. Explorers who have succeeded carry the secrets unarticulated with them.

Rather than take up the tasks (and the terror) of facing our diversity, we have preferred to try to homogenize the outer casings of every psyche, to create a wholly typical and uniform Middle America, the better to "communicate." In the unexplored regions, great shifts of emotion sometimes occur: rage suddenly gathers, and we are surprised. What they appear to be on the surface—dressed alike, bland, nice neighbors, inoffensive—Americans in the depths of their psyches are not. But what are they?

It is one of the tasks of an electoral campaign to find out.

Who are we, we Americans, under these stars, with the wind of the evening on our faces? Diverse, yes. But in how many effective political shapes?

4

Unseen Power

The communal convulsion of choosing a president is a privileged route to the many worlds of the American people. Elections "legitimize" the exercise of concentrated power. Each citizen is called on to examine his own symbolic world and to place its weight behind the symbolic world of one of the candidates. (Or to abstain.) No other pilgrimage sheds so much light on the crosscurrents, stirrings, and clashing symbols in the many American publics.

The election of 1972 was exceptionally revealing in this respect, because only at critical turns in our history have basic symbols been so in conflict. The fulcrum of the election, indeed, did not seem to be located in economic conflicts or in contrasting schemes of social organization. It was centered in symbolic perception. The election was decided, in the words of Joseph Duffey, former chairman of Americans for Democratic Action, by issues of "cultural politics." It was a declaration of national self-knowledge. Mr. Nixon even in his inaccessibility seemed to

understand better than any Democrat the actual contours of the
"civil religions" of America. Senator McGovern in several key
instances stepped outside the bounds of basic structural symbols
and was repudiated, often passionately.

An analysis of the civil religions actually operative in America
was introduced to wide discussion (among scholars at least) by
Robert N. Bellah, a sociologist who had earlier studied Asian
societies. His is a potent conception, highly illuminating in the
day-to-day activities of presidential politics. It is not the whole
truth about presidential politics, but it is a much larger part of
the truth than our customary pragmatic prejudices let us see.
Three prejudices, in particular, block our intelligence.

First, the current language of politics confers on such words
as "image," "symbol," and "charisma" misleading connotations
from the world of advertising. When a presidential candidate
strides at dusk through a huge shopping mall, shaking hands, he
is surrounded by the nimbus of television lights. Ordinary people surprised in their occupations catch a sense of excitement,
and look—with a certain skepticism or a certain awe—at this
presence from another world, a world perhaps more "real" to
them than that of their own flesh, the world of the television set
and the movie screen. "He's taller than in his pictures." "Isn't he
good looking!" "How does he keep his tan?" They compare
what their eyes briefly see to the world their imaginations daily
dwell in. When we speak of image, therefore, we are bound to
think of "the selling of the president" and the deliberately nur-
tured illusions of videotape.

But such words also point to psychic levels more fundamental
than this, to one level in particular which the image-makers
must take for granted, an indispensable substratum without
which their work would have neither coherence nor emotional
power. Central, unforgettable experiences of American history
have given rise to basic metaphors in our national consciousness:
virgin newness; the birth of a nation; lawlessness; the restless
pull of frontiers; oppression in field and factory; the Civil War;
foreignness; action and violence and will; empire; hard work;
con men and hucksters; the deeply nourished desire of many to
be "good." Unless foreign observers know of these experiences,

they can scarcely understand some of our discourse or the images of our advertising or our activities.

This substratum of vivid, turbulent experience smolders as active energy in the memories of Americans. It bursts into flame whenever political leaders of genius breathe on it. Transcendent claims of liberty, equality, justice glow underneath the ash.

Second, when they hear the word "religion," many educated persons can't help thinking of illiberal experiences they have had with clergymen, with creeds and catechisms, with symbols that needed to be woodenly "explained" (symbols, in other words, that no longer symbolize). The word "religion" is understood too narrowly by many Americans, not least by many concerned with politics. So where Bellah uses "civil religion," I often substitute the phrase "national self-understanding." Like him, I mean by this not merely private beliefs but *public* rituals and *institutionalized* ways of speaking and proceeding. In chapter sixteen, a precise definition of the concept "civil religion" will be offered; at present, a rough equivalency will serve. Each reader has his (her) own vision of America which, from time to time, he finds publicly celebrated. These public institutionalizations of a vision of the nation constitute a civil, secular religion.

There is more than one such self-understanding among us. There is more than one set of favorite rituals, texts, and activities. There is more than one morality, more than one kind of political conscience. Being a liberal rather than a conservative is not like belonging to a church. But it is like living within a different sense of reality, living out a different story with one's life, responding to a different set of symbols. Being a liberal or a conservative—or a radical—is not merely a matter of having different facts at hand or of holding different moral principles. One's whole imagination, person, life-project are involved. It is more like cherishing a different understanding of the nation and of self. In this sense, being a conservative rather than a liberal is *like* belonging to a different religion. But religion in America is somehow confused with belonging to an organization; and thus "religion" is too weak a word for our political commitments. For many, politics is *deeper* than religion.

Third, it is difficult, as we have seen, to keep from saying *"merely* symbolic." Yet the candidate with the most money and the largest (even most intensely committed) organization does not always win. The realism and structural power of symbolic forms is not to be underestimated.

Symbolic forms have had power even over persons who thought they were supreme pragmatists: over John F. Kennedy, Lyndon Johnson, Everett Dirksen, and Richard Nixon, to name a few. But how can we call these symbolic structures—so obvious in the conduct of others, so hidden and implicit in our own—into clear consciousness? How can we speak of these structures with precision, accuracy, and fresh illumination and yet not falsify the power their very tacitness and elusiveness confer upon them? I do not want to trivialize them by trying to put them into words.

Resources in the national self-understanding now lie fallow and untended. It is as though the nation is bottled up, imprisoned in too constricted a form of its own self-understanding. Its experiences seethe, the skins of old symbol systems are not sufficient to contain them. The inner pressure is intense. We struggle to find even a small escape hatch, to imagine a more ample and more accurate symbolic channel for our communal life. Consciously or not, we labor toward a creative social theology— not merely an economic game plan or a social scheme, but a set of symbols that will liberate the energies of the heart.

A starting place for such an inquiry lies in the odd duality of the office of the American president, in a glimpse of the necessary elements of symbolic power, and even in the strangly revealing, somehow poignant and tragic career of Richard Nixon.

5

Egalitarian and King

"The truth is," the historian Henry Jones Ford wrote in 1898, "American democracy has revived the oldest political institution of the race, the elective kingship. It is all there: the precognition of the notables and the tumultuous choice of the freemen. . . . That the people have been able to . . . make good a principle which no other people have been able to reconcile with the safety of the state, indicates the highest degree of constitutional morality yet attained by any race." Whether the achievement of an elective kingship makes our nation superior is another matter; but that what we elect is a king must be grasped with sufficient seriousness.

It is one thing to have a prime minister, a general manager, a spokesman, a statesman. It is another to have a king, through whose liturgical *persona* shine the agency and values of all the people. The two roles clash. Because we in America try to be so pragmatic in our interpretations of our own conduct, because we do not like to be caught being mystical, sentimental, or in-

volved in ritual, we are inclined to overlook the kingly role. We
thereby deceive ourselves. We surrender more power than we
realize.

Attorney General Stanbery told the Supreme Court in 1867:

> Undoubtedly so far as the mere individual man is concerned
> there is a great difference between the President and a King;
> but so far as the office is concerned—so far as the great ex-
> ecutive office of this government is concerned—I deny that
> there is a particle less dignity belonging to the office of Presi-
> dent than to the office of King of Great Britain or of any
> other potentate on the face of the earth. He represents the
> majesty of the law and of the people as fully and as essen-
> tially, and with the same dignity, as does any absolute mon-
> arch or the head of any independent government in the
> world.

The inauguration of a president now resembles the coronation
of a king. Perhaps it is no surprise that the first Catholic president heightened the nation's sense of liturgy. His inauguration,
alone among the others, is vivid in the common mind: a slow
smoky fire as the Cardinal from Boston grated onward, the
troubled eyes of the Yankee poet laureate, the Eastern politicians' top hats—it was Irish New England on the stage. So also
his stately, caissoned funeral. The Catholic sensibility, being
ancient, is attuned to royalty, and royalty is the oldest political
institution of the human race.

Royalty—the human heart ceaselessly reinvents it. It brings
unity and simplicity to the image of government, power at a
single source. Television has only heightened the ancient hunger. Its cameras need a single actor, seek the symbolic event as
the desert hart seeks water. "The American president," Clinton
Rossiter writes, "is the one-man distillation of the American
people." If you want a picture of America in action, if you like
to focus on "the Great Decisions," only one actor listed under
our *dramatis personae* requires full and constant camera.

At the inauguration of Washington in 1789, all the American
adults had been subjects of George III. Even after Bunker Hill,
the prayers of the army chaplains fervently asked blessings "on

the king." Almost a year after Lexington, in January, 1776, General Washington presided over an officers' mess in which the king's health was celebrated nightly. Even in the midst of hostilities, Washington sent his troops, not against the king's troops, but rather more delicately against "the ministerial troops." Over a third of the colonists remained loyal to the Crown, resisting the Revolution. For almost all, the sense of being one of the king's subjects did not end suddenly, on a given day, at a given hour. The habit of royalty was strong.

As the constitutional convention met, one great difference between Britain and America stood out: here there was almost no sense of nation for a ruler to symbolize. America was a weak confederation of autonomous and mutually jealous states, led by wealthy men more or less dominant in their respective territories. There was little question of a strong executive. Obloquy was hurled, instead, against "King Congress."

John Adams wanted symbols of dignity and power to surround the office of the president: "Take away thrones and crowns from among men," he wrote in 1790, "and there will be an end of all dominion and justice." He hated the plain, managerial title "president." He was contemptuous: "What will the common people of foreign countries, what will the sailors and soldiers say, 'George Washington, President of the United States'? *They will despise him to all eternity.*"

Those of "high-church" tradition have tended to value the explicitness of royal symbolism; those of chaste rational or Puritan tendency have preferred the plain, unostentatious symbolism of capitalism: from Salem sobriety in dress to the gray flannel suit of the anonymous manager. Jefferson, for example, disdained the pomp of Washington's inauguration. For his own inauguration in 1801, he "unostentatiously walked from his boarding house"—as Professor Wilfred Binkley describes—"over to the Capitol to deliver his inaugural address to the two houses assembled in the Senate Chamber." It was not the spirit of poverty that motivated him nor even egalitarianism, but rather a rationalist's distrust of imagination, an Enlightened Man's confidence in the simplicity of reason left to itself. The political effect of Jefferson's rational ways was a decline in the power and meaning of the office of the presidency. The power of Congress dwarfed the presidency until Andrew Jackson marched on Washington.

Jackson viewed himself as singularly representative of the people. Government until then had been in the hands of landed and wealthy men, not only in the federal Congress but also in the state legislatures. Jackson was the first president elected by the newly enfranchised ancestors (it is sobering to recall) of the millions of lower-class voters of the South and West who 143 years later, in 1972, cheered George Wallace—rough, vulgar, unlettered, resentful, exuberant. John Quincy Adams of Boston called his victorious opponent a "barbarian who could hardly spell his own name."

The people, however, found in Jackson reason to begin to love the presidency as an image of themselves. Ironically, but predictably, the more egalitarian the base of participation, the more deeply felt was the tug of royalty. Binkley describes Jackson's tour of Adams' New England:

> The acclaim with which President Andrew Jackson was greeted by the populace heralded a revival of the symbolism of the presidency. His journey to New England in 1833 illustrates the point. Entering Philadelphia on a white charger, provided for the occasion, the aging warrior accepted the obeisances of the crowds for five hours as they filled streets, windows, and roofs, and the reception continued for four days and nights. From New York City Jackson wrote, "I have bowed to upward of two hundred thousand people today." His passage through Connecticut was a continuous ovation. "Across Rhode Island cannon boomed from town to town as if New England were a battle line," and receptions overlapped each other. In Boston he was "received with all the show of honor which we paid to Lafayette," wrote an astonished citizen. And Harvard outdid itself in conferring upon Jackson the degree of Doctor of Laws.

The common man—to use a dated phrase—trusts a ruler he can love more than he trusts committees or colorless executives. Perhaps Harry Truman of Missouri better than any president before or since powerfully combined the common man's manners and a bond of affection worthy of a king, while eschewing pomp and circumstance: the very model of how to transform the outer symbol from one culture to that of another without losing its emotional power. Yet perhaps even Truman's success was felt more heavily after he left office than before and more affectionately in the Middle West than in the East. At his death, he benefited by comparison with Nixon, and the liberal Eastern press extolled him.

William Seward, Lincoln's Secretary of State, told a British journalist: "We elect a king for four years and give him absolute power within certain limits, which after all he can interpret for himself." The office of the president—a crucial fact—is not clearly bounded. In the absence of clarity, he can do what he can get away with doing. By his own imagination and personal *élan,* he decides himself what the office means. Against all checks and balances, the president retains powers of counterattack, subterfuge, direct appeal to the people, subtle pressures of many kinds. His power is not exercised in a vacuum by any means, and it is not absolute. But it is difficult for even well-informed and studious citizens to penetrate through what the president *says* to what he is actually *doing.* The development of the war in Vietnam is only an instance of presidential power in operation far beyond public gaze; the lag between policy and public discovery is often two years or more. In executive power, the president is all too like a king of old, especially and perhaps fatally in foreign affairs.

Yet it is the president's symbolic power that is most underestimated today. Once let him lose the trust or the affection of the people, as Lyndon Johnson did in 1968, and his many other powers begin to wilt. Once let him establish his right to the symbolic power, his "mandate," as Richard Nixon did in 1972 (perhaps even without actually winning emotions of trust or affection), and his powers in other matters advance enormously. Not least, his foes become most cautious of some sudden thrust of his that might effectively isolate them outside the current symbol system. Contrariwise, let him squander that symbolic power by ill-considered actions, and even the advantages of his electoral "mandate" can evaporate. *Hubris* exacts retribution.

Thus, the American monarch rules, not by blood but almost wholly by symbolic power. When the king is riding a crest of approbation he is in greatest peril. The ancient maxim holds: *who strikes the king must kill.* His foes hold back, watching closely for the first false step. When he violates the public symbols—FDR trying to "pack the court," LBJ crying "peace" while dispatching bombers, Nixon permissive to crime in White House operations—the blows fall with little mercy.

Symbolic power is the precondition of pragmatic power. There are many realistic, practical programs proposed every year that haven't the faintest possibility of passage because they are not symbolically acceptable. A "hard-nosed" thinker may have contempt for the role of symbolism in politics: it is obscure, irrational, unenlightened, and unmeasurable. But a different conclusion is just as plausible and more probably correct. Politics is primarily the art of understanding the symbols actually operative in society and learning how to make them issue forth in action. It is the art of persuasion. It is the art of governing, not rationalists, but people. (The hard-nosed are people, too, and are just as profoundly moved by symbols as all other humans are; but perhaps by *different* symbols.)

In January of a presidential election year, how much is certain about who will be the candidates in November? Twelve good men in the opposition party jockey for position. Who will touch the chords that arouse the people? Who will articulate best what a majority longs for? There is something corrupt about the need of a candidate to "sell" himself to the people. But there is also something noble about the system that requires it. How shall a man of historically unequaled power be chosen? Especially when people demand that he reflect the moral qualities that flatter them? "The president," James David Barber writes, "is expected to personify our betterness in an inspiring way, to express in what he does and is (not just in what he says) a moral idealism which, in much of the public mind, is the very opposite of 'politics.'" So he must be political and not political at the same time. For it is one of the pecularities of the major American symbol system that "politics" and "morality" are opposites and lie in separate realms.

At the start of a campaign, we do not know where the feelings and judgments of Americans lie. What do they think is just and fair? Are they content or ready for major change? Do they feel included or excluded? What are their grievances, resentments, hopes, needs? Do they want to be inspired or merely left alone? ("Reason I'm for Wallace," a man at a bar in South Milwaukee told two Wallace workers who were resting their tired feet in March 1972, "he's the only fella in the whole damn bunch ain't gonna do nothin'." Trapped between pleasure and dismay, the Wallace girls smiled.)

There is a destructive use of symbol-making, too. One can try to surround one's opponent with the symbols of recklessness, corruption, or sin. Thus, the Democrats in 1964 coupled the image of the atomic mushroom cloud with the name of Senator Barry Goldwater; and in 1972 "dirty tricks" included false letters asserting sexual misconduct, ethnic slurs, and other accusations against Democratic candidates. Such mud-slinging would not make sense, however, except against the background of deeply cherished symbols: that a president ought to be a moral person, dependable, a man of reason. Thus, the use of manufactured symbols (pro or con) pays implicit deference to a deeper level of genuine symbols, to the tutored expectations arising out of a people's history.

A politics based on "image" is to a politics based on symbols what manipulation is to liberation. A politics based on attractively manufactured images is based on getting from the people whatever can be gotten from them. A politics based on identification with the profoundest symbols latent in a people's life is a politics that seeks to release and to enlarge psychic energies that are the people's own. In the first case, the susceptibilities of the people are the means to the manipulator's purpose. In the other, the spiritual life of the people is the candidate's goal and guide. People rightfully feel used by most politicians. By a few politicians, the people feel liberated—released, uplifted, led.

Premature closure can arise from a candidate's attempt to

impose upon the people his own moral symbols. With all good intentions, a candidate can appeal to "the best that is in the people," but get it wrong; the people do not recognize themselves in his symbolic pictures. He means to express their dreams, but he cannot ring the changes. This was, it seems, George McGovern's deficiency in 1972. America has a vaster, more diverse symbolic geography than, even with all good will, McGovern discerned.

If a president once gains a symbolic identification with people, he can bring them to entertain, or to do, things they might well otherwise resist. That is, he can *lead*. Eisenhower was free to discredit Senator Joseph McCarthy as no Democrat could have been. Nixon was freer than a liberal to negotiate with China or Russia and to support for a season bolder programs of welfare reform, like the Family Assistance Plan. David Burke, until 1970 the administrative assistant of Senator Edward Kennedy, described the Kennedy impact on Massachusetts: "Take quite conservative Catholics in Dorchester and Worcester and Fall River and lead them to vote their consciences." The same constituencies that in other states in November 1972 were about to reject George McGovern decisively, in Massachusetts handily endorsed him. The Kennedys have provided a symbolic framework within which political issues in Massachusetts now are framed.

Symbol systems have built-in capacities for transformation and transcendence; that is how they survive down through the years. Symbols that one leader turns back upon themselves in narrowness, resentment, and xenophobia, another leader opens as with a wand, makes to flower and to grow. It is the task of leaders to lead. One talent required is to diagnose the symbolic resources of one's people, enter into them, and transform them to meet the demands of the time. Harold Laski wrote in *The American Presidency*: "The president must not be too far ahead of his time if he is to be a successful president. . . . To get anywhere, he must win understanding; to win it, the policy he pursues must never be so remote from the views around him that he cannot get that understanding."

In *The Federalist* (LXIV), John Jay described the ebb and flow of symbolic life:

> They who have turned their attention to the affairs of men must have perceived that there are tides in them; tides very irregular in their duration, strength, and direction, and seldom found to run twice exactly in the same manner or measure. To discern and to profit by these tides in national affairs is the business of those who preside over them; and they who have had much experience on this head inform us that there frequently are occasions when days, nay, even hours are precious.

In 1907 Woodrow Wilson tried to describe the president's access to symbolic power and its translation into pragmatic effect:

> The President can dominate his party by being spokesman for the real sentiment and purpose of the country, by giving direction to opinion, by giving the country at once the information and the statements of policy which will enable it to form its judgments alike of parties and of men.
>
> His is the only national voice in affairs. Let him once win the admiration and confidence of the country, and no other single force can withstand him, no combination of forces will easily overpower him. *His position takes the imagination of the country*. He is the representative of no constituency, but of the whole people.
>
> He may be both the leader of his party and the leader of the nation, or he may be one or the other. If he lead the nation, his party can hardly resist him. His office is anything he has the sagacity and force to make it.
>
> Some of our Presidents have deliberately held themselves off from using the full power they might legitimately have used, because of conscientious scruples, because they were more theorists than statesmen . . . The President is at liberty, both in law and conscience, to be as big a man as he can.
>
> His is the vital place of action in the system, whether he accept it as such or not, and the office is the measure of the man—of his wisdom as well as of his force. [Emphasis supplied.]

Electing a president, we elect the chief symbol-maker of the land, and empower him in the kingdom of our imaginations as well as in the executive office where he supervises armies, budgets, and appointments.

6

Five Elements
of Symbolic Power

Symbolic power contains at least five components.

First, there is the degree of *identification* or *inclusion*. To what extent does a person, looking at the president, say "we"? This factor was decisive in 1972.

Second, there is the component of *interests*. To what degree do the president's speech, action, and being suggest knowledge of and concern for one's own interests? Contrast the symbolic power of Robert Kennedy and Richard Nixon among blacks; not necessarily the statistical profile of what they actually did, but how they lent their own identity to the dramatization of interests—*that* symbol created political weight.

Third, there is the component of *action*. To what degree do the actions of the president awaken actions in the general populace, whether of cooperation, of laissez-faire, or of resistance? It is possible for a president, John Kennedy perhaps, to awaken great excitement even while actually doing little; or, on the contrary, in other areas to do a great deal without arousing any interest or concern at all.

Fourth, there is the component of *moral fulfillment*. To what degree does contemplation of the person who is president convey a sense of admiration and inspiration, making one as pleased and complacent as if one had seen one's own best image in the mirror, drawing one along in imitation and in striving: "God! I'd like to be like that."

Finally, there is the component of *authority*. To what extent does the candidate seem to know what he is doing, to be in charge, to be able to direct the whole nation with steadiness and skill? This factor, too, was influential in 1972. Sometimes educated people belittle the need to respect authority, picturing it as a need for a "father figure," making it seem immature. In truth, in any corporate enterprise, from a college faculty to Joe Namath and the offensive unit of the New York Jets, confidence in leadership is a mature and realistic desideratum. Since in their own symbolic world educated liberals have aversion to the daily realities of authority, more confusions exist concerning this component than any other.

What makes some people feel secure with one leader and others insecure is sometimes a function not of his authority but of his identity, interests, and actions. Bobby Kennedy was adjudged "ruthless" and all too capable of acting with authority, but it cannot be said everyone felt secure at the prospect of his election. Eisenhower was denounced by activists as a "do-nothing" and "mere father figure," but his capacity to command was not really the issue; rather it was *his* judgment against theirs that more lasting good is done by less presidential agitation. The component of authority measures whether people believe that the politician in question is a *leader*. The other components measure whether they are drawn to his *kind* of leadership.

The American president reflects the people that choose him, but not precisely as a mirror does. They want to identify with him not only as they actually are, but perhaps more so as they are in their ideal form. America was founded by people who (according to ideology) wanted to be saints, joined by millions of others who had to agree (via the sacred rites of "Americanization") to become "new men." Being reborn is a fundamental American metaphor. And so our king must be very priestly and as demanding as the prophets of old. We expect him to chastise us and to challenge us. The call for sacrifice is a ritual still lively and effectual among us. Even Nixon in 1972, while lulling us and affiirming that from his privileged overview the fevered fears of the 1960s were overwrought, hid behind appeals to moral renewal, to "the hard road" called for by ancient virtues. In choosing a president, we choose a symbol of our better selves. We do so because that has become the nature of the office, as it is an irrepressible need of the human heart: to find public models of inner aspirations. We are liable to affirm in him our own illusions.

No little of the president's power derives from the sacredness in which his office is naturally, inevitably held. For a while Richard Nixon shared that sacredness. From the first, this thought offended some like a sacrilege. It was not his management alone that offended. It was "what he stood for." For them, two symbols were in conflict: the symbol Richard Nixon and the presidency of the United States.

7

Making the Most
of Improbable Talents

It must be difficult to be the president of the United States and to know that the two most influential papers in the nation, *The New York Times* and *The Washington Post,* hold you in naked contempt and frequently show it. It must be difficult to assume that those professors whose views figure in the journals of influential circulation despise you. Lyndon Johnson once agreed to a White House conference for intellectuals set up for him by Professor Eric Goldman. Intellectuals, he found, know how to hate a guy. Is any group more given to cutting down inferiors?

Nixon, some say, should not have been petty about the criticism he received from some professors and the media. Over 80 percent of the papers of the nation consistently endorsed him in his national campaigns and (until 1973) editorially supported his actions as president. In the main, professors seemed on his side. Why should he have persisted then in dividing the vast reaches of "Middle America" (which extend into every region of the land) from the "Northeastern liberal establishment"? Why not "bring us together"? Those involved in moral warfare (for that is what it is, a contest for what shall count as moral in the public mind of America) seldom recognize the moralism and divisiveness of their own public statements. The position of each group seems to it so obvious that failure to see it is attributed to deliberate malice or to such unbelievable obtuseness as one is entitled to hate.

In some quarters, Nixon has long been hated with a passion. Of few public officials has it been so easy to express contempt without apology and with the certainty of corroboration. FDR was vilified, JFK has since his death been savaged, LBJ was degraded in *Macbird*. Still, if Spiro Agnew had written a speech half so crude as Philip Roth's book about Trick E. Dixon, how outraged would many be? Commonly, those on Left or Right are blind to their own excesses, while deliciously aware of those of their opponents.

By 1972, Richard Nixon stood higher than before in public estimation. Many had come to admire his courage. Some had a new esteem for him, sufficient to make them question the convention of looking down on him. They would again have worked to defeat him. They believed him to be horribly wrong in some decisions—as in the Christmas bombing of Hanoi in 1972—and they opposed his domestic political program (or lack of one). His aloofness from Congress and the people was disturbing. They knew they must keep closest check on him. But they took him to be a serious and strangely consistent person, lacking neither intelligence nor (in his own phrase) "a lead butt" and stubborn will.

William Appleman Williams in *Some Presidents* followed the prevailing literary convention. That convention proposes that there *is* no real Nixon, simply an emptiness, a cipher of expedience: "Almost everyone who has tried to make sense of Richard Milhous Nixon has acknowledged serious doubts about the value of the effort, admitted spells of boredom and outbursts of anger, and confessed recurrent frustration in finding and understanding the man. . . . It is a shell game without any pea." Bruce Mazlish seems more correct in his *In Search of Nixon*: "Nixon *has* always been himself, and that self has been steady and consistent throughout his life." It is an ambivalent, complex self. Professor Mazlish is not a supporter of Nixon, yet he writes: "Much of that 'self' and many of these traits are, I would concede, admirable. . . . Many of his specific policies and programs are laudable. There is much to applaud in the thirty-seventh President of the United States."

For a brief time, a new trend seemed under way. Theodore White expressed a favorable change of attitude toward Nixon in 1968. John Osborne also surprised many by writing at the end of *The Nixon Watch* (1972):

> There Mr. Nixon is, in the Presidency, changing with it and growing in it in ways dimly and uncertainly perceived, but somehow attractive in a sense that nothing about him attracted me in 1968. . . . I have a feeling that the Presidency has been good for Richard Nixon, in a distinctly therapeutic way. . . . Nixon the President seems to me to have become a stronger man, a more decent and credible man, than Nixon the congressman, the senator, the Vice President, and the candidate allowed himself to be. It is as if the Presidency enabled and encouraged him to afford a showing of strength, a level of decency that his character did not require and his circumstances did not permit in the prior time.

Revisionism is common in our history. William Appleman Williams has written in stunning praise of Herbert Hoover, "the little boy from Iowa," and Dwight Eisenhower, "the boy from Kansas." Williams' villains are "white Northern liberals" and "liberal orthodoxy." He plainly likes the solid Midwesterners, except for Harry Truman.

Nixon, of course, is no solid Midwesterner. He is a Californian, which perhaps means rootless. So thick are the clouds of invective around the man—"used car salesman," "lacking in all principle," "mean, petty, expedient," "robotlike"—that the first time he broke through to me as a human being, I confess, was in a brief sequence in a viciously anti-Nixon movie. There was a shot of him as a young law student at Duke, and suddenly I saw in him a score of students I have known: tense, uncertain, striving, determined despite his many drawbacks to "make it."

Who could have singled him out then? Most of the thousands of his contemporaries would make it, by comparison with their fathers, but modestly: notable lawyers in their small towns, nice incomes, modern suburban homes. It is easy to make fun of the "squalor" of their lives. But what they do and how they live beats, by far, sweating in the mills or mines or shops or barns their fathers sweated in. They travel, they read (a little), their children have the best, or almost the best, of everything. America has, quite tangibly, been good to them. Horatio Alger's basic tale is not an untruth; it is a deeply embedded, functioning form of life: poor boys by the thousands do end up as college professors, editors, newscasters, bank presidents, congressmen, judges, and presidents.

But *really* poor. A temperamental father, severe, beaten down, unpredictable. A brother who dies a rending, difficult death from tuberculosis, and then a second—two beautiful, healthy children in early pictures, surrounding Richard in age, one older, one younger. (In the same period, wealthier scions bathe in hot springs and recover.) The bleakness of a small-town store in the Depression: *Bonnie and Clyde* and *The Last Picture Show*. In a fairly amoral and wide-open state, backward and far removed from the powerful East, where "east," indeed, can mean Carson City.

Take a gangling, fairly gawky young man with no pretty television face, wound up tight as a drum and tormented by his own spontaneities, with no special heroism or even wounds from the war to boast of, no money, no significant connections, with no "farm belt" to make him a favorite son, neither high-Wasp nor low-Wasp nor thickly Irish (no tribal constituency, then, for whom to be the spokesman) and place him down in an age soon to be known as the age of television and charisma and the new politics. Richard Nixon was in 1946 no Ronald Reagan. Not photogenic, not at ease, not a showman. Conveying always the sense of inner torment and tightly wound self-control—hiding something, pent up, not easily trusted. One of those grinding, determined young men with pimply faces and carefully brushed hair of whom in any given year hundreds of thousands throng business schools, schools of engineering, and law schools, stale sweat in the worn armpits of their standard suits—none of the flash that captures the attention of girls or student body newspapers, no glamour, no aura of the free, swinging athletic body, no natural aristocratic command of the social graces. By dint of hard work, he would succeed like hundreds of thousands of others (his brother, even). But symbol of the power, diversity, grace, and past of the United States of America? A hundred thousand others more likely.

Nixon, so a man who once worked for him describes, is like a golfer who has no natural swing, no special grace, no power in his wrists—only a fierce desire to master golf, because it is a necessary instrument of his ambitions. So ten hundred thousand practice strokes. Again. Again. Until he need not be humiliated. Short, jerky, mechanical swing but steady, down the fairway. No arc nor grace nor awesome flight but plunk, plunk, with total concentration and control, a managed and workmanlike and dogged round within reach of his companions. Embarrassing. A triumph of will. A triumph of self-control. A thousand such triumphs required every day.

A quick study. Always learning. Swift, darting eyes. Recording information no words could ever exhaust, studying, breaking down into analytic, imitable parts. A wise man learns from his mistakes, but a Richard Nixon—sensing a terror, a danger, a void—learns from everything. In college, the young have always hated fellows like that. While they are having fun, he is calculating. No one will get close to him. A loner, he nevertheless doesn't believe in introspection or "psychologizing." Rather, in calculation, in analyzing every circumstance, in devotion to a "lead butt," in forced self-confidence. Push ahead. Analyze shyness, nervousness, gawky looks. Accept. Push ahead.

Our culture supports the ego of such a human type. It is a culture of will. And action. Of self-control, of mastery, of the exertion of the power of the head over the movements of the body. Master the earth. The triumph of spirit, of the *will*. And not exactly the Nietzschean will-to-power. Not the heroic, pagan superman. But the pragmatic decipherer of the labyrinths of social-political-economic systems: climbing through the brambles, over rocks, avoiding the sudden chasms, deciding correctly at the great crises where the irrecoverable ways divide. There is a kind of heroism involved: not Promethean, not the Germanic Thor, but the niggling little pragmatism and patience of the god who will, at last, disconcert everybody by finding the secret door, the hidden cave, the way out of the labyrinth in which the Fates had thought him imprisoned. He did it.

Thus a great surge of confidence. With an abiding sense that the world is brutal and unfair. A harshness toward those who were unsparing of him. A need to control and to make sure that the Great Escape is not squandered, he will relentlessly demand a loyal administration as closely locked in his mind's control as are the muscles and reflexes of his own body. Reality, too, is perceived as hostile and punishing. So often his fingers have been burned. His reading of the social-political-economic system in which we are all equally confined is, however original and illuminating, often false. He misgauges its resistance or its venom: it lashes him. Eyes more furtive next time—flashes of anger, thunderclap of warning—his will executed more subtly thereafter; but not dissuaded. Thus, he exploded when the Senate twice rejected his Supreme Court nominees. Slowly the Court fell under his power then.

So also the "self-defense" of bugging his associates, unparalleled efforts at political espionage, and gargantuan collections of cash. In a close election (as in late 1971 seemed very likely), he would have no reliable friends in the major media (television news, the national magazines, the *Times,* the *Post*). They would look for scandals, promote "leaks," encourage the stealing of documents. They would try to humiliate him. He would be portrayed as Evil, the villain of the traditional puppet show, dark, stiff, malevolent. They would try to defeat him.

Nixon's fear seems often to be corroborated by events. In his portraits, his enemies are very powerful; the odds are always on their side. Yet paranoia, even when accurate, leads to miscalculation. Trying to build impenetrable protection, with pre-emptive espionage against his foes, his administration vastly overreached. His symbolic stature crumbled through errors of his own; his estimate of his enemies' power was exact.

Yet after long years of being burned, his personal sense of
reality was attuned to the intricacies and vectors of force in
the interlocking and elaborate American labyrinth. The education of Richard Nixon, could it be retraced, would reveal a map
social scientists might pore over for years to come, tracing
through it the contours and the fault lines of this most fascinating
of societies. Lct them not neglect the thousands and thousands
of beef dinners with the cold potatoes and limp salads and
canned fruit cups in every county seat and Grange Hall and
sports arena of the heartlands of America: the names, the
faces, the relationships, the tastes, the dreams, the angers, the
spites, the social barriers, and status signals. Does any man in
America know the political surfaces of their lives better than
Richard Nixon? It is much to be doubted.

So diverse a land! Alive with a not-ideal people, small and
petty and sweaty, faults as large as the land they inhabit, the
land—Mencken wrote—of the third-rate. Look on America and
see, if we may paraphrase Isaiah 53, there is no comeliness in
her, no beauty. *That* taste of reality is sweet. By comparison
with it, dreams are bitter, illusions savorless. To see the people
as they are is grace.

Richard Nixon lacked the grace of reading hearts. He knew
only the political surfaces of people, as well as any man.

It is a greater grace by far to make flow for them channels
in which to realize what is yet imprisoned and distorted within
them. It is Nixon's deficiency that finding his way out of the
labyrinth has been so consuming a task that his idea about what
is best in the people is, by comparison with other ideas of his,
unsophisticated and avuncular. It is not, as some assert, that
he does not offer "moral leadership." It is, rather, that his moral
leadership has always been of a sectarian sort, no longer real
even for the actual living members of its sects. His task was
easy, though. All he had to do was hit closer to the mark than
the media Left was hitting.

While the media Left has wandered farther and farther from
uneducated people, so full of its superiority that no one seems
to remember where the uneducated people are, Nixon has meth-
odically entered the unguarded vacuum. He has only had to

touch the surfaces, sprinkle raindrops in the desert of aspiration, so thirsty were millions for even remotest recognition. In some peculiar way, Nixon is not "in touch." He has made an effort, in that stiff way of his.

And they, the people, cautiously, not trusting, after a lifetime of opposition against him, backing into it as it were, in sufficient numbers voted for Nixon to present him in 1972 with the most unheartfelt landslide in history. The lonely law student had long ago set aside rewards of the heart as unobtainable. Stoically, with satisfaction, he made do with one of the two greatest proportions of hard, cold votes in the nation's history.

He had seized the dominant symbols of the American civil religions while they were left unguarded, clutching them to him like the unlikeliest scout striding out from the bushes to "capture the flag." The outsider, the prisoner, the condemned man was suddenly chosen priest, prophet, king—the tabernacle his. David did no more gleeful a dance before the ark. Muscles in his heart, long constricted, must have leapt. This much he could never have expected. No wonder *hubris* mushroomed from the deeps.

Thus, Richard Nixon became the primary incarnation of the nation's self-understanding. And thus the Watergate scandal, burgeoning out of lifelong fear, exploded the dream—the dream not only of his own self-esteem, the dream also of the people, obliging them to see in the rippling circles of political slime an image of themselves: bright young professionals without any conscience except professional loyalty, for survival turning on each other like cats in an alleyway. Nixon's efforts to return America to a nostalgic past ended in a vision of our real past: a clawing contest for power, in a lawless land, among confidence men and hired guns, with cool disregard for the restraints of civilization.

Yet the symbols of the presidency, revealed differently in the life of each president, go far beyond the tragedy of Richard Nixon. Some Americans expect so much of presidents they do not wish to see feet of clay. For others, these same expectations make the sins of presidents not merely sins but *sacrileges,* evoking far beyond mere blame, biting outrage.

Richard Nixon was in a good position to glimpse in advance the sacredness of the role he was to undertake. In 1967, in preparation for the campaign of 1968, he received a memo on the subject. To that and to the liturgical or ritual character of presidential actions, we now must turn.

8

A Professional's Memo

The psychic power inherent in the president's office derives directly from the people. The president is obliged to make ritual pilgrimages among them—to touch them, to "press the flesh" as Lyndon Johnson put it—to complete the electric circuit of his symbolic connection with them. At least every four years, the campaign pilgrimage reopens this fundamental symbolism. The people get to "know" their president, and he them. Their approval, at the crowning symbolic conclusion of the campaign, "legitimizes" his later economic and administrative decisions.

A campaign is a symbolic "long march," a *rite de passage,* not practical in dollars-and-cents, perhaps not even practical as an "education in the issues," but symbolically indispensable. If the people cannot see the president's personality torn and tested, how can they trust their lives, fortunes, and honor to his decisions? A presidential campaign is an *agon.* How do the candidates bear up under its tortures? It is a blood rite. The candidate suffers *for the people's sake.* They select which candidate has most united himself to them.

In a column in the *New York Post,* Max Lerner caught a
glimpse of the underlying realities:

> The whole thing becomes an elaborate exercise in what Ir-
> ving Goffman has called "ritual face"—the way a man must
> appear in public, whatever his interior confrontation with
> himself—the tortured process of acquiring, losing, and saving
> some image of political salvation. . . . Running for Presi-
> dent . . . has become a punishing ordeal . . . compounded
> of . . . political hoopla, commercial greed, personal megalo-
> mania, and national bread-and-circuses. . . . The Presi-
> dential office is itself an ordeal. . . . A man has to be
> stretched on a rack, tempered in a fiery furnace, to see if he
> has the stuff of survival in him.
>   Give the voter some reflective chance to assess and re-
> assess each madman who offers himself for the sacrificial
> ordeal. And pray for the health and sanity, as well as the
> survival power, of the men who make it.

Say, if you will, that electoral campaigns are "merely" symbolic. Something powerful is going on. A single word may destroy a man (Romney's "brainwashed"). The big spenders don't
necessarily win (Lindsay in Florida). A man's personality may
crack (Muskie's tears in New Hampshire; Nixon's outburst in
1962). Symbolic violations may exclude a healthy, popular,
and able candidate (Kennedy at Chappaquiddick). Assassination may intervene (the attempt upon Wallace in 1972). The
underdog may surprise virtually everybody (McCarthy in 1968;
McGovern in 1972). "Intangibles" are many.

To run for president, a person must show great capacity to
raise money. Still, despite the amounts of money involved, we
spend less every four years to determine who will fill the most
powerful office in the world than we spend annually to determine
which team will win the national football championship. (The
religions of football and of politics meld more profoundly in our
national psyche than the exchange of metaphors suggests: game
plan, campaign, field general. Even their financial base is more
parallel than meets the eye: corporate profiteers, regional events,
fan participation.)

To run for president, a person must show great organizational capacities. But "organization" is a matter of morale and motivation as well as of bureaucratic charts, funds, and lines of command. The organization must have symbolic access to a wide range of voters. Committed workers cannot win if their plans encounter indifference or hostility among the people.

So, not least among prerequisites is a sound instinct for the current expectations of the national self-understanding. Required is not only a reading of the "popular mood," but also of the symbolic structures underlying that mood. One might read the mood correctly but violate certain expectations, taboos, or forms, and thus forfeit the public's trust. These expectations, taboos, and forms may not seem "rational," but there is no denying their effectiveness. One might have many millions of dollars in a campaign chest, a splendid organization, vulnerable opposition, and nevertheless forfeit all advantage.

The landscape and the laws of America's symbolic life are so little defined that practical politicians usually discover them the hard way and by accident. So oriented are they to what is "practical" that they often speak sheepishly and even defensively about symbolic realities. They seem to feel that symbolic realities are "emotional" or "irrational." In fact, these symbolic realities are the interpretive structures according to which people understand their own experience. What is more "real" than that? Or more closely related to understanding? Symbolic realities are rational and reasonable and intelligent. *All* thinking is symbolic. *All* acting is symbolic. *All* language is symbolic. It is part of our peculiar rationalism that we find it awkward to bow to this humble but universal demand of human intelligence and morality.

Not all symbolic attempts to interpret experience are equally accurate or acceptable. Like hypotheses, symbols may be tested against the experience they seek to interpret. They may be criticized, modified, or rejected. If we approach symbolic realities in a quasi-scientific, practical way, perhaps they will not seem so threatening.

Politicians with long experience on the national scene learn how to work with the civil religion and its variants. Thus, Ray Price, an experienced adviser to Richard Nixon, wrote a revealing memorandum for the Nixon staff in 1967. In this remarkable document, Price seems apologetic and embarrassed about so unpragmatic a matter as a national symbol system. He gives the issue a "practical" edge by suggesting how image-makers and public-relations persons might make use of it.

"Politics is much more emotional than it is rational," Price begins. It would be more accurate to say "more symbolic than pragmatic." "And this is much more true of presidential politics." He continues:

> People identify with a President in a way they do with no other public figure. Potential presidents are measured against an ideal that's a combination of leading man, God, father, hero, pope, king, with maybe just a touch of the avenging Furies thrown in. They want him to be larger than life, a living legend, and yet quintessentially human; someone to be held up to their children as a model; someone to be cherished by themselves as a revered member of the family, in somewhat the same way in which peasant families pray to the icon in the corner. Reverence goes where power is.

But sometimes power goes where reverence is. As Lyndon Johnson felt reverence slip away in 1968, he felt his power slipping too.

We shouldn't credit the press, Price continues, with a greater leaven of reason than the general public shares: "The press may be better at rationalizing their prejudices, but the basic response remains an emotional one." "Prejudices"? Merely "emotional"? To look at the matter as Price does is to be embarrassed that humans have moral needs, that the feeling of commitment and dedication is as necessary as air, that humans require a sense of purpose. People expect more of a president than practical skills. One may "manipulate" that expectation and treat it as a weakness to be exploited. It is also a strength in the people, ultimately prompting them in revulsion to spew out the demagogue. To treat with contempt the longings of a people for a measure of self-transcendence is to invite their bitterness. They do not like to be "taken." Of course, Price is trying to break through the merely practical biases of his readers, to get them to take symbolic matters seriously:

> Selection of a President has to be an act of faith. It becomes increasingly so as the business of government becomes ever more incomprehensible to the average voter. This faith isn't achieved by reason; it's achieved by charisma, by a feeling of trust that can't be argued or reasoned, but that comes across in those silences that surround the words. The words are important—but less for what they actually say than for the sense they convey, for the impression they give of the man himself, his hopes, his standards, his competence, his intelligence, his essential humanness, and the directions of history he represents.

But how do the people judge a candidate, his "standards," his "essential humanness," or harder still "the directions of history he represents"? In the light of standards they themselves share, through an image of what a good human being is as they see it, by the direction of history as they feel it coursing in their own lives and plans. All these inclinations of theirs are socially shaped, socially inculcated.

The image of what a "good" president is is shaped by experiences with past presidents. The people have "a presidential instinct." They may admire a person for many qualities. But a good president? That's a farther, more narrow gate to enter.

The American president functions as king, prophet, and priest because America functions as a secular religion. Being an American is a state of soul. Yet it is not easy to define what this "being American" is. We are far from being all alike. To speak about "Americans," without noting how many disparate groups there are among us, is to be isolated from reality. There is not some vast mass of "Middle Americans." There is no homogeneous majority of "Silent Americans." Go and see—this people is enormously diverse.

Yet no member of any minority is unaffected by the experience of America. Two men may be "black brothers," but the one from Ethiopia or Nigeria will be the first to note that the other—from Atlanta or Cleveland or New York—is utterly American, not African. A Polish-American may not feel he has been recognized for his true value in America, may feel in some respects like an "outsider," but a visit to Poland will soon assure him that he is no longer simply Polish. A white Southerner may feel every day the contempt of the white Northern liberal, yet in England discover acutely that he is without doubt a "Yank." Italo-Americans born in Brooklyn distinguish themselves sharply from those thousands of Italian-Americans who continue to immigrate to Brooklyn each year, and who come as literate persons, secure in their cultural and political identity.

America is a corporate experience. We come into this experience from different locations and at different times, with different perceptions and different preparation. Each of us knows a different America. Yet that corporate experience in which we all participate is unlike any other on the face of the earth.

A nation from its inception undergoing traumatic experiences of loneliness, revolution, slavery, depression, global adventure, assassination, guilt, space exploration, defeat—such a nation is a crucible of vivid experience which none escape. We are, each in our different ways, American *because* we have been through these things together. In their light, we are prepared to evaluate "the directions of history" our presidential candidates represent.

At every turn in our national life, the symbols and images of our national self-understanding are invoked. In the light of our civil self-conceptions, investors fan out around the world, troops are dispatched, national interests are weighed.

A contest for the presidency is a contest for several symbolic centers of America. It is a contest for the souls, imaginations, and aspirations of Americans as much as for the nation's levers of power. It is also a contest between national self-images. Not infrequently citizens will vote against their self-interests, coldly and economically defined, for the sake of symbols more important to them. To call such behavior irrational may be to miss the fact that humans do not live by bread alone. And it is possible, of course, that in reaching for bread they may receive instead a stone. Fundamentally, in choosing a president people choose—now more pragmatically, now more symbolically—what satisfies themselves. Criteria for what is necessary to satisfy them are supplied by an instinct learned and nourished by the history of the national self-understandings active among us.

The Price memo of 1967 continues:

> Most countries divide the functions of head of government (prime minister) and chief of state (king or president). We don't. The traditional "issues" type debates center on the role of the head of government, but I'm convinced that people vote more for a chief of state—and this is primarily an emotional identification, embracing both a man himself and a particular vision of the nation's ideals and its destiny.
>
> All this is a roundabout way of getting at the point that we should be concentrating on building a received image of RN as the kind of man proud parents would ideally want their sons to grow up to be: a man who embodies the national ideal, its aspirations, its dreams, a man whose image the people want in their homes as a source of inspiration, and whose voice they want as the representative of their nation in the councils of the world, and of their generation in the pages of history.

Winning the loyalty of hundreds of thousands of volunteers, workers, and doorbell-ringers is beyond the competence of the candidate as mere manager or mere executive. It is a task for the candidate as symbol-maker. The presidential candidate must evoke a huge symbolic response, issue significant symbolic rewards. People must feel that what they are doing is good, worthy, and important. The criteria for what counts as good, worthy, or important for the nation and for themselves are not any criteria whatever, blown about by the winds. The main lines of those criteria have already been established by our history. To these we shall turn in Part Three.

At present, we must note how the structure of presidential life is inescapably symbolic.

9

The Liturgy of Leadership

George McGovern ran for office as a man of candor, a politician unlike other politicians, a person unconcerned about image. *That* was his image. There was a kind of naïveté built into his attempt; indeed a naïveté of two kinds.

First, it is impossible *not* to have an image. A candidate has only limited exposure; he must reach over two hundred million citizens; no one can look into his soul.

A national politician has the attention of a substantial public —on network television, for example—for a very small number of hours a year, usually in very short segments of thirty seconds or, perhaps, three or four minutes. Senator Muskie was given two half-hour shows by the Humphrey campaign in 1968. His greatest exposure probably came in the brief talk he gave the eve of the congressional elections in 1970, during the half of a football game, back-to-back with President Nixon. More than anything else, those few minutes probably fixed his reputation in the public mind. Add several more hours for appearances on

"Meet the Press" and similar shows, and accumulate the number of minutes he made the news each month in 1971—it is not an overwhelming exposure.

Granted a finite exposure, what does the politician choose to show of himself? No matter what he selects, even if it be un-rehearsed and spontaneous, it *is* a selection. His twenty-four-hour-a-day self will never be wholly public. A segment of his life will have to stand in the public mind for the whole.

Add the inattention, indifference, and inaccessibility of millions of citizens. How to reach an electoral majority? (Not all citizens vote, some may be counted as safe, others as immovably op-posed.) Still, how to reach them? And when, with many efforts, one does reach various voters, what actually "comes through"? A man may *want* to project *X;* but is *X* what the perceivers perceive? Ray Price, President Nixon's speechwriter and ad-viser, said in his 1967 memo:

> We have to be very clear on this point: that the response is to the image, not to the man, since 99 percent of the voters have no contact with the man. It's not what's there that counts, it's what is projected—and, carrying it one step fur-ther, it's not what he projects but rather what the voter re-ceives. It's not the man we have to change, but rather the received impression, and, his impression often depends more on the medium and its use than it does on the candidate him-self.

Price stresses that the demands of the medium "depend more on the medium than on the candidate himself." In the last decade, all of us have learned how the medium of television distorts our sense of reality, how reliance on television injures as well as helps. Television creates fads—"the youth culture"—and just as soon jettisons them. It announces "God is dead!" just before we are in the midst of an evangelical revival. What is true? What isn't? Only a thin selection from reality gets through.

Television is not alone in generating misconceptions. Even precise, technical language is read differently by different readers. The language of law is not what the laws *say* but what the public through the courts *hears*. Thus, James Madison in *The Federalist* (XXXVII):

All new laws, though penned with the greatest technical skill
and passed on the fullest and most mature deliberation, are
considered as more or less obscure and equivocal, until their
meaning be liquidated and ascertained by a series of particular discussions and adjudications. . . . The use of words is
to express ideas. Perspicuity, therefore, requires not only that
the ideas should be distinctly formed, but that they should
be expressed by words distinctly and exclusively appropriate to them. *But no language is so copious as to supply
words and phrases for every complex idea, or so correct as
not to include many equivocally denoting different ideas.*
Hence it must happen that however accurately objects may
be discriminated in themselves, and however accurately the
discrimination may be considered, the definition of them may
be rendered inaccurate by the inaccuracy of the terms in
which it is delivered. And *this unavoidable inaccuracy* must
be greater or less, according to the complexity and novelty
of the objects defined. When the Almighty himself conde-
scends to address mankind in their own language, His meaning, luminous as it must be, is rendered dim and doubtful
by the cloudy medium through which it is communicated.
Here, then, are three sources of vague and incorrect definitions: indistinctness of the object, imperfection of the organ
of conception, inadequateness of the vehicle of ideas. Any
one of these must produce a certain degree of obscurity.
[Emphasis added.]

The problem is not merely public and political. Husband and
wife, parents and children, do not understand each other lumi-
nously. We perceive each other even in our most intimate relations through images or symbols. We try to replace faulty symbols with more accurate ones, struggling through misunderstandings with faltering honesty. To each other we are images, shad-
ows flickering in a cave, even in each other's arms. Does Eleanor McGovern really understand George; or Pat, Dick, or anybody, anybody?

Excluded even in the most intimate relations, limpid understanding in more distant relations is impossible. We have no
choice but to try to discern the larger outlines of character and
action. Human affairs are necessarily symbolic and dramatic. To
try to act without generating an image is like trying not to have

a shadow or like pretending to be invisible. *No one* is going to see the "real" person. They will see only a creature of flesh and blood engaged in speech or action, interpreted according to the capacity of the perceiver.

The second naïveté, perhaps a hypocrisy, on the part of George McGovern was to pretend not to depend on images. Public office is liturgical. Necessarily and properly so. An official does not act, should not act, is not expected to act solely in his or her private *persona*. He or she acts chiefly, and perhaps solely, as a public officer, representative of the people, in a role marked out by law and tradition. To have a government of laws, not men, is precisely to hold in check human spontaneities: to establish a part, a role, a voice. It is to create a public drama in which assigned players take up assigned parts and play them with whatever ingenuity and originality they can muster. The official may "be himself" in order that the official role not be dead but alive. Each holder of the office may draw out of it possibilities not before realized in it. In this sense, the existence of a public dramatic form does not eliminate personality. Far from it, it channels, deepens, ordinarily fulfills personality, gives it outlet and scope. But at a price. The private person now belongs to the public. Public action follows different laws from private action, is part of a quite different drama altogether. Not to respect this difference is to confound one's private needs with the demands of office, to confound rule by men with rule by law.

The presidency is not at its occupant's whim. Vast room for different sorts of persons is provided, of course, but the office belongs to the people, not to the incumbent.

There are, then, public expectations based on law, custom, and tradition for what the president may or may not do. No doubt the latitude for invention and novelty is huge. But accountability is never absent. Perhaps in private life laissez-faire obtains, but in the presidency a person acts of, by, and for the people. As "liturgy" comes from Greek words meaning "worship on the part of the people" and as a priest at the Eucharist is not just good old Joe Murphy but the representative of the people before God, so the man who would be president must learn the part, recognize those possibilities within the official role that suit him, and note well the subtle and unwritten stage directions built up by past performances as public expectations.

For candidates, there must come, at some point, an inner click of comfort in the role aspired to. Suddenly one feels like a president, talks like a president, sounds to others like a president. One's own self-image, one's symbol of oneself, has got to alter. Only then do words and actions become convincing. Otherwise the gestures may be technically correct, yet everyone senses the lack of *authority*. Television is sometimes merciless in subliminally conveying a man's inner disposition in this respect. In 1960, Nixon was hungry, Kennedy in good humor and in charge. Who, on television, looked like a president? A crucial question. In 1972 McGovern to many seldom looked like a president, did not exude the sense of competence.

To speak of the presidency as a liturgical role is not to speak of pretense or falsity. It is to suggest that the presidency requires a presidential person. It is a role that forces the private man to become what he has not been before. At ten minutes before the hour, a man is simply Jack or Harry or Dick; but once the oath is taken, that man is "Mr. President." Our voices do not change out of primitive awe, but out of the sound recognition that a new drama is now underway. When this man acts henceforward, the drama is not his alone, not private, but public and corporate —the people of the United States act in him. He incarnates in one person all of us, our numbers, our power, our past, our deficiencies, our hopes.

We may wish it were otherwise. But he is *king*—king in the sense of symbolic, decisive focal point of our power and destiny. He is *prophet*—prophet in the sense of chief interpreter of our national self-understanding, establishing the terms of national discourse. He is *priest*—priest in the sense of incarnating our self-image, our values, our aspirations, and expressing these through every action he selects, every action he avoids.

We have handed over to this human, this public *persona,* a great deal more power perhaps than our Founding Fathers were conscious of. Because he is not descended of royal family, wears neither ermine nor crown, bears no title of nobility, is bounded somewhat by Congress, somewhat by the courts, and somewhat by tradition, public opinion, and indeed by inertia—because of such constraints, he is not exactly an absolute monarch. But what monarch of the past, surrounded by jealous lords, would not at an instant surrender his crown for the power and functions this man has?

Part Two

MORALISM
AND MORALITY

The Presidency is not merely an administrative office. That is the least part of it. It is preeminently a place of moral leadership.
— Franklin Delano Roosevelt, 1932

The central thesis was, and is, that the Liberal Movement both religious and secular seemed to be unconscious of the basic difference between the morality of individuals and the morality of collectives, whether races, classes or nations. . . . This distinction justifies and necessitates political policies which a purely individualistic ethic must always find embarrassing.
— Reinhold Niebuhr, *Moral Man and Immoral Society* (1932, 1960)

10

Being Moral and Being Practical

Gusts of December wind were blowing a stiff, dirty candy-wrapper scratching across the runway when in 1971 a straight, tall, self-contained man, his head slightly inclined, eased himself down the ramp from the Eastern shuttle at La Guardia. He was wearing a tan raincoat, a dark red and blue tie lay against his broadly striped shirt. Tanned of face, his thinning black hair wind-blown, Senator George McGovern smiled a slow, engaging, country-boy's smile and for the one-hundred-thousandth time extended his smooth strong hand. His manner was slow and serious. While aides gave him a few instructions, he pursed his lips. Then he climbed into a waiting car with the thousandth reporter he had talked to the past twelvemonth and was sped toward Manhattan. "He appears," the correspondent for *The New Yorker* later wrote, "so plainly honest, kind, sincere, and good that he makes other people feel rotten by comparison."

It was the end of 1971, and after a full year of campaigning to become a symbol of return to moral idealism in America, George McGovern was still gathering only 3 or 4 percent in the

57

polls. Nevertheless, in a two-way race with Richard Nixon he was running 38 percent. (There is a time-honored Democratic clubhouse maxim that *anybody* can get at least 33 percent of the vote.)

"We're concentrating on the organizational effort," the junior Senator from South Dakota told the reporter, "and we're out in front of everyone else in grass-roots organization. The aspect of politics that interests me the most—and is the most fun—is the development of ideas and issues [this by way of differentiating himself from those politicians who find talk of ideas and issues boring, unproductive, and vastly overrated] but I've learned that without careful organization you don't get very far. I have a lot more confidence than I had last January, when I embarked. I've really worked Wisconsin, New Hampshire, Florida, California (extensively), Oregon, New Mexico, and Nebraska—all key primary states. We've got to either carry them or do very well in them. I've gone to hundreds of small, informal meetings—sometimes eight or nine a day—at which I'll speak for ten minutes, then field questions." By the next month, he had been in Wisconsin eleven full days. He had his best organization there.

What the senator did not tell the reporter was far more significant. He had just been completing one of the most neatly arranged coups in primary caucuses ever engineered in American politics, and he had done it in the traditional Yankee manner: under the cover of superior morality. He had chaired the committee that wrote the new party rules, and his staff grasped their complexities and implications better than anybody.

But even that very day he showed he knew, like any politician, how to exploit an audience. No issue had so scarred the college student as the war in Vietnam, for the student by the very act of being in college is vulnerable to pangs of guilt about other young men dying in his place. He is safe, while the great struggle of his generation rages halfway across the world. In the auditorium of Hunter College, McGovern delicately awakened and exploited that feeling of guilt, that feeling of loss. He spoke of the eighteen thousand young Americans, like themselves, who had died while Nixon was in office and they were in school. "As we meet here, bombs are falling." Images of bursting rosebuds. He spoke of defenseless victims of American power. (*American* power, *their* power, they being privileged, powerful, responsible people who would feel the shame and the responsibility precisely because, despite their disclaimers of powerlessness, the American system belonged to them. Many others in America, not sharing their privilege, decidedly did not feel potent, in charge, responsible.) His voice rose. "To me, that is a moral outrage that should stir the conscience of every American." Moral relief, prolonged applause.

"If I were President," he continued, "my first act would be to terminate the war." Then, in the oldest traditions of American politics, he offered a realistic, concrete boondoggle directly in their self-interest: "And the second would be to declare a general amnesty." There was, once more, long applause.

Thus the Senator made amnesty an electoral issue. He did so while a very disagreeable and unpopular war was still going on, while young men not in college were still being sent to Vietnam and while some 30,000 veterans of Vietnam, without benefit of college education, were looking aimlessly for work. Perhaps some wiser statesman might have argued that there is only one effective way to declare an amnesty: to wait until much later when, outside the din of controversy, by executive order, in connection with some patriotic or religious holiday, such a declaration would be widely hailed as magnanimous. A wise man might have argued that the best way to bring amnesty into discredit would be to make it an electoral issue, subject to all the passions, resentments, recriminations, and frustrations of the worst wartime experience of the nation's history.

Amnesty is an important moral issue. Put correctly, it could help to reconcile the nation; but to raise it in the context of a partisan electoral campaign is twice wrong. Such a tactic invites political polarization on an issue that might carry virtual unanimity if approached in a bipartisan fashion. Second, such a tactic awakes the ancient American lust to make moral issues the cutting edge of politics. It invites one faction to imagine that superior morality inheres in its partisan position. It makes morality a symbol of partisanship rather than of universality.

Students, in this case, crowded around the man who had just made them feel both guilty and superior, while an aide told the reporter with forced political savvy: "After a thing like this, we get about two hundred names of people who want to work for him. That's what counts."

To view McGovern this harshly is, of course, unfair. For on that fatiguing December day, George McGovern also spoke of his experiences as a bomber pilot in World War II. He had flown from an airfield near the Adriatic through some of the heaviest flak of the war. He was then twenty-two. With becoming understatement, he now recalled that most of the men who trained with him and flew with him did not come back. "I made a pledge that if I survived I would devote the rest of my life as best I could to the cause of peace."

Over the years George McGovern had borne the grinding daily work of politics. He had proved he had that practical approach to idealism which impelled him down the long, messy route of politics: no necessary choice for a religious idealist in the Methodist tradition, who had been taught that politics is the realm of compromise and corruption. He did not enter into the intrigues of politics with the sheer delight of hundreds of eager young Irish Catholics in every city of the Northeast. He had to argue his way into such a choice, almost as a penance, almost as a religious mission, the fulfillment of a vow.

Senator McGovern had borne bone-wearying days for almost two full years now, away from his family, in strange places, always with strangers, suffering a traveler's stomach, without a cheering section to goad him on, made light of—almost ignored —by the national press. So, in quite self-mortifying ways he was *dedicated*. With a kind of quiet lambency too, a halo he kept around his presence of something Norman Mailer was later to perceive as tenderness.

Yet presidential politics is a winnowing art. It does require salesmanship—makes a man go public, makes him exploit his convictions, even his tastes, turns him inside out while the public gazes on his soul. It is a quest for power, on which in the end one goes naked and undisguised. Can a decent man seek the job? One's intention, some will argue, makes a difference. If one seeks power not for its own sake, but power for the sake of peace or justice or reform or something noble . . . but that is a dangerous way of thinking. For then the quest begins in purity, proceeds by imagining the horrors of the opposition's evil (otherwise, what is the difference?), and ends in demonology.

Better, no doubt, to look for good and evil everywhere, in everyone. Better to keep a keen eye on where the power is, what the latent and the manifest interests are of every person, every group. Better to track both the moral symbolism and the practical calculations of advantage. Politics is the architectonic art, larger even than ethics, shaping priorities for whole communities and every individual within them, establishing within the state the context for all thinking and doing, encouraging here, inhibiting there, shaping the lives of all—shaping writers, reporters, commentators, parents, police officers, educators, workers. Presidents are, to paraphrase the comment St. Augustine made about bishops, the enemies of the people: *Praelates inimici Ecclesiae.* For they can never be good enough to release all the creativity they might; their every fault limits, imprisons, wounds the psychic climate of the state.

So McGovern was neither more corrupt nor less for his many calculations. What is odd, rather, is the extent to which he and his followers masked their ambitious deeds, no doubt even from themselves. They swathed themselves in the ample flowing gowns of moral purpose, while doing what political instinct drove them to do. The "new politics" is the old politics using new moral symbolism according to the tastes, affectations, and scruples of a new educated class.

To understand the meaning of the American presidency in the 1970s, therefore, it is extremely important to look behind the appearances—more exactly, to look *at* the appearances, seeing what was there all the time—and to grasp precisely the shape and import of the two constitutive networks of every political action: what the act symbolizes and what it effects. The symbolic network McGovern generated at Hunter was one of guilt and redemption. The effective network was a constituency wooed by promise of tangible relief, volunteers signed up, money collected. One network necessarily depends on the other.

Within any given nation, both the symbolic resources and the effectual resources are limited. Not every sort of symbolic appeal moves a constituency. Not every desired effect is attainable. The political leader moves within a straitened world of "hard realities," including the hard realities of available symbolic materials. Politics is "the art of the possible" precisely because not all things *are* possible. Finding the ones that are is the subject of no known science, and will never be. Science considers general laws; in politics, every day brings singular, unlawlike contingencies. Yet cultural traditions do persist. Symbolic patterns that guide perceptions are communicated wordlessly generation after generation. Laws of inertia apply. In an age when the media have commercial reason to stress what is "new," intelligent self-defense requires skepticism about the depth and the reality of "change."

For change itself is a powerful symbol. It is an important symbol for the educated, mobile, affluent, managerial class. This class grows larger year by year in America. Its careers depend on rapid social change. It is the class that executes change, promotes change, and is deliciously aware of the changes to which its own power and influence are hostage. It has given the word "change" a moral connotation of powerful political significance.

To understand the current relations between morality and moralism one must grasp the character of this growing class of voters, the "constituency of change." One must also grasp the symbolic heritage on which it draws.

11

The Constituency
of Conscience

The election of 1896 was in curious ways a precursor of 1972. Against utterly improbable odds, "the prairie populist," William Jennings Bryan, emerged from the Democratic convention in Chicago as the party's nominee. His nomination split the party. Urban bosses and established money men shuttled between the formation of a third party and a contemptuous neutrality. At the Chicago convention, legions of Southerners and Westerners who hated "Wall Street" and "the East" screamed their unsettling enthusiasm. William McKinley, meanwhile, following the cigar-chomping advice of his New York partner, Mark J. Hanna, coolly stayed home in his big house on a shaded corner in Canton, Ohio, letting the voters come to him, counting on the stable citizenry of the big states to bring in his majority.

Bryan, for all his populistic leanings, could not seem to find the language of the factory workers and urban Democrats. Indefatigably, his wife at his side, he gave ten and twelve talks a day, his voice gone at night, exhaustion lining his face, up again the next morning. It was, he said, a campaign of Good against Evil. The choice was between "the interests" and "the people." He wanted to end the "windfall profits" of the speculators. Just before the election, economic conditions began to ease. The vote came in: 7,107,822 for McKinley; 6,511,072 for Bryan.

McKinley spoke for the traditional, stable civil religion; Bryan, for simmering resentment. McKinley loved the staid Protestant pieties; Bryan, evangelical fervor.

But at this point there is a crossover. Bryan expressed the hatred among farmers and miners for those powerful forces that came into their regions, extracted their wealth, and left the outlands mired in poverty; he expressed their hatred for the corporate leaders and financiers, who grew fabulously wealthy and endowed libraries, cathedrals, and universities from whose towers they looked down upon the uncivilized, uncouth men of the interior. Hatred for the Northeast was intense. In 1972, Nixon inherited this side of Bryan's constituents and symbols, while McGovern inherited the other side.

To understand this ironic crossover is to understand how a "new class" arose from the new administrative apparatus of the industrial state, from the new technology given impetus by World War II, from the huge expansion of the universities, from the modern philanthropic foundations, from the national offices of the churches, and from the concentration of the media in the Boston-Washington-New York-Los Angeles metropolis.

David Bazelon has described the emergence of this new class. Richard Hofstadter traces its beginnings in *The Age of Reform*. Michael Harrington and others have extolled it as "the constituency of conscience," the class of voters "of principle" and "reason" and "compassion." That is to say, liable to be Left-liberal.

From the beginning, this class rejected Richard Nixon. After his graduation from law school, Richard Nixon went to New York with two of his classmates seeking positions. Two were accepted, Nixon was not. The third man out went home to Whittier.

When Nixon went to Washington with the Office of Price Administration, he disliked the Eastern attitudes he encountered. When Nixon was the congressional prosecutor of the Hiss case, he was led to resent what he saw of Eastern education, snobbery, class loyalties, and "spinelessness." The Eastern press, he felt, did not treat him fairly. They were savage with "outsiders"; they protected "their own."

The concentration of the media in the Northeast and Hollywood provides for the other regions of America a sense of oppression with which Nixon identifies. Many of the avant-garde ideas and opinions and values pressed upon them and him—by universities, magazines, television, and the cinema—seem pressed upon them by a culture in which they do not share, a kind of superculture, national in scope, permeating major universities and organs of the media and symbolically localized in the Northeast. Everywhere one goes in America, one hears the constant drumming of resentment against the cultural bias of the Northeastern media. It is not now Wall Street that is the symbolic magnet, but the television networks and print commentators (as President Eisenhower dramatized in the convention of 1964). Regional hostility is still a powerful force in American life.

Yet the demarcation between "Northeast" and "the heart of the country" is not geographical; it is based on liberation through education. Ordinary outlanders resent the educated and are amply resented in return. The educated believe *they* are the besieged minority, oppressed by the overwhelming weight of Middle America, struggling to "liberate" here a street, there a playground, here a successful political party.

Thus, two different cultures, each with many variants, have sprung up in our midst, each fed by its resentment of the other. It is not just a matter of years in school—think of Nixon himself —but of attitudes. Fissures go far beyond long hair, bellbottoms, opposition to the war, Charles Reich's three kinds of consciousness. Region, class, ethnicity, religion, and interests of economics and status tangle the skein.

What one group takes to be real, the other takes to be irrelevant. What one group takes to be moral, the other thinks immoral. What one group thinks admirable and exciting, the other holds beneath contempt. What one thinks the heart and marrow of freedom, the other finds an ominous sign of impending totalitarianism. Each fears the other as a destroyer of civilization.

Neither the new class nor Middle America is a solid bloc. Depending on the issues or the persons who catalyze action, most Americans may lean one way or the other. What makes political analysis especially difficult is that key words fall into codes that are understood in several different ways. Ask people if they think the police should "crack down" on criminals and a majority says "yes." Typically conservative, one shrugs. Ask further if they oppose no-knock entry and prior detention and if they support better provenance and other improvements in prison, experiments in the rehabilitation of prisoners, and the like, and a majority still says "yes." Amazingly liberal. Thus, the sloganizing of code words makes opinion polling extremely deceptive. Consider, for example, such code words as "busing," "law and order," "civil rights," "peace," "welfare," "work ethic," "compassion," "hopes as against fears," "moral leadership," "divisiveness." Yet such sloganizing does supply a rough index of who lines up *rhetorically* on which side. Is it more satisfying to you to side with "the silent majority" or with "the constituency of conscience"? A great deal depends on the company you keep. Yet many Americans pride themselves on being outspoken whatever group they're in. In every group it is in vogue for some to be "independent," to believe themselves superior thereby, and to enjoy being rejected, like Socrates. A nation of minor heroes, fighting against odds.

Who belongs to the left wing of the new class? Some artists, engineers, advertising men, social workers, poverty bureaucrats, architects, cameramen, reporters, teachers, librarians, students, young lawyers and doctors and clergymen, pacifists, child-care specialists, computer designers, swinging businessmen, talk-show emcees, foundation officers, editors, opinion samplers, consultants, planners, efficiency technicians, psychiatrists, college-trained union officials, educated housewives, outspoken athletes, about half the movie stars, and a general and admiral or two. Such persons are (supposedly) not easily swayed by the political symbols or political institutions of the past. They are "independent." They are "issue-oriented." They are interested in ideas. They are good at organizing themselves and raising money. They have time for "causes." They have created a demand for "a new politics."

A good share of that class is stocked by liberal Republicans, now trending Democratic. One of the favorite symbols of the new class is "issues." Are they indifferent to symbols? They practically invented charisma and they loved Camelot.

George McGovern's campaign aide, Gordon Weil, thought it of enormous symbolic importance that a huge directory of "McGovern on the Issues" be prepared early in 1972. "It's all there," he said with pride. "We've declared exactly what we're going to do. No secrets. Everything public." To some, such a symbol was exciting and provocative. They didn't read it all or intend to hold McGovern to all of it. It was a symbol.

Senator Edward Kennedy once received more than three hundred letters after his wife Joan attended a White House reception in a see-through blouse, but only eight or ten after serious public hearings before one of his committees. Recounting this contrast, the Senator seemed to be trying to be shocked, trying to believe that issues are—*should be*—important to people. For he is obliged to be more interested in ideas than his brothers were, more idealistic, less frankly cynical. Despite Chappaquiddick and present criticisms of his maturity, he starts with higher status among the new class than John Kennedy had before his election. But surely he knows in his blood that issues have never been important to large numbers of people, that the mail about his wife's dress was typical.

The rational description of a problem and a programmatic solution means more to professionals than to the public. Citizens—including managers and engineers—need most a story to live out, a drama to take part in, villains to oppose, a tradition of heroism and idealism to carry forward.

Presidential politics is necessarily a morality play. As in the theater a tiny detail can be the symbolic pivot of the plot, so in politics even a see-through blouse can focus all the energies of vastly different conceptions of the moral. A telephone call by John Kennedy to Martin Luther King's wife in 1960 was worth a one-foot pile of issue papers.

Still, serious consideration of "the issues" has become a symbolic act in presidential politics. John F. Kennedy established the clipped, precise style of the new pragmatists, rattling off statistics and drawing up swift decision procedures to lay before the people: "My judgment is . . ." or "We'll have to make a determination on that." Kennedy's performance cut through much of the resistance against him; his crisp discussion of "issues" was a sign of a new energy and style. It energized the new supermarket vote.

The era of the four-point program and the eleven-point proposal roared in on a tide of eager young university professionals carrying attaché cases through government buildings. The tide was already running out when George Wallace began to joke that inside each busily carried attaché case was . . . a peanut butter sandwich.

When Adlai Stevenson tried to "talk sense" to the American people, he seemed uncommon, rare, attractive only to "eggheads." But a crisp and intelligent discussion of issues is now required of a presidential candidate. It is one more symbolic performance he must master. Yet if it is the only one he masters he will bore many. For the discussion of issues is only talk. He must show his capacity to dominate events. A candidate does this by choosing actions that draw on every symbolic resource he can awaken in the hearts of the people. Chief among the latter is the people's sense of what is moral. In the past five or six years, the most common national dilemma has been, indeed, what meaning to attach to that word. Nixon has grasped this point—and the struggles over it within several constituencies—far better than his opposition. This is how he first established, symbolically, his right to represent the nation. Painful as it must seem to many moral people, particularly after Watergate, he captured the word "moral" for the culture he represented. The men around him were from the *other* side of the new class— practical, crew-cut, moral in their fashion.

12

That Word "Moral"

Adlai Stevenson showed that a quiet, urbane, intellectual style could hold over 40 percent of the Democratic vote, even in 1952 and 1956, against a great and admirable military hero. But what a relief, after Eisenhower's meandering syntax, to have Kennedy's wit and grasp of fact and terse professionalism. Kennedy gave the educated the mantle of morality and progress and leadership. And jobs. Washington swarmed with bright young lawyers fresh from law school, eager graduate students, confident professors of the social sciences. Many who had never before thought much about government service "got religion," the religion of the new class for almost a decade being politics. Many lives were changed.

Eisenhower had had to fight against the widespread view that "politics is a dirty profession." But after 1960 the table of values tilted and the word "moral" slid to the corner of the young activists, the best and the brightest, the new generation born in this century and eager to get on with "progress." The inactive, silent ones would become moral if they followed their

69

better-educated, enlightened, professionally trained leaders, who knew what was right and had only to solve the technical problems of getting there. Camelot was a time of pure thoughts and high hopes.

At first, the New Frontiersmen went easy on the word "moral." *That* was the kind of word John Foster Dulles was always using. It suggested Richard Nixon's telling the audience of the Great Debates that he disapproved of Harry Truman's language. What constituted the new morality of the New Frontiersmen was their studious avoidance of the word. They were professionals. Experts. Men of technique. Those were days for celebrating the secular city, its rigorous respect for the profane and the pragmatic and the mobile. Farewell to the morality of the rural culture of the past.

Subtly, however, the word "moral" began to creep back into political usage, now no longer in praise of the virtues of the individual, but in praise of social movements.

Bred on egalitarianism, the new class gradually wished to deny that it constituted an élite. It examined its secret thoughts to weed out vestiges of élitism. (Mental hygiene is important to the new class; having one's consciousness "raised," being "informed," winning the accolade "sophisticated" is a high responsibility.) Is there not a law of human societies, all societies even the most intimate, to suggest that élites there will always be? The question is not *whether*, but *what kind?* And every élite embodies a new morality.

Early in 1963, John and Robert Kennedy violated one of their own cardinal political tenets. Concerning a pressing social issue, in the face of a brilliantly led social movement, they modified their vaunted pragmatism, their caution, their habitual demystifying of problems. Tardily but effectively they made the civil rights movement a "moral crusade." What Eisenhower had done for the war in Europe they did for the war against racial discrimination.

In mid-1963, President Kennedy moved beyond pragmatism; race, he declared, "is a moral issue . . . as old as the Scriptures . . . as clear as the Constitution. . . . A great change is at hand, and our task, our obligation, is to make that revolution, that change, peaceful and constructive for all." Robert Kennedy, far more than John, carried this direction forward.

Because America is preeminently a nation struggling to be moral, this sudden shift in the Kennedys' attitude was widely applauded. Guilt was vast. If there *are* moral issues, racism surely qualifies. A war of unconditional surrender was launched on racism—soon to be defined as "white racism." The enemy was defined in terms awakening guilt: racism was seen to be a sin, not only a sin of the private heart but also of institutional structure. First of all, people needed to be made aware that what they had accepted as normal was not normal but sinful. To rid oneself of guilt became the motive force of social change. Examine consciousness for hidden remnants of racism (and, later, sexism). Impure attitudes need not apply.

Thus, Bobby Kennedy passed from being the pragmatist *par excellence,* the hatchet man, the tough-minded Boston Irish kid, the ruthless, dangerous influence at his brother's right hand, to being a leader of the new abolitionists, a hero of the kids of the new class, a voice of political morality in avant-garde America. How personally torn he was in the long months of 1967, between the tough pragmatism of his past and the new moral leadership he was being asked by activist Al Lowenstein to exert! For opposition to the war in Vietnam had become the new moral cause, and Lowenstein was trying to persuade first Kennedy, then McGovern, and finally Eugene McCarthy to oppose Lyndon Johnson in New Hampshire.

The traditional American itch surfaced once again; the issues of 1968 came to be defined in moral terms. Antiwar leaders, especially, drew on moral imperatives.

The new class was the constituency Robert Kennedy had come most to cherish, the constituency not just of Harvard but of "the young." Bobby wanted to lead them, he wanted to be out in front; yet the earlier Bobby, tutored not by the civil religion whose basic forms are Protestant but by the school of Boston Catholic realism, now felt trapped. To challenge the leader of his own party, in the person of the man he himself had vetoed as his brother's vice president, would be to exhibit pushiness, personal ambition, and conniving. The project seemed quixotic. He had been taught that politics is not the place to score moral points but to win and that after one has won, moral deeds are the way to greatness. Each in its time, because life is like that. "What's the point of raising hell," John Kennedy had said, "unless you can win?" The American Catholic civil religion diverges from the dominant Protestant type.

Eugene McCarthy knew that there is a time for the politics of winning, but also a time for the politics of witness. And that several states—New Hampshire, Wisconsin, Oregon, and California—were especially ripe to feel the muscle of the new class. Not as some moralistic crusader, but quietly, in a deliberately understated way—one recalls vividly how disappointed most journalists and academics were with him in January and February of 1968—McCarthy gave the national self-consciousness a new expression. *Substantively,* he avoided evangelism, avoided the passions and certainties of the preacher, and seemed to prefer to complicate rather than to uncomplicate moral discussions. He too was Catholic in his symbols, a different sort of Catholic, his Benedictine College and Minnesota Irish against Kennedy's Boston Irish and University of Virginia. McCarthy disliked the intense moralism of the later Kennedy years; he disliked the harsh pragmatism of the Kennedy underside; and he disliked the Kennedy-style organizers: the lawyer-engineers. As the primaries progressed, reconciliation between the Kennedy troops and the McCarthy troops became impossible. Symbols—important symbols—outweighed pragmatic calculations. The refusal of the Kennedy forces to rally to McCarthy guaranteed the nomination of Humphrey, which neither wanted. So solid is the reality of symbols.

Most of the new class had preferred McCarthy. Bobby had complained that Oregon, which he lost, was one big suburb with none of his kind of people. Supporters of Kennedy were, in moral terms, on the defensive. Even Bobby, in Indiana, having a bowl of spaghetti all alone in a restaurant after midnight, seemed puzzled and forlorn when he saw an old friend with four McCarthy kids. Later, Kennedy probed the kids for several minutes. He wanted to know *why* they preferred McCarthy. It troubled him deeply that they did.

On into 1969, on television and in the press, the word "moral" belonged to the educated young and the active. The very fact of being young seemed to carry a certain moral superiority. It was as though the young must be morally better than the old —otherwise, where is progress? The nation must be drawing closer to the saintliness it ardently desires (the McCarthy theme: "When the Saints Come Marching In"); otherwise, all that faith in Dr. Spock and in years and years of education would seem to be misplaced.

A benign faith in social progress is at the very heart of the American sense of reality. If America does not get better year by year, how can we justify the agonies inflicted on the Indians, the centuries of slavery and injustice, the shame engendered in immigrants, the deaths and injuries inflicted daily upon workers in the mines and mills and factories of the land? So much suffering simply for material gain? The thought is intolerable. It is our national self-understanding that our future will be better than our past, our children better than ourselves.

The sons and daughters of the new class, in ten or twenty of the most prestigious universities, became the style-setters of the late 1960s. They raised serious questions most of their teachers had been neglecting. They prompted a critique of liberalism and precipitated intellectual stirrings whose energies are still alive. Their contributions were many and valuable, their mistakes flamboyant. In public discourse, they captured the word "moral" and brandished it so successfully that all others were placed on the defensive. Television made them seem more numerous than they were, made a fad seem to be a trend, traded outrageously on a speeded-up version of the national mythos. The media decide where reality is, "where it's at." Television, whether under élite control or through commercial laissez-faire, has metaphysical power.

When by a narrow margin he became president in 1969, Nixon had two large symbolic problems: how to neutralize the one remaining Northeastern establishment implacably hostile to himself—the media—and how to recapture the word "moral" for his own constituency. He temporarily solved both problems with one speech. On television.

13

Vietnam: More Moral Than Thou?

"The best and the brightest" got us into the war in Vietnam, says David Halberstam. The Northern liberal orthodoxy, writes Professor William Appleman Williams, was pounded into "Ol' Lyndon's" brain, taught him by his betters, and *that's* why "Ol' Lyndon" did what he did in Vietnam.

If the intellectual left wing of the Democratic party contributed to getting us *into* the war—the best and the brightest of them—and later they thought it was all a mistake, is there some chance that their later passion for immediate withdrawal was also a mistake? Many citizens did not trust the judgment of educated élites.

The question gains in poignancy if you were among those who were puzzled by conflicting reports out of Indochina from 1962 to 1965 and hurried out to buy David Halberstam's book-length report *The Making of a Quagmire*. China, much more mysterious to us then, was predicting a tide of wars of liberation around the world. Halberstam gave advice which many must have made the basis of their own judgment at the time:

What about withdrawal? Few Americans who have served in Vietnam can stomach this idea. It means that those Vietnamese who committed themselves fully to the United States will suffer the most under a Communist government, while we lucky few with blue passports withdraw unharmed; it means a drab, lifeless and controlled society for a people who deserve better. Withdrawal also means that the United States' prestige will be lowered throughout the world, and it means that the pressure of communism on the rest of Southeast Asia will intensify. Lastly, withdrawal means that throughout the world the enemies of the West will be encouraged to try insurgencies like the one in Vietnam. Just as our commitment in Korea in 1950 had served to discourage overt Communism border crossings ever since, an anti-Communist victory in Vietnam would serve to discourage so-called wars of liberation.

It was, apparently, reasonable to hold this view in 1965—wrong, perhaps, but not irrational or evil. By the time Nixon took office in early 1969, many including Halberstam had changed their minds. Because the price had become too steep? Because new information had emerged? Because the *way* the United States sought its ends—the *means* it employed—were cruelly disproportionate? (This last represents my own view.) But some Americans had *not* changed their minds. In their view, getting a girl pregnant is bad enough; abandoning her is no improvement. The responsible and courageous path was to see the commitment through—give South Vietnam a chance to remain independent of North Vietnam. The "two Vietnams," as even Bernard Fall called them. It is one thing to disagree with the Johnson-Nixon point of view; it is another to call it—and not only polemically, but righteously—immoral.

During 1968 and 1969, the momentum of morality belonged to those who wanted an end to the war. "Hawks" seemed embarrassed. On October 15, 1969, huge antiwar rallies were held all around the nation. Another moratorium was planned for November 15, and then for every month thereafter. Those who had cornered President Johnson now picked up Nixon's scent. Mr. Nixon's immunity on the issue of the war had been expended.

On television, Mr. Nixon is often heavy in his moralism, obvious in his denials of any and every conceivable wrongdoing, eager to seem moral, just, wise, and strong. The medium flatters some personalities (Eugene McCarthy, John Kennedy) and penalizes others (Mike Mansfield, Hubert Humphrey). Nixon's small, analytical, active eyes do not reflect the repose and almost lazy self-contentment that television makes attractive. His controlled movements do not reflect ease, warmth, relaxation. In the magnified intimacy of the tube, we encounter a most unintimate man, a loner, introspective. Watching him on television, from however neutral and dispassionate a perspective, is not a calming, soothing, pleasurable experience. One's stomach begins to move in response to his nervousness, one feels his efforts at control, one is fascinated by the prospect of sudden breakdown and eruption. In the background, as it were, is the music of gathering tension. Even when the President sits calmly in a dark blue suit, before a blue backdrop carrying the presidential seal, the private emotional conflicts behind his self-control generate nervousness in one's own stomach.

On the night of November 3, 1969, in advance of the second moratorium, Mr. Nixon at long last took before the people his own understanding of what was at stake in Vietnam. He did not blanch at the high level of technological destruction required to carry out the policies he enunciated; he did not talk about that at all. (It is one thing for a nation to carry on a war of high terror fully aware of the awful moral costs. It is another to keep reality at a distance, out of sight and out of mind, to congratulate oneself on moral purposes, without regard to the brutal means employed.)

In 1968, according to Gallup, over 60 percent of the public had come to believe that the war was a mistake and should be ended. Nixon had said during the campaign that he had a plan to end the war. It would have been relatively easy for him, both as a new president and as a man with impeccable anti-Communist credentials, to end the war on almost any terms; he could not credibly be accused of "appeasement." Nixon the pragmatist, Nixon the poll-watcher, Nixon the expedient, one would think, had every reason to emulate Eisenhower's achieve-

ment in swiftly ending the Korean war. Nixon surprised a great
many cynics by showing that he was not the man they thought,
but a man of ideology, a man of rigid principle, a man of considerable political courage. He released to the press a letter from
Ho Chi Minh, in which Ho outlined the "correct" solution in
Vietnam: not a compromise solution, guaranteeing independence
to South Vietnam, but in effect a concession of American defeat.
Many in America might have accepted. Not Nixon.

Speaking slowly and with great clarity, so that even a fourteen-
year-old could understand (the level at which for many years
Hollywood films were carefully aimed, a level that so irritates
the more highly educated) Nixon showed he grasped plainly
what was being asked of him:

> There were some who urged that I end the war at once by
> ordering the immediate withdrawal of all American forces.
> From a political standpoint, this would have been a popular
> and easy course to follow. After all, we became involved in
> the war while my predecessor was in office.
> I could blame the defeat, which would be the result of my
> action, on him—and come out as the peacemaker.

Nixon then rehearsed the official view of why we were in
Vietnam in the first place. We were invited in to help halt a
revolution supported from outside South Vietnam. (Nothing
here about the failed elections of 1956 or the explicitly tempor-
ary division into North and South. Nixon assumes, rather, that
many in South Vietnam *want* independence from North Vietnam. He assumes too that North Vietnam cherishes historical
dreams of dominating all of Indo-china.) He then faced the
question in which he must make a decision: "Now that we are
in the war, what is the best way to end it?"

In world politics, what men intend to happen seldom happens
as they intended it; often, the reverse. Actually, then, in moments of decision one is swayed more by what one feels about
the past, more by one's own psychic nature, more by what feels
comfortable and sound, than by clear knowledge of the future.
How, one might ask, will my choice stand up in history books?
What is the American thing to do, in line with America's past?

Here one's own grasp of the national self-understanding weighs most heavily. What are the underlying structures of the American people at their best, not their mood of the moment but their continuing best judgment of themselves? You do not find the answers to these questions in recent polls, but in the permanent structure of the people's character: institutionalized and habitual and not likely rapidly to change. Nixon discerned the following four characteristics.

First, Americans do not think of themselves as great soldiers or conquerors or first-rate militarists; there is no civic pride in war-making here, as in Sparta or Germany or even in the British Imperial Service. Americans *need* to think of themselves as instruments of peace. The national psyche does not want a "war department." The national psyche does not covet the symbolism of wars of expansion, wars for territory, wars of domination or colonialization. This national self-understanding may be flatly inaccurate—we may be more militarist than we dare face—but it remains a powerful symbolic reality. Its moral power, indeed, has been indispensable to the peace movement. Peace is in tune with the national self-understanding. The moral weight of popular sentiment was slowly—yet with remarkable ease—shifted to the side of peace.

Nixon wanted the national self-understanding on *his* side. So *he* made *his* cause the cause of peace, too.

> Let us all understand that the question before us is not whether some Americans are for peace and some Americans are against peace. The question at issue is not whether Johnson's war becomes Nixon's war. The great question is: How can we win America's peace?

Second, Nixon discerned, the United States is a nation of "manifest destiny." The shots fired at Lexington were "heard round the world." The personal freedom shared by citizens in the United States is still a model for the rest of the world. Not only that, so great a gift demands that we help others attain it. Freedom is indivisible. No one is free while others are slaves. (The Left as well as the Right draws nourishment from this self-understanding. Sympathy for the revolutionary forces of the

Third World moves some; sympathy for governments opposed to Communism moves others. The national mission is the same.) It is not very American to promote decadence and indifference. Our activists try to *spread* "liberation." They say we must not act as an arrogant, powerful nation. (Why not? What would be more typical of a wealthy, powerful nation? It would not be moral.) Thus, President Nixon too relies on an image of American moral destiny:

> For the United States, this first defeat in our nation's history would result in a collapse of confidence in American leadership not only in Asia but throughout the world. . . .
> In my opinion, for us to withdraw from that effort would mean a collapse not only of South Vietnam but Southeast Asia. So we're going to stay there.

The United States has never suffered defeat in war. It is important to some that God has been ever with us, that right has always triumphed. If the United States is capable of deliberate moral wrong-doing—"Three American presidents have recognized the great stakes involved in Vietnam and understood what needed to be done"—then all reason for self-confidence is gone. How, in the future, could we claim to be the leader of nations? How could we look others straight in the eye, confident in our own high moral standards? Our bluff would have been called. In the future, no one would worry about our verbal threats. We would have less moral weight, would have to rely on naked force. Even if we came with armies, they would know we lacked perseverance. We would never be able to trust ourselves, to trust our own determination. We would fall into the habit of losing, giving in as soon as costs mount. We'd be quitters. If we lose respect for ourselves, nine-tenths of our power in the world is gone. For our power is mainly moral and symbolic. That is what we cannot squander.

Of course, there are many rebuttals to this way of understanding America. Our purpose now, however, is not to criticize but to uncover Nixon's understanding of the structure of our national psyche, which follows nicely his understanding of his own psyche. In significant ways, he and the nation are in tune. Professor Mazlish writes:

> Nixon's basic vision of himself is as a high-principled, fair-minded man (of greatness), who is constantly being unfairly attacked and smeared by his opponents (mainly communists and crooks), and who is his own severest critic. Much of this self-image, we must admit, corresponds to the image of self-righteousness projected by America as a whole; this correspondence is undoubtedly a part of Nixon's political success.

The third feature of the national self-understanding perceived by Nixon is the nation's impatience. About this flaw, it is permissible to be critical. It is a fault about which Americans enjoy blaming themselves, as one might blame oneself for being too attractive to the other sex.

> We Americans are a do-it-yourself people—we're an impatient people. Instead of teaching someone else to do a job, we like to do it ourselves. And this trait has been carried over into our foreign policy.

Nixon, of course, intends to counter this impatience.

The fourth feature of the national self-understanding is a defense-mechanism against many of the soft and idealistic qualities we attribute to ourselves: Americans should bargain only from strength. Yankee traders are known the world over for their special approach to bargaining. With clear, honest eyes, they put the most moral possible glow over anything they do—but they drive a flinty, cold bargain. It is as though the candor on which they pride themselves is a weakness, and they fear being taken advantage of; so they calculate opposing strengths close to the vest. A nation of river gamblers, tutored by poker as the Russians are by chess or the English by cricket:

> I have not, and do not, intend to announce the timetable for our program, and there are obvious reasons for this decision which I'm sure you will understand. As I've indicated on several occasions, the rate of withdrawal will depend on developments. . . .

An announcement of a fixed timetable for our withdrawal would completely remove any incentive for the enemy to negotiate an agreement. They would simply wait until our forces had withdrawn and then move in. . . .

Along with this optimistic estimate, I must in all candor leave one note of caution. If the level of enemy activity significantly increases, we might have to adjust our timetable accordingly. . . .

If the level of infiltration or our casualties increase while we are trying to scale down the fighting, it will be the result of a conscious decision by the enemy. Hanoi could make no greater mistake that to assume that an increase in violence will be to its advantage. . . .

The President speaks confidently of "obvious reasons . . . which I'm sure you will understand." He knows the structure of traditional American experience. The perfidy and treachery of other peoples, by contrast with the candor of Anglo-Saxons, is a pervading theme of our national life. He looks straight into the camera and calmly speaks of our "candor" and desire to be "completely clear." He says it as a matter of fact: "If I conclude that increased enemy action jeopardizes our remaining forces in Vietnam, I shall not hesitate to take strong and effective measures to deal with that situation." Just at that point he is at his calmest: "This is not a threat. This is a statement of policy. . . ." In the American character there is a traditional and profound ambivalence about blackmail. We prefer to call it by other names— candor, frank discussion—and because this tradition is so deep we count on one another to "understand." No use being vulgar about it. Intelligent people know force when they see it. All very neat. Classically American. The understatement of Marlon Brando, Humphrey Bogart, John Wayne, Gary Cooper. Talk quietly, carry a big stick.

Nixon is so certain that he has the American tradition on his side that he now moves in for the closing kill. He wants to show in a few last paragraphs that *he* is at the very center of the national self-understanding, at the heart of truth and morality as the American tradition presents them, and that his opposition falsely uses the banners of morality for something outside American experience and values. By all signs, a majority wants the war over with soon—period. And the majority is growing, in the government, among businessmen, housewives, doctors, lawyers. Within three months over 70 percent of the construction workers in New York will declare themselves in favor of total withdrawal by December 1970. But Nixon is penetrating to something deeper than the issue of the war, to the people's inherited conception of America and the presidency. He is sure that on this point he has a great majority with him. If he can stand as the symbol of what that majority feels and believes, he can swing them—against their own private opinions—on the war too. It will be a powerful speech indeed if he can reclaim the American tradition of morality so that it supports his war policy. Such is the power of a president to call into being what doesn't actually exist, "a silent majority" in favor of continuing the war. His conclusion is in this respect, brilliant, however sickening it seems to those whose sense of America is different.

"My fellow Americans," he begins with serenity, "I am sure you can recognize from what I have said that we really only have two choices open to us if we want to end this war." He *knows* a majority wants to end it. He doesn't fight them, he joins them. "I can order an immediate precipitous [sic] withdrawal of all Americans from Vietnam without regard to the effects of that action." The typical American impatience. "Or"— and here he mentions the twin option—"a negotiated settlement, if possible" or "our plan for Vietnamization, if necessary."

> I have chosen this second course. It is not the easy way, it is the right way. It is a plan which will end the war and serve the cause of peace, not just in Vietnam but in the Pacific and the world.
>
> In speaking of the consequences of a precipitous withdrawal, I mentioned that our allies would lose confidence in America. Far more dangerous, we would lose confidence in ourselves. Oh, the immediate reaction would be a sense of relief that our men were coming home. But as we saw the consequences of what we had done, inevitable remorse and divisive recrimination would scar our spirit as a people.

Nixon was recalling here, perhaps, the recriminations after the "fall" of China or after Yalta. The costs of the war to families that lost sons, to a military that had been humiliated, and to an immature nation like our own could not be far from the mind of one whose own career had dealt in powerful resentments which he did not invent. That there is meanness and vengeance in the people—"ain't no hate like Christian hate"— he well knew.

> We have faced other crises in our history and we have become stronger by rejecting the easy way out and taking the right way in meeting our challenges. Our greatness as a nation has been our capacity to do what has to be done when we knew our course was right. . . .
> For almost 200 years, the policy of this nation has been under [sic] our Constitution by those leaders in the Congress and the White House elected by all the people.
> If a vocal minority, however fervent its cause, prevails over reason and the will of the majority, this nation has no future as a free society. . . .
> I respect your idealism, I share your concern for peace. I want peace as much as you do. There are powerful personal reasons I want to end this war. This week I will have to sign eighty-three letters to mothers, fathers, wives and loved ones of men who have given their lives for America in Vietnam. . . .
> I have chosen a plan for peace. I believe it will succeed. . . . if it does succeed, what the critics say now won't matter. If it does not succeed, anything I say then won't matter.
> I know it may not be fashionable to speak of patriotism or national destiny these days, but I feel it is appropriate to do so on this occasion.
> Two hundred years ago this nation was weak and poor. But even then, America was the hope of millions in the world.
> Today we have become the strongest and richest nation in the world, and the wheel of destiny has turned so that any hope the world has for the survival of peace and freedom will be determined by whether the American people have the

moral stamina and the courage to meet the challenge of free-
world leadership.
Let historians not record that, when America was the
most powerful nation in the world, we passed on the other
side of the road and allowed the last hopes for peace and
freedom of millions of people to be suffocated by the forces
of totalitarianism.

"Stamina," "courage"—words of the frontier. We were weak
and we were poor. How many millions still remember! The
Depression turns round and round in millions of memories. Today, now that we are rich, will we forget others? Minds of
Poles, Czechs, Lithuanians, and others flash to cousins never
met, nieces and nephews and brothers- and-sisters-in-law. The
grand drama of the forces of individualism confronting vast
forces of collectivism still moves imaginations. Not a literal
drama; history is too complicated for that—people know about
dictatorships in the "free" world; for goodness sake, they know
that Daley "stole" Illinois for Kennedy; they are not purists.
And the memory of Kitty Genovese in New York is vivid too,
stabbed again and again, crying out in the night while many,
inside and warm, allowed her last hopes to be suffocated by the
night. The Nixon conclusion, "the forces of totalitarianism," is
too heavy. Momentarily it recalls the ideologue of former years,
Tricky Dick. He has almost let credibility slip away.
   In the very next phrase, he recovers. He conveys to millions
a sense of importance, moral diginity, and high purpose—a cama-
raderie too in silence. Not boisterous, not pushy, but civil and
decent and trustworthy. He does not command, he asks. The
symbol of the presidency is made central. He is the people.
What happens to him happens to them.

> So tonight, to you, the great silent majority of my fellow
> Americans, I ask for your support. I pledged in my campaign
> for the Presidency to end the war in a way that we could win
> the peace.
>   I have initiated a plan of action which will enable me to
> keep that pledge. The more support I can have from the
> American people, the sooner that pledge can be redeemed.

For the more divided we are at home, the less likely the
enemy is to negotiate in Paris.
 Let us be united for peace. Let us also be united against
defeat. Because let us understand: North Vietnam cannot
defeat or humiliate the United States. Only Americans can do
that.

We remain invincible because our cause is right. We can fail
our cause. Our cause will never fail us. The ending will be profoundly religious—not Christian, not Jewish, but civil, secular,
American. Saints, traditions, institutions, doctrines, relics will be
evoked. A holy history is, in hushed tones, called to mind. Not
Nixon's personal idiosyncrasies, not his political necessities—
nothing less than the entire American pilgrimage in search of
just and lasting peace is involved. In accordance with psychic
structures already embodied in the people Nixon addresses, he
serves only what is already sacred to them.

Fifty years ago in this room, and at this very desk, President Woodrow Wilson spoke words which caught the imagination of a war-weary world. He said: "This is the war to
end wars." His dream for peace after World War I was
shattered on the hard reality of great power politics. And
Woodrow Wilson died a broken man.
 Tonight, I do not tell you that the war in Vietnam is the
war to end wars, but I do say this:
 I have initiated a plan which will end this war in a way
that will bring us closer to that great goal to which Woodrow Wilson and every American President in our history
has been dedicated—the goal of a just and lasting peace.
 As President I hold the responsibility for choosing the
best path for that goal and then leading the nation along it.
 I pledge to you tonight that I shall meet this responsibility
with all of the strength and wisdom I can command in accordance with your hopes, mindful of your concerns, sustained by your prayers.

That night and the next day, the White House lines crackled
with calls and wires. There was no "silent majority" out there,
but there was a repressed and hungry minority, famished for
public moral approbation. Their civil religion was now properly

reestablished. White House aide Patrick Buchanan, in his book *The New Majority,* cited this speech as the critical turning point of Nixon's first administration; others formed the same judgment as they listened. Nixon had made the central symbol of our nation—"moral"—his.

The November moratorium was more frantic but less successful than the October one. Nixon had cut the heart out of the idea. For it was predicated on the growing respectability of protest, bringing in ever-new constituencies that had not before been seen in demonstrations. The President established the idea that those who do not demonstrate are on his side, a "silent majority." He made new recruits for further demonstrations carry burdensome symbols around their necks: not only would they be expressing a moral protest against the war, now they would also be expressing their unwillingness to support the President, they would be branded as a minority, and they would be linked to the young war protesters of the last four years. Over 60 percent of the people might be against war. But asked to rank groups on a scale, 33 percent of the people gave "war protesters" the strongest negative rating available. Even 56 percent of those opposed to the war gave "war protesters" a negative rating. The protesters were perceived as outside the national self-understanding. Even if you strongly opposed the war, you now also had to choose between standing with the President or standing with *them.* With such negative emotions running high, many antiwar citizens preferred not to associate with war-protesters.

The moratorium movement fizzled out by December. Its leaders closed down their offices two months later, just in time to assure Nixon no organized opposition when suddenly, after two private screenings of the movie *Patton,* in April of 1970, he ordered the startling invasion of Cambodia. The almost total success of his speech of November 3 had lulled him into believing the antiwar movement dead. Effectively cut off from its base in the civil religion, wilted, it was splashed into new life by his arrogant invasion of a neutral nation. This time *he* had stepped out of bounds. RE-ELECT LBJ, the bumper stickers said. HE KEPT US OUT OF CAMBODIA.

14

The Rise and Fall of Liberal Moralism

In his second term, Nixon's ability to capture the language of morality for his own purposes gave him symbolic potency far more extensive than he gained by mere deals or manipulations. It is a fundamental law of American politics that whoever speaks with the power of morality on his side gains enormous practical power and puts his opponents—even if more numerous, wealthier, and better placed—on the defensive. Characteristically in his career, Nixon has represented a minority of Americans. His ability to attract votes on a national scale hovered at about 42 percent as reflected in the comparative polls between him and Muskie in 1971. He set out to establish himself as a majority president—indeed, as the architect of "a new majority" that would last for the duration of this century—by capturing the symbols of morality proper to one after another of the nation's "worlds." The United States, Walt Whitman said, is "a teeming nation of nations." Nixon set out to identify himself with a majority of them. One of his targets was urban Catholic working men and women.

The Catholic experience in America is not the same as the Protestant or Jewish experience. Catholics have been especially eager to show how adaptable they are to America. Traditional American symbols have a certain power over the consciousness of many Catholic working people, not just the lower-income groups, but many too in the modest suburbs of Queens and the new suburbs of Chicago's northwest side. Before trying to uncover the various national self-understandings operative in the Catholic population, it is useful to be clear about two main currents within American moralism.

There is a traditional moralism in America. There is also a relatively new variant. The two are intimately related in a way that made it possible for Nixon to oppose the form that seemed most anti-Catholic and to identify with the form that seemed most benign and comfortable. He did so not by promises, but by letting the new variant collapse of its own miscalculations.

The traditional moralism holds that the United States is a uniquely good nation. "I know America," President Nixon said in 1970, "and the American heart is good." The new moralism holds that the United States is an immoral nation, racist, militarist, and counterrevolutionary. According to the traditional moralism, it is wrong to "bad-mouth" America. According to the recent variant, it is wrong to be "coopted" by her. The first preaches "patriotism"; the second preaches "resistance" and "revolution."

Even to draw the contrast in this way seems like an exercise in nostalgia, a reprise of the language of the 1960s. The power realities on which the rhetoric was based were poorly grasped.

The key constituency in the Democratic party is composed of working men and women, particularly urban Catholics and Jews in neighborhoods like those of Queens, the Bronx, Chicago's south side, Milwaukee, Parma (Ohio), Warren (Michigan), and South Philadelphia; but it is also composed of coalitions of farmers and workers in states such as Minnesota. These constituencies are the key to American politics not only because of their number, but also because in economic matters they are more liberal than the population as a whole, yet conservative on matters relating to family and neighborhood.

This constituency usually votes Democratic, but it sometimes votes Republican. The Democrats have tried to hold these groups since 1932 by getting them to vote "their pocketbooks." The Democratic party has claimed to be *their* party. But, on the other hand, in national and statewide elections since at least 1952, such voters have proved remarkably independent. With discrimination, they have given a good share of their support from time to time to Republican presidents (Eisenhower and Nixon), senators (Scott, Percy, Javits, Saxbe, Taft), and governors (Rockefeller, Romney). The words "independent voter" often suggest the image of college-educated, affluent, enlightened persons. But if we mean by "independent" those voters who over the past twenty years have voted now Republican, now Democratic, many working people are independent voters, especially in presidential elections.

Traditionally in politics, Catholic voters have been on the "wrong side" of moralism. The abolitionists of the Civil War period happened to have too many links to anti-Catholic movements to win the trust of Catholics; too many sons of Catholic working men took the places in the draft vacated by the sons of rich men who could pay to send a substitute. Campaigns to "reform" city machines and to end "corruption" in city government have for generations borne an anti-Catholic, anti-immigrant edge. The American Protective Association before World War I unleashed an army of "loyal Americans" who filed three million complaints about "un-American activities." The battle to maintain "pure Americanism" ended in 1924 with restrictive legislation against Catholic and Jewish immigration. Then came Prohibition. In short, the words "reform" and "morality" in American politics have, to the Catholic ear, a decidedly dangerous ring. The following reaction is typical: "The minute I hear 'reform' or 'morality,' I know someone's out to get me, even if I don't see how. I'm going to have to pay for it." "Reform" and "morality" are uncomfortably close to being traditional code words for "anti-Catholic."

From the perspective of the pipefitter in Pittsburgh or the telephone linesman in Queens (and perhaps of lower-class Wasps as well), the new moralism of the Left echoes the old moralism of the Right. The distance from John V. Lindsay, silk-stocking reform Republican, Mr. Morality, to John V. Lindsay, liberal Democrat, is no distance at all. The old moralism had two sources: élite Republicanism of great wealth and fulsome moral statement and smalltown Republicanism of Protestant patriotic superiority. The new moralism seems to attract the old Republican élite and to make common cause with the liberal universalists of the airwaves and the universities: not just a few "eggheads" (1950s) but millions on millions of "long-hairs" supported by the "knowledge industry." Under either moralism, working men and women are the traditional targets at whom the preaching fingers jab: "You pigs are the ones to be reformed. You're the problem."

The constituency of conscience inherited a symbolic tradition anti-working people and anti-Catholic in tone. Orthodox Jews, like orthodox Catholics, have also felt insistent pressure from the liberalizers. Perhaps the tone was antiorthodox, rather than specifically anti-Catholic; the educated tend to like romantic rebels but not those who remain loyal and faithful and unbending. People are free to be different but not *that* different.

John Kennedy had given millions of working people confidence that at last *they* were symbolically represented. In this trust, they followed his and later Lyndon Johnson's leadership on the most sweeping government-sponsored social reforms on behalf of blacks and the poor in the nation's history. It was important that the symbols of the "war on poverty" were Catholic —Michael Harrington wrote *The Other America* under the stimulus of the Catholic worker movement, and Sargent Shriver regularly announced its programs in a distinctively Catholic idiom. Priests, nuns, laymen, and Catholic college students were swept by enthusiasm for building and celebrating a new "secular city." It was a time to move out from intramural Catholic concerns and fulfill one's yearnings for peace, justice, and "the reconstruction of the social order" (Leo XIII) in the "modern world" (the Vatican Council's "Schema XIII"). The sudden, brilliant symbolic confluence of "the two Johns"—John XXIII and John Kennedy—exploded Catholic awareness and Catholic energy into every sector of social and political life. Consider Mario Savio and Tom Hayden, Michael Harrington and John Cogley, Robert Kennedy and Eugene McCarthy, Wilfred Sheed and Sissy Farenthold, Daniel Berrigan and Garry Wills; the 1960s were a time of unparalleled Catholic influence in American politics and culture.

Yet the larger movement of Catholics toward the Left was predicated on the trust which ordinary working people placed in John Kennedy and his brother Robert. (Edward Kennedy does not seem to share the same trust. The crowd enthusiasm he evoked in 1972 might have been in honor of memories, in contrast to George McGovern, or for other reasons; it might or might not have been a pledge of future political support.) John Kennedy and Robert Kennedy conveyed a sense of realism, toughness, and reliability. With them, working people felt a bond of identity. Their large families, their sufferings, their setbacks, their political entanglements and compromises made John and Robert Kennedy seem true to life. The more some of the Left called Robert Kennedy "ruthless," the more trustworthy he seemed to the workers of Gary, black and white. In this often absurd and bitter world, working men and women can trust men who have known loss, failure, and heavy opposition and yet who remain, no less, winners. (For fighting back from his own losses, failures, and heavy opposition, Nixon also has won respect.)

When John Kennedy ran for office in 1960, one key group of Democrats slow to support him was the intellectual Left. *The New Republic,* not long before election day, carried an article entitled "Tweedle-dum or Tweedle-dee." In 1968 in many circles, those who supported Robert Kennedy were treated as "unclean" by the affluent, educated supporters of Eugene McCarthy. Yet, once in power, John Kennedy won the hearts of the intellectual Left all too easily. The Kennedys became the chief political spokesmen for the intellectual Left. Only after Robert Kennedy turned down the race against Johnson in 1968 did George McGovern and Eugene McCarthy feel free to seize leadership on the Left.

By 1972, Edward Kennedy had come to seem more the candidate of the Left than the candidate of working people. He was

not so thoroughly identified with the new class as George Mc-
Govern had become. But he was no longer as solidly trusted by
working people as his brothers had been. The political symbols
with which he surrounded himself, his language and his moral
tone, were no longer those of this brothers. He is ensnared in an
idealized image of his brothers. Whereas in the flesh, they were
tough Boston politicians who also happened to have ideals and
visions, in legend, the moral language had come to dominate.
Edward Kennedy found himself laden with moralistic sentiments
and poses, against which Chappaquiddick is in uncomfortable
contrast. His presence still has electric power; working people
do not hold Chappaquiddick against him as harshly as the more
educated do. Working people are at once more cynical and
more forgiving. But they do dislike the moralism of the Left.

For the programs of the 1960s often seemed to working
people to be exclusively aimed at benefits for *some* among them
—for the minorities of race, black, brown, or red—at the expense
of others. Often the programs were not themselves divisive; but
the language and the symbols through which they were articu-
lated seemed to be so. Thus, "open admissions," which in reality
gave new opportunities to the sons and daughters of Poles, Italians, and others, often had the public *appearance* of being established solely for blacks. Such symbols were unnecessarily divisive. And the Kennedys are properly made to bear some of
the blame for the moralism of the 1960s.

Issues in the 1970s are no longer where they were in the
1960s. Powers and interests are different. Grievances and hurts
occur at new places. Above all, the high moral language of the
1960s—civil rights as a *moral* issue, Vietnam as a *moral* issue,
amnesty as a *moral* issue—suffered the fate of all moral language
in politics. Moral language was converted to the political uses
of some constituencies. It was reduced to being one political tool
among others. To many, it seems to have become merely a
hypocritical mask for partisan politics. Moralists in politics—according to ancient and penetrating wisdom—are not to be trusted.

15

Beyond Niebuhr:
Symbolic Realism

In 1972, Nixon capitalized on McGovern's poor handling of the symbols of morality. At the height of his power Nixon did not place the language of morality and politics on a stable basis. The President's language about morality remained sectarian and regional. Even among some who were sympathetic to his politics, it was not convincing. Billy Graham is a popular man; but he does not symbolize the moral views of all Americans.

Second, Nixon's past record, emphasized by his enemies and boasted of by his friends, exhibited classic American pragmatism. Nixon has always been, to those who establish the national moral tone, an outsider. He has never been trusted. Such moral stature as he attained prior to the Watergate scandals depended more on the discrediting of the morality of the Democratic Left than on his own image of integrity. He was extraordinarily vulnerable to the whiff of scandal.

Third, and most important of all, Nixon has not fashioned a set of moral symbols capable of advancing the nation's self-understanding. He rests his moral claims on symbols inherited from the past—American power, responsibility for freedom around the world, hard work, patriotism, good citizenship. Meanwhile, great energies seethe. Many long to break free from these traditional symbols, to expand the American self-understanding. Enormous political power awaits the man who gives shape to gathering cultural energies.

The key symbol is morality. Which party can best convey a moral cutting edge? Which represents superior morality? American energies always seek this symbol.

Among Americans of this century, Reinhold Niebuhr (1892–1971) was perhaps the greatest moral teacher. In *Moral Man and Immoral Society, The Children of Light and the Children of Darkness,* and *The Irony of American History,* he established a vocabulary for criticizing the innocence, pretension, and moral arrogance that have marred American life in every generation. Niebuhr opposed moralism wherever he found it, and he found it not only on the Right, among such preachers as Carl MacIntyre and Billy Graham, but also on the Left, among those religious and secular liberals who put their trust in reason, progress, and the perfectability of man. In both camps, Niebuhr noticed, moral claims mask class interests. In both camps, the role of power and violence in human affairs is overlooked and the intractability of social interests is wished away. Political affairs, he thought, are more irrational than a rational people easily admits, more two-sided than moralists care to emphasize, more "ironic" than the innocent suspect.

One of Niebuhr's most penetrating axioms is that the morality governing conduct between individuals is quite different from the morality governing social groups. The individual as an individual and the individual as a member of a social group fall under two different (although related) moralities. In neither the individual nor the social sphere is it enough to *claim* to be moral. In both spheres, that claim will be measured by others more harshly than by the self, and ultimately it will be measured by an undeceivable God. It will be measured by the quality and intent of one's actions, by their appropriateness in the circumstances, by what interests they represent and which powers they strengthen, and by their consequences.

In the individual sphere, it is exceedingly difficult for one human being to pass judgment on another with full certainty that his judgment is accurate, fully perceptive, and complete. In the social sphere, this difficulty is multiplied many times. Not even sociologists claim to have mastered the general forms of social processes. The moment-to-moment and unrepeatable shapes of social processes in conflict are virtually impenetrable. Our ignorance about the effects of particular social interventions is vast.

Social groups necessarily act in large, symbolic and relatively gross ways. Every law that is passed fails to provide for countless possible contingencies; laws that seem well conceived can, in practice, cause unforeseen harm. Every speech a political figure gives is subject to unpredictable magnifications. Every social program mobilizes some resources, but also sets in motion unpredictable counterreactions.

In politics, calculation is not aimed at scientific precision. It is quite a gain if one minimizes possible sources of damage, for there are an infinite variety of ways things can go wrong. Only by getting every factor right (often by inspired combinations of guesswork, serendipity, and ignorance) can a project succeed. Complete success seldom occurs. If it should, alertness is more than ever called for, because success inspires rivals to mask their countermoves. Niebuhr, therefore, stressed the "ambiguity," "irony," and "irrationality" of politics.

In trying to reach a moral judgment about political actions, it is a useful maxim to listen with special attentiveness to the judgments of one's political enemies. "In my truth," Niebuhr used to say, "is bound to be some error; in his error, some truth." Since hostility blinds, the area of our greatest blindness is likely to lie somewhere in the area of our opponent's strength. We can safely assume that our opponent is more accurate in his perception than we would like to admit.

Niebuhr's thought can be carried forward in several important respects. In setting up an opposition between the rational and the irrational, Niebuhr obscured something important: our most rational decisions include many elements that are really non-rational; therefore, attention to nonrational factors can be highly intelligent. Assume for the moment that classical philosophic debates (between the rational and the irrational, the cognitive and the emotive, the normative and the descriptive) recur because *both* sides of each couplet are always present. Then the issue becomes, Are there better tools for cutting into reality? The use of words such as "symbol," "national self-understanding," and "sense of reality" is an attempt to find glimmers of illumination and reason in the nonrational.

Let us, for example, attend carefully to what happens in our *imaginations*. Each of us works within our own imaginal world. This imaginal world is in part socially derived. The deepest feelings in the pit of our stomach; our sense for which arguments are relevant and which bits of evidence are weighty; our image of the setting of an action, the actors, and the plot; our instinctive feelings for what is good and what is evil; our guiding model of human fulfillment or human alienation—these we did not invent in psychic isolation all by ourselves. Our family, our native region, our present social location, our intellectual and symbolic traditions—such social factors have shaped the construction we place upon (or "discover" in) reality. In a pluralistic country, we find several entangled symbolic worlds competing in our consciousness. Nixon's favorite symbols may have a comforting obviousness for some; they may make others throw slippers at the television set.

Even while sharing one social symbolic world, of course, individuals weave individual variants of their own. But in America, we tend to exaggerate how individual we are. We seldom measure how much of what we think, imagine, and feel is socially derived, how thoroughly we reflect social institutions of various kinds. Ironically, when we *do* perceive how socially derived our consciousness is, we tend to feel ashamed, as though we should be wholly autonomous, as though it is not natural for humans to be thoroughly social animals. Even the autonomous individual is a socially derived ideal, realized through supporting social institutions.

In America, most individuals live in more than one symbolic

world. The grandchildren of Jewish immigrants from Poland almost certainly retain elements from the ways of perceiving passed on by their grandparents and parents; but they have also assimiliated materials from the other symbolic worlds in which they participate. They may be unconscious of the differences between the several symbolic worlds they move into and out of, for it is common to find Americans whose inner symbolic geography is not clearly mapped. Some of their perceptions, some of their reactions to certain political symbols, may surprise them. Some disconcerting materials are repressed.

National politicians become painfully aware of their own symbolic limitations. In Maine, "down East" stories are captivating; but the same stories told in Pittsburgh and Albuquerque fail to win appreciation. In the upper Midwest, the long, slow, quiet ways of McGovern may be perceived (even by opponents) as conveying a certain courage; in the taverns near the mills of Pittsburgh, these quiet ways may be perceived as weak. The Kennedy oganization's slickness is an asset in regions where lack thereof shows lack of polish; but in Oregon it can rub the wrong way. One may say "Chicanos" in Los Angeles, and "Latinos" in New York, but it is best to say "Spanish-surname" in New Mexico. For blacks, "quota" is a word guaranteeing that at last they will be let *in;* for Jews, "quota" carries memories of how they have been kept *out;* for Slavs and Italians, to speak of "quotas" is to violate a taboo. They *know* they've been kept out, but their general policy is not to draw attention to it, while silently proving their capacity for breaking in.

In Watts, on the day Angela Davis was acquitted, George McGovern faced a sea of happy, jubilant blacks at a picnic rally. The news of the acquittal was barely an hour old. Hot rock whipped spirits high. McGovern told the crowd he wanted to lead the nation back to its ideals of 190 years ago. Not many in the crowd wanted to go back *there.* The longer he spoke, the more the mood of the occasion flattened.

Would it be permissible for Zorba the Greek to cry in public? If we may believe Dostoevsky's novels, not a tree grows in Russia unless a man cries on it. But if you run for the presidency of the United States, it is better to have "masculine" emotions.

All moral judgments are guided by symbolic materials. Moral statements are not merely propositional and abstract in form. Moral statements acquire their concrete meaning within social symbolic worlds. If someone tells you that it is a fundamental principle of his to keep promises, you won't know how to rely upon his promises until you perceive the *story* he is living out, the *image* he has of the arena of social action, the *progress* he imagines for various actors through it, and the concrete *symbols* through which he perceives the circumstances and style of promise-keeping. There are utilitarians whose symbolic world is functional and atomic and whose pledge to keep a promise carries with it a warning: "unless grave inconvenience arises." There are persons of an old-fashioned sensibility for whom a promise is a vow, whose image of social interdependence is so strong that if they promise something you may stake your life on it, even if its cost to them is high. In politics, it is essential to grasp the symbolic world within which the maker of promises lives and has his being.

Morality, in a word, concerns a way of life. Your morality is not simply a record of your actions, described in generalizable moral statements. Your morality includes the timing, the intent, the feeling-tone, the style and manner of your actions; it includes the sense of reality that infuses your actions, the story of your life of which your actions are incidents or episodes or turning points, the symbols which guide the instinctive decisions you make as you act (cautiously or boldly, gently or passionately, in trust or in outrage, apathetically or with design). When everybody shares the same culture and social class (that is, when they participate in the same social symbolic world), then the larger lines of good and evil may comfortably be taken for granted. But in a pluralistic society, each person may (within limits) *choose* the social groups and institutions to which he or she will belong. One chooses one social construction of reality rather than another.

Not only the actions included *within* a way of life, but that way of life itself, are choices subject to moral criticism. *What kind of human being do your choices cumulatively make you?* That is the fundamental moral question.

Because human beings are not minds alone, but embodied persons, imaginal materials help constitute their moral identity. We are not merely rationalists, creatures of pure intelligence and solitary will. We are historical, social animals, participants in finite cultural traditions. Each of us carries around with us a symbolic world as real and influential upon our actions as our hands, our heads, our hearts. The skills with which we read, or drive an auto, or cast a vote have not been developed by ourselves alone, but by our ancestors down through many generations. A long history has shaped our emotions, our perceptions, our deeds. Our ancestors made choices not for themselves alone, but for us as well; and our choices will continue to reverberate in the lives of our children. To respect another, therefore, is not merely to respect the individual our eyes see before us, but also to make contact with the social history that has formed his or her symbolic world.

It is odd that these notions, while widely accepted (staples, even, of anthropology, history, and sociology), are poorly realized in practice. Population experts try to export techniques into another culture as though that culture had no weight or legitimate resistance of its own. Teachers in our urban schools address the young faces in front of them equally, as though each did not come from a different cultural history, as though those diverse cultural histories had no reality to be noted, nourished, and advanced. Writers quibble with one another's words as if all words on white pages came from identical backgrounds and were aimed in identical directions. Not often in America do persons feel as though others see them as they are, in their social and cultural finitude. Too often, rather, we treat one another at face value, impersonally, without social, historical, or cultural depth. An ironic outcome of our exaggerated individualism is that it diminishes us as human beings.

The cult of individualism distorts political and social realities. Falsely, each is divided against each. Each unnecessarily accepts alienation and loneliness as natural. What many glory in as the ultimate authenticity—the sweet taste of their own otherness—is, from another point of view, false consciousness.

Social symbol systems, however secular, generate an important type of religion; that is, if we take the word "religion" to indicate not churches or ecclesiastical traditions in the Western style, but a distinctive public sense of reality. Niebuhr's later work, for example, *The Self and the Dramas of History,* draws our attention to the store of images and symbols available in the collective imagination of a people. Our historical, imaginal nature requires that we carry such finite symbolic worlds with us, both as persons and as societies.

Two benefits derived from approaching American politics through the study of cultural symbol systems: the interrelation between morality and politics becomes easier to grasp and the distinction between moralism and morality becomes easier to draw.

Every social symbol system declares a moral choice. It defines one way of life against others. Thus, to boast of having a "pragmatic" standpoint and to attack the "moralism" of other points of view is *also* to take a moral position.

Every person is subject to criticism from others, concerning his way of life. Each way of life is but one selection, from among many, of what human life might be like. The inadequacies of one chosen way of life are legitimately pointed out by those who have chosen another way. There is no nonmoral, objective, neutral position.

Any criticism of another's way of life is implicitly a declaration of how life *ought* to be lived.

Similarly, every political choice *ipso facto* raises *moral* issues. For political choices aim at shaping society this way, rather than that. And what reasons can be given why one choice ought to be preferred to another? Such reasons inevitably involve a view about the identity of man.

Conversely, every moral choice *ipso facto* raises *political* issues. Human beings are social animals, and even deeds done in private are part of a general social reality. The organization of life that allows "private space" within which individuals may do as they please is *also* one political system among many. Sophisticated social systems may purchase the allegiance of citizens by offering, in effect, "bread and circuses" so that public structures will not be questioned. It is appropriate to ask, however, What must happen to others elsewhere in this social system for me to have this private space within which to do as I please?

In a word, then, what is moralism in politics? Moralism imitates morality, uses moral language, projects moral aims. But it has two characteristic deficiencies. First, moralism disguises the power base and real interests of its own constituencies. Those afflicted with it tend to portray their opponents not only as politically mistaken, but also as immoral. They tend to reduce political choices to moral choices; and to believe their symbols of morality are morality itself. And yet doesn't pluralistic experience teach us that to differ, even fundamentally, about human identity and concrete practicalities is no sure sign of turpitude? Those, for example, who think of themselves as members of a "constituency of conscience" usually don't notice that a society organized according to their conception of justice will find them in positions of high political status and their leaders in positions of power; and the same is true of those who think of themselves as participants in a "silent majority," composed of the "good, law-abiding" citizens in an increasingly "decadent" time. Political partisanship nearly always carries moralism with it, trying to pass itself off as true (and higher) morality.

Second, this kind of moralism, whether political or personal, places excessive confidence in human reason or in some form of individual piety, while overlooking the intransigence of social interests, the uses of overt and covert power, and the ironies and intractabilities of social organization. One phrase, in particular, reveals such moralism in operation. It occurs when a speaker intones, "If only . . ."—if only men tried harder, if only they had more love in their hearts, if only they would be more reasonable, if only they would get out the vote. This is a big "if," because its function is to appeal for unusual, heroic effort, whereas social organizations must be constructed to allow for *ordinary* efforts and *characteristic* inertia. People usually don't wish to think too much about the social machinery of their lives; they want the machinery to purr quietly in the background, while they get on with the business of living. (Those whose passion it is to work on the social machinery, of course, find the indifference of the multitudes scandalous, at least as scandalous as young clergymen find the apathy of their flocks.)

Moralism of this sort must be distinguished from "moral inspiration." Army officers, coaches, team captains, teachers, parents, corporation managers, and political candidates must, necessarily, inspire their followers. Genuine moral inspiration draws on symbolic resources already *in* others and makes them feel that they are becoming more fully themselves. Conversely, moralism speaks *down* to others, exhorting them to some supposedly higher but alien self. George McGovern, it seems, created in many Americans the impression that he was preaching down to them and calling them to symbols he thought they should share, even if they didn't. He did not get inside the people. He failed to speak *for* the people. He couldn't find the keys to their several and complex aspirations. Richard Nixon clung to rather hackneyed themes that won little enthusiasm but offered widespread and comforting recognition. He used ancient public motifs skillfully. He seemed to inhabit some middle zone between sincerity (these really *are* his values) and moralism (he recited them *because* they were familiar, trusted, lulling). He did not awaken a fresh moral power already dormant in the people. He tried to comfort their restlessness by repetition of the fragments of the old national faith.

Several civil religions are powerful in American politics. Sorting some of them out is our next task.

Part Three

THE CIVIL RELIGIONS
OF AMERICA

The McGovern phenomenon had been something more than a movement, something more than a party coup. It had been a rhythm, a sound in the hearts of millions of Americans, a rhythm that came to crest that night in Miami. . . . And then, after that, the magic left. The music which moved the McGovern phenomenon was the oldest music in American life—the music of the religious ones, of the American crusaders, the abolitionists, the good-cause people, the cold-war people, a music that inspires some and frightens others. On the long march of the American people to the uplands, most have usually been willing to go along. . . . At Miami the music began to frighten people.
—Theodore H. White
The Making of the President 1972

16

The Nation with the
Soul of a Church

G. K. Chesterton once described America as "a nation with the soul of a church." It is a nation "founded on a creed," committed to values no nation can fully achieve. Our basic national scriptures are texts to which after errant wanderings we return again and again in order to renew ourselves. Right and Left try to prove that the other is betraying the nation's fundamental convictions. Each tries to prove it loves the "true" nation more. Thus Norman Mailer brooded about what he saw in Miami in 1972:

> *In America, the country was the religion.* And all the religions of the land were fed from that first religion which was *the country itself,* and if the other religions were now full of mutation and staggering across deserts of faith, it was because the country had been false and ill and corrupt for years, corrupt not in the age-old human proportions of failure and evil, but corrupt to the point of terminal disease, like a great religion foundering. [Emphasis added.]

The religion of America is not Christianity. It is not Judaism. There are many theories about what it is. Professor Sidney Mead calls it "the religion of the Republic." It is, Robert Bellah says, "the civil religion"; or John Dewey, "the common faith"; Will Herberg, "the American way of life"; John E. Smylie, "the nation itself." Conrad Cherry has collected some basic documents of this national religion in *God's New Israel* (1971).

The country as the religion—the theme is an old one. Walt Whitman wrote of it in the preface to the 1872 edition of *Leaves of Grass,* a hundred years before *The Greening of America*:

> The time has certainly come to begin to discharge the idea of Religion, in the United States, from mere ecclesiasticism, and from Sundays and churches and church-going. . . . The people, especially the young men and women of America, must begin to learn that Religion . . . is something far, far, different from what they supposed. It is, indeed, too important to the power and perpetuity of the New World to be consigned any longer to the churches old or new, Catholic or Protestant—Saint this, or Saint that. . . . It must be consigned henceforth to Democracy *en masse,* and to Literature. It must enter into the Poems of the Nation. It must make the Nation.

Most Americans do not take America's corruption, evil, or powerlessness as simple matters of fact, as inevitable. Most are shocked and they protest when life in America is not morally beautiful. America is a vessel of salvation, the bearer of transcendent hopes, as for Italians Italy, say, is not. Foreign observers such as Gunnar Mydral frequently comment:

> America, relative to all the other branches of Western civilization, is moralistic and "moral conscious." The ordinary American is the opposite of a cynic. He is on the average more of a believer and a defender of the faith in humanity than the rest of the Occidentals. It is a relatively important matter to him to be true to his own ideals and to carry them out in actual life. . . . Compared with members of other nations of Western civilization, the ordinary American is a

rationalistic being. . . . These generalizations might seem venturesome and questionable to the reflective American himself. . . . But to the stranger it is obvious and even striking.

In order to describe the anomaly of racism in America, Myrdal had first of all to isolate the American creed. If that creed were racist, there would be no anomaly. He found its tenets more "explicitly expressed" than in any other nation of the world.

The schools teach them, the churches preach them. The courts pronounce their judicial decisions in their terms. They permeate editorials with a pattern of idealism so ingrained that the writers could scarcely free themselves from it even if they tried. . . . Even the stranger, when he has to appear before an American audience . . . finds himself espousing the national Creed, as this is the only means by which a speaker can obtain human response from the people to whom he talks.

After a visit to America, G. K. Chesterton tried to answer for himself, What makes America peculiar? His answer: "America is the only nation in the world that is founded on a creed. That creed is set forth with dogmatic and even theological lucidity in the Declaration of Independence. . . . It enunciates that all men are equal in their claim to justice, and that governments exist to give them that justice, and that their authority is for that reason just." These are staggering notions. The United States thought of itself, Chesterton divined, as a "home for the homeless." It had the unique idea of "making a new nation literally out of any old nation that comes along." America even aspired to offer a pattern for "a new world" and to make of each raw human individual of the rest of the race "a new man."

No one church was allowed to become the official guardian of the central symbols of the United States. Instead, the nation itself began to fill the vacuum where in many cultures a church would be. The nation became its own unifying symbol system, the chief bestower of identity and purpose.

A candidate for the presidency of the United States does well to recognize that he is running for a religious office. The national religion is, to be sure, quite pragmatic and secular. His concerns will be power, vested interests, money, jobs, and other utterly mundane affairs. Still, America conducts itself like a religion. A candidate had better understand that.

There are those, of course, who say that the religion is weakening. Some young blacks, for example, have become defiant. In 1968 at the Olympics, two raised clenched fists during the playing of "The Star-Spangled Banner," and in 1972, two others chatted casually, as though that anthem were not *their* symbol and the usual forms of respect not *their* form. A white housewife in San Jose told *The New York Times* that she now hates to say the pledge to the flag, it "means nothing" to her, what it says "isn't true," especially "those words about justice for all." "Above all else," President Nixon intoned during his second Inaugural Address in 1973, "the time has come for us to renew our faith in America. In recent years, that faith has been doubted."

Isn't the language of "faith" an odd language for a wholly secular, managerial state? Such a state, more than any other, requires faith. For unless they believe in something, invest their dreams in it, how will people be led to make sacrifices for it? The weaker the churches become as symbol systems, the heavier the symbolic weight that must be taken up by the state. In the twentieth century, nations are everywhere becoming politically religious; politics is regarded as a means of salvation. Words once used for religious matters—"commitment," "dedication," "purpose," "principle," "conscience," "witness," "sacrifice," and "prophecy"—are now used frequently in reference to political behavior. Many altogether secular and agnostic persons reveal in their political pursuits both the kind of passion and the intensity of passion one used to think of as religious. One wonders whether politics can support such hopes, what will happen when disillusionment descends. "If you desire a purpose in life," Prime Minister Heath told some of his idealistic constituents, "don't come to me. Kindly call on your archbishop."

In America, belief in the nation is especially deep. On the

dollar bill appear the words, *Novus ordo seclorum*: "The new order of the ages." We dreamt here of a "new world," separated by oceans from the Machiavellian corruptions of Europe and Asia and Africa and Latin America. *We* were "the last best hope of mankind." *We* were charged with "setting an example for the world." *We* were a "good, generous, compassionate people." We thought of ourselves (not quite consciously, which would have been arrogant, but just below the threshold of consciousness) as unusually candid, clear-eyed, innocent, good-willed, young, strong, brave, true. The tall cowboy with the white hat. *Foreigners* were the untrustworthy ones.

Today even our cynics manifest the reverse side of the same faith. Few are the black militants or youthful revolutionaries or middle-aged radicals who accept racism, militarism, corruption, or official lying as a matter of course. True cynics, by contrast, do not expect government to be trustworthy. They do not expect justice in society. Of empire they do not ask sensitivity. Calm in their cynicism, they feel no excess of emotion, no bitterness, no anger. Our cynics are not true cynics, but more intense believers than the rest of us. Our doubters are disappointed lovers.

A social system is easy to take for granted. One wants it to be personal, just, warm, compassionate, liberating. But society is not a loving father, nor does the state offer a loving God. (The price true religion asks for such gifts is that one live in the thin air of the transcendent.)

In June, 1940, when Nazi armies had overrun Paris with ease and were massing for assault on England, Walter Lippmann told his Harvard class reunion: "You took the good things for granted. Now you must earn them again. It is written: For every right that you cherish, you have a duty which you must fulfill. For every hope that you entertain, you have a task you must perform. For every good that you wish to preserve, you will have to sacrifice your comfort and your ease. There is nothing for nothing any longer."

In those days, the threat was external. Today America is a land without adequate symbols. The experiences of its people and the aspirations many feel find no legitimate public outlet.

The faith of many is narrow, naïve, immature. Want of means and resources is not our dilemma. Our own imagination is our enemy.

We need to reconstruct our national project. Having conquered the frontier, worldwide enemies, space, we must at last face what we have spent so long avoiding: we must face each other.

17

The Innocence Lingers On

Some people hate the word "America." They are embarrassed by its songs and public rituals. They believe themselves to be "international" and do not think of themselves as American. They hate "The Star-Spangled Banner" and everything that smacks of patriotism. The major issues of the world, they say, are not "American" but "human": the consciousness of women, the development of the Third World, overpopulation, the environment, and so forth. In the eyes of some, concepts like "nation" and "patriotism" should be stricken from the language of a moral person. Some forget that humans are incarnate, finite, rooted, and that universality and local belonging are not contradictions.

The detached observer, sympathetic to their point of view, notes nonetheless that moral fervor continues. "Amerika" is condemned as passionately as Sodom and Gomorrah ever were. The war in Southeast Asia is called "immoral." Racism is regarded, not as a characteristic of every human culture, but as a vice in the soul (and in institutions) to be confessed, repented of, uprooted now, and fitting restitution paid. The new "secular" attitudes have an even higher intensity than the old religious ones. They consist of "consciousness-raising," "radicalization," "conversion." Their locus is in consciousness, perception, and way of life. Confession of guilt is prominent. Amendment of ways is strictly enforced. The discipline is communal—bands of "brothers" and "sisters" quickly detect deviations, want of purity, infidelity. A passion for innocence inflames. A Great Awakening has occurred. Persons who in an earlier generation would have been conventionally devout became "political." Politics was for a brief time—before apathy reappeared—a new religion.

In the hot summer of 1960, *Life* magazine and *The New York Times,* moved by a sense of urgency, published jointly a series of articles on "The National Purpose." The mood of the time was stifling silence. The nation's energy seemed spent. "What has happened to the American Dream?" William Faulkner asked. "We dozed, slept, and it abandoned us. There no longer sounds a unifying voice speaking our mutual hope and will."

At the gate of his Gettysburg farm, Eisenhower was small-town America, the good fruit of generations of solid and reliable and energetic people. Yet his way of life seemed no longer hopeful, contained no visions or surprises. Dreams, symbols, purposes seemed flat. "The public mood of the country," Walter Lippmann wrote, "is defensive, to hold on and to conserve, not to push forward and to create. We talk about ourselves as if we were a completed society, one which has achieved its purpose, and has no further great business to transact."

George F. Kennan raised yet another motif of this remarkable public confession, intended by eminent molders of public debate to awaken the nation. Did his words penetrate beneath the rush of trucks on the highways, the hurrying of aimless crowds in the cities, the sleepiness of rural towns?

> If you ask me whether a country—with no highly developed sense of national purpose, with the overwhelming accent of life on personal comfort, with a dearth of public services and

a surfeit of privately sold gadgetry, with insufficient social discipline even to keep its major industries functioning without grievous interruption—if you ask me whether such a country has over the long run good chances of competing with a purposeful, serious and disciplined society such as that of the Soviet Union, I must say that the answer is No.

This last sentence hangs in the air like the breeze of a sleepily hot July picnic before a cyclone of passion and despair. Yet even as these essays appeared, John F. Kennedy was invoking the lure of the frontier, the old desire to "get moving," the old longing (as he told the American Legion) "not to be number one *if*, not number one *and*, not number one *but*, but number one *period.*"

There are several ironies. Among the ten essayists of 1960, none was a black. None was a Catholic. None was a woman. The symbolic power of the Anglo-American civil religion was flickering down. Like virgins charged to tend the flame, ten guardians were asked to blow life into it.* The undertow was sadness.

But just then the young Catholic presidential candidate from Boston was showing that the traditional civil religion was alive in him, that he could infuse it with new power and a new feeling of vigor. He showed that he could modify the civil religion in several new ways in regard to blacks, Chicanos, Indians, and other excluded ones. The civil rights turmoil that Gunnar Myrdal had predicted in 1941, as a necessary and inevitable expression of "the American Creed," began to unfold more rapidly in 1961. Activity exploded.

In his Inaugural Address, Kennedy went beyond nationalism to speak to all the citizens of the world. He began the long process of forging an international symbolism. Against those who thought him a callow youth, he added guarded but bellicose warnings. Millions in the world understood. He was more popular outside the United States than within.

But the very purpose and energy of Camelot seems to have

---

* In addition to Faulkner, Lippmann, and Kennan, the other writers in this series were John K. Jessups, James Reston, Clinton Rossiter, John W. Gardner, Alfred Wohlstetter, Archibald MacLeish, and Billy Graham.

furnished a false second start. Many of those then most excited by the vistas of a new generation coming to power in 1961 are now the most bitter and publicly cynical. Some of their later disillusionment with JFK may be a way of keeping pain away. If we can deny that those days were hopeful, touched with wit, laced with vigor, liberating of the best within us, we can blame something else, not ourselves. Some uses of revisionism are latent.

Whatever the ultimate judgment of history, the administration of John Kennedy was important for revealing dramatic limits in the civil religion. He opened up America beyond merely Protestant symbols. That was a watershed.

Max Lerner points out in *America as a Civilization* that there is more than one American tradition.

> Actually, there are four great separable migration families that moved to the American continent. The first was probably from Asia—that of the men who formed the strain of the American Indians. The second was from the British Isles and western Europe. The third was from Africa—the Negro strain. The fourth was from Mediterranean, central, and eastern Europe, from Asia, from Latin America and everywhere else—the polyglot ethnic strain. Nevertheless, there were pressures to select one of them (the British-West-European) as *the* "American" one.

Of course, that selection seemed altogether sensible. Eighty-two percent of all whites in America in 1790 were British-Americans, most of the others west Europeans (French, German, Dutch). Does length of time in America make a group more "American"? By the test of time, the most "American" stocks are the American Indians, the descendants of Jamestown and Plymouth, the Spanish of the South and West, and the descendants of the early Negro slaves. Lerner notes:

> European stocks are more "American" not by the fact of long settlement but by the fact of being European (West European, *not* Mediterranean or Slavic). . . . The West Europeans have run the show in America since early times

and have therefore made the rules and set the admission price. They feel more at home and have made others feel less at home.

By breaking the bonds of Protestant metaphors, Kennedy's presence as President sent shockwaves through America's self-understanding. In at least three ways, the inherited civil religion soon showed its inadequacy. First, the old civil religion did not provide us with a self-understanding that was truly pluralistic, that included all equally. Its institutions, rituals, holidays, and daily symbols excluded the Irish, blacks, Indians, Orientals, and southern and eastern Europeans. No black, Jewish, Oriental, Indian, Slavic, or Italian president has been elected. Can an atheist represent the nation's self-understanding? As for over a century only males had suffrage so also the symbols of the civil religion are mainly masculine.

Second, the traditional civil religion has been less than universal. It has tended to make the nation itself the object of reverence, as though to become a kind of "American Shinto." There have from the beginning been elements of universality and genuine internationalism in the American dream, respected by many abroad who have deep esteem for America. Myrdal himself wrote:

> The American Creed is the common democratic creed. "American ideals" are just humane ideals as they have matured in our common Western civilization upon the foundation of Christianity and pre-Christian legalism, and under the influence of the economic, scientific, and political development over a number of centuries. The American Creed is older and wider than America itself.

Yet the national self-understanding remains ambivalent about the mission of the United States in the world. Isolation and empire have both been national passions. The nation should stay disentangled; *and* it should be an example to other nations; *and* it should fulfill its responsibilities to freedom around the world; *and* it should help to liberate the poor and the oppressed. Kennedy summed up all four motifs in his own person. He felt the pressure of all four. Had he lived, he would have been forced, as we now are, to choose among them.

Third, the traditional national self-understanding offered America little instruction in how to admit to evil, corporate and individual; how to accept defeat; how to live in a world of scarcity, limits and fragility; how to aspire to a tragic sense of life. As a civilization, America has never experienced total and irretrievable failure nor occupation under a foreign army nor a sharp and embittering break in its history. Thus, Max Lerner writes, "America as a civilization has been far removed from the great type-enactment of the Christian story, or the disasters of Jewish history or of the Asiatic empires; it has not suffered, died, been reborn." The key elements of Christian and Jewish perception have never quite seemed true to Americans.

Then the assassination of Kennedy in Dallas introduced the experience of the absurd. Millions were drawn against their wills into the emotions of Greek tragedy: youth, death, meaninglessness, no voice to break the silence. Intelligent people sought some "explanation." To accept the view that history is irrational required resources some did not possess. Another decade's experience would instruct them in life's irrationality.

In these ways and others, the national self-understanding has been too narrow. But if one form of the civil religion breaks down, there is no choice except to construct another. If there is to be a degree of national coherence, purpose, and vitality, *someone* will create unifying symbols and institutional forms. To gain emotional power, such forms must carry forward the passionate memories and sufferings of the past. Far more powerfully than we suspect, most of us carry around the elements of these forms in our hearts.

Those on the Left are sometimes reluctant to admit that the civil religion is alive in their own attitudes. The image by whose light they condemn the present realities of American life is, however, remarkably like the image that governs "The American Creed."

Suppose, for example, that America were an explicitly racist country, not only in practice but also in creed. Whites have enough power to live up to a creed that would command slavery or total and unrelenting subjection or concentration camps or extermination. The American creed posits instead the inalienable rights of each person to equality, justice under the law, and liberty. In between these two extremes falls the practice. But only in the light of the creed do our reformers criticize our practice.

Or let someone say, with hostility and contempt, that America is "Amerika"—militaristic, imperialistic, oppressive. A cynical answer might be, *So what?* Isn't it a normal, inevitable pattern for any great energetic world power to dominate others with all necessary military power? But such cynicism is not the common response in America.

Henry Fairlie, a British political writer for *The Spectator* did offer in *The New York Times Magazine* to lead "A Cheer for American Imperialism." He argued that an empire "has no justification except its own existence." An empire should never contract nor try to rationalize all its accumulated commitments nor be too much faulted for its waste of life and treasure. Empires happen. What matters, Fairlie argued, is that the American empire is uniquely benevolent, devoted to individual liberty and the rule of law. Fairlie himself was once freed from a Yugoslav jail simply because he threatened to call the American Consul. "Sublime," the Britisher commented. To which Senator Fulbright, in *The Arrogance of Power,* exclaimed: "What romantic nonsense this is."

America, Fulbright argued, has a traditional responsibility to set a humane, liberating example for the other nations of the world, and must resist the temptations fallen into by other world powers in the past. But where did we get this "traditional responsibility"? Fulbright implies that we are not like other nations. The course of empire in Asia, Greece, Rome, Spain, France, Germany, or England, for example, is not the standard for our behavior. We expect more of ourselves. For the arrogance of power shall we then substitute, with all due modesty, the arrogance of virtue?

This pattern of expectation is utterly revealing. Take an American writer of the Right, who will deny that America is a "sick" nation; or a writer of the Radical Left, who peels back one by one the historic injustices and oppressions of our national life. They both hold up an especially bright standard for the nation. One says America *is* "uniquely benevolent" among the nations. The other holds America to a uniquely high standard, while debunking her present intentions and accomplishments. Neither denies the national ideals.

In *God and Man at Yale,* William F. Buckley, Jr., debunked the liberal professionals. In *The Greening of America,* Charles Reich also debunked them. Debunking is an American passion. It flourishes where ideals are cherished. (The present book in part depends on it.) Decadence and fatalism—as in *La Dolce Vita* or *Satyricon,* perhaps—mirror in reverse the hope and moral energy of America. The ritual response called for by the American civil religion is not resignation, indifference, or satiety. Confronted with evil, our ritual response is: what can we *do* about it? (Like, start a committee.) How puzzling, naïve, and touching this response seems to others. We practice an extraordinary faith in the power of action.

No religion can be adequately reduced to a creed or a list of values. But there are several attitudes toward action that grow out of the American experience. Immigrants have had to assimilate these attitudes. Foreign visitors have to adjust to them. Going abroad, some Americans become aware of them in themselves. They figure prominently in our electoral processes.

"America was promises," wrote Archibald MacLeish in 1930. The most salient attitude of the American self-understanding is its sense of expectation and, naturally enough, its sense of disappointment. Almost all central symbols of the American self-understanding are dual, in exactly this pattern.

1. *Movement ahead and stability.* The Constitution was designed to preserve the power of the wealthy, the landed, and the socially established from the enthusiasms of popular will. On the other hand, the Declaration of Independence and the Bill of Rights set forth the ideal of full equality under law. Two images of America were conjured up: stable, continuous, practical, unrevolutionary; and restless, subject to popular passion and will, risky, rebellious. The American civil religion is *both* republican *and* democratic.

2. *Lovers of law, and lawless.* Americans, as Gunnar Myrdal pointed out in *An American Dilemma,* are uncommonly skilled in negotiating basic moral-legal conflict. Ordinary citizens are accustomed to *not* living up to ideals. They don't surrender the ideals, but they don't hesitate, when other habits or interests press upon them, to shrug their shoulders and do what seems to them practical. Among Anglo-Saxon Protestants, dry-laws and other efforts to legislate ideals into reality accustom millions to honoring the law in principle while flagrantly doing otherwise. Among Catholics, long traditions of casuistry, a certain alienation from dominant American Protestant ideals, and an attitude toward the secular state as a merely *administrative* agency (speeding in traffic was never "sinful" the way missing church on Sunday was), work to the same effect. Those whose traditions spring from the rational humanism of the Enlightenment show distaste for unenforceable laws; but they too appeal to "civil disobedience" as a device for refusing to obey laws of which they do not approve. Americans, Myrdal comments, are uncommonly lawless in their practices and derogatory of law in rhetoric. Yet they are quickly stimulated by pet grievances to say in regard to others: "There ought to be a law against that!"

3. *Dream and skepticism.* America is, in Max Lerner's phrase, deeply involved in the "metaphysics of promise." Americans understand almost everything in the light of the "fact" that life will be better in the future. America is a "new world." It was "conceived" in ideals and "dedicated" to propositions. Few other nations are to so great an extent a creation of consciousness. Most earlier nations grew out of a long past, drew their nourishment from history, moved forward by the strength of *what they had been.* America is drawn almost wholly by *what will be.* It is a land of dream, expectation, impossible possibilities.

Yet a very strong conservative bias corrects the utopian dreaming. Perhaps because almost all Americans are of lower-class origins, a strong practical instinct defends them against the hucksters of dreams. Each remembers what it was like when times were *worse.* Moreover, America shows upward mobility, but countless examples of downward mobility too: people who once were prosperous or neighborhoods that once were elegant, now fallen on harder times. Hence, not all dreams are sweet dreams. To be able to dream of success is also to have nightmares of failure. The slick salesman of the Brooklyn Bridge, the fiery preacher who promises a land of honey, the merchant of useless nostrums, and the perennial promises of politicians—these are well-established images in the consciousness of every citizen who has ever traded for a house or a car.

A nation of dreamers breeds cynics and skeptics. Americans want guarantees that they will not lose what they have. New arrangements must leave past gains unpenalized. New proposals must inspire confidence in actual general improvement. While American society is uniquely open to change, it sets high standards of practicality and hardheadedness. The ideal American dreamer is a person of demonstrated practical accomplishment. Americans keep a sharp eye on what changes may mean to their pocketbook and their status.

4. *Equality of opportunity and inequality of status.* Part of the lure of America is the expectation of a genuinely classless society in which the taxi driver has as much right to his opinions as a professor (including the right to explain them in detail). Thus, in the movie *The Emigrants,* a family that has migrated from Sweden is surprised to find their riverboat apportioned in three decks: for the partying rich, the poor whites, and the slaves. The son of a grocerystore owner and the son of a restaurateur can become president and vice president of the United States. But "upward mobility" is upward only when stratification persists.

Given these internal contradictions in our attitudes, frank recognition of class realities is often considered bad form. When Sargent Shriver visited mills, mines, and foundries during the campaign of 1972, some journalists contrasted his Cardin suits and Gucci shoes, his healthy tan and trim good looks, with the begrimed overalls, bad teeth, and hacking coughs of the workers. But perhaps the workers took these class discrepancies for granted, without envy. In that sense, they do not believe in equality. The real world is not one of equality. Life *is* unfair. On the other hand, every worker can believe that someday some son of his will beat one of Mr. Shriver's sons in some field of human accomplishment.

So one American feeling for life is that there *is* a class structure and that with hard work, talent, and luck a person *can* rise. In Europe, many worked for centuries under conditions of serfdom. Here they worked, for the first time in their family history, for *themselves.* That alone has been a great source of dignity. It includes the possibility of failure. There is pride in every step beyond failure: a roof over one's head, food to eat, schooling for the children, a good neighborhood. More affluent Americans may look at row houses in Queens and feel distaste or even mockery. People living in those houses may marvel that by their own hands they have come so far to such orderly beauty, privacy, and luxury.

5. *Guilt and hope.* As Myrdal found, Anglo-Americans recognize that for blacks and some others opportunity is far more limited than for themselves. Nearly all white Americans, Myrdal wrote, experienced the situation of the black as a legitimate moral accusation. The American creed is honored by open admission of culpability. The situation of the black is taken as a sin and scandal. Yet Americans believe in the power of their own creed; in time, with practicality, the immorality will be removed. "Americans believe in their own ability and in progress," Myrdal concluded. "They are at bottom moral optimists."

For most Americans, the American system has been tangibly benevolent. They therefore tend to underestimate the sheer evil of racial inequality, the damage done to the psyche of individuals, the depth of rage. Believing in "progress," they have an insufficient grasp of the deep and systemic obstructions in the path of blacks. In jobs, housing, education, and health care, inequities demand not just "progress" but a wholesale reconstruction. Liberals have enormously underestimated the social disruption the American creed calls for (disruptions, they too easily imagine, in the lives of *others.*) Other Americans, beginning to catch a glimpse of what will be required, are understandably gripped by fear. It is not only a "racial" fear, fear of blacks as blacks, but a systemic fear. If the system is rearranged, what treatment can *they* expect from the system's managers? They do not fear blacks nearly so much as they distrust the planners and the managers. There are regional and ethnic memories behind such distrust.

6. *America as Number One—and humble too.* Finally, a symbol no presidential candidate can hope to evade is the ethnic-economic pride of America as the world's leading power and moral presence. The pride is ethnic, because it is based on a long tradition of belief in the superiority of Anglo-Saxon institutions of liberty and law. Our drama of human history depicts the formal drama as developed nations versus underdeveloped nations, free nations that respect the rights of the individual versus nations that coerce the individual. Our drama of history concedes us first place in the world's moral competition. Since at least World War II, we have *also* wished to be first in military power. It is, however, difficult for us to admit that we wish to be an imperial power just for the pleasure of power. We have to believe we are *Numero Uno* for the sake of others. Moral to the end.

We must not only be better than Spain or France or England or Russia in our behavior; we must satisfy the absolute demands of our own creed. Not only "better than others," but as near to being perfect as we might.

These are among the symbols presidential candidates must come to terms with.

18

The Civil Religions

Jean-Jacques Rousseau suggested two centuries ago that the decline of the old religions would require the emergence of a new religion. In the name of progress, the world would return to an ancient social form: the state would become the church. Since *Protestant, Catholic and Jew* (1960), Will Herberg has been the most consistent discerner of just such a drift in American life. The great American religious institutions, he argues, have fewer and fewer "edges," make less and less difference, mute their voices to a rapidly increasing sameness. The content of their witness is "the American way of life," the lived reality of a new religion, neither Protestant nor Jewish nor Catholic. Afraid of diversity, we have gradually raised a genial, rather liberal sameness into an orthodoxy. Herberg believes that this new American religion functions like the state religions of ancient Greece and Rome. A somewhat more hopeful view of the civil religion is championed by Robert N. Bellah:

> While some have argued that Christianity is the national faith, and others that church and synagogue celebrate only

the generalized religion of "the American way of life," few have realized that there actually exists alongside of and rather clearly differentiated from the churches an elaborate and well-institutionalized civil religion in America.

Both Bellah and Herberg try to look at American life as an American anthropologist looks at a New Guinea tribe or a lost Latin American civilization. In any society, what are the unspoken symbolic unities that hold its centrifugal energies together? What symbols allow all to participate, perhaps unconsciously, in a single cultural life?

The strength of Herberg's thesis arises from the actual behavior of middle-class Americans and their spokesmen. One imagines rings of suburban houses expanding irresistibly over the rolling hills of New Jersey, Connecticut, Illinois, and other states. The strength of Bellah's thesis arises from certain "central" documents and ceremonies in our national history, in particular the rituals and the formal addresses of presidential inaugurations. Bellah takes a rather "high-church" view of the American liturgy. Herberg looks at the practical men-in-the-pew, broadminded and liberated: the Methodist who drinks a little, the pleasure-exploring Calvinist, the secularized Catholic, the non-Jewish Jew, of whom our literature speaks so contentedly.

There is a conservative component in this American way of life. One finds, for example, a resistance to "permissiveness." There is, on the other hand, a liberal component. One does not expect major conservative figures like John Connally or Barry Goldwater or William F. Buckley, Jr., to be world-renouncing; on the contrary, one expects them to be broadminded, to enjoy sports cars and yachts, to be understanding of modern codes of behavior. Mrs. Loud of Santa Barbara, in the television documentary "An American Family," tried not to reveal feelings of shock or surprise, no matter what she encountered. She tried desperately to be modern. Even the Reverend Billy Graham manages to be an acceptable religious symbol under both conservative and liberal administrations precisely because, even as an evangelist, he is modern in his methods and his presence. His "crusades" are well-conceived media campaigns, masterpieces of organization. He wears a business suit and speaks with all-American sincerity, not unlike thousands of coaches, promoters, and salesmen across the land.

"Every functioning society," writes sociologist Robin Williams, "has, to an important degree, a common religion. The procession of a common set of ideas, rituals, and symbols can supply an overarching sense of unity even in a society otherwise riddled with conflict." This overarching sense of unity is *not* composed merely by some "lowest common denominator." It is a *distinctive* unity, a way of perceiving and acting that copies no other in history. According to its own self-understanding, America is a nation of destiny and innocence. Our national values are regarded as benchmarks by which we measure the "development" of other nations. National heroes (Washington, Lincoln, FDR, Martin Luther King) are venerated. Our national history determines the future of humankind.

Even a pilgrimage with one's children to Disneyland will teach one much about the American psyche: a sense of universal mission and prettified international relations; an elective system (laissez-faire) of entertainments; a pervasive sense of virtue and uplift in a well-lighted place, where evil, corruption, lust, gambling, misery, power, and oppression have been resolutely swept from view; a place where a Supreme Being is discreetly alluded to and patriotism made the central unifying theme; a place where sanitation is achieved by an efficiency unrivaled anywhere in the world. ("It's so incredibly clean!" one marvels.) Shrines of immaculate, innocent perception, as if the American way of life were a design to cleanse all evil from the face of the earth with hygienic thought and determined will. A conspiracy against the dirt and confusion of older worlds: *Novus ordo seclorum.* "In our beginnings, God smiled on us: *Annuit coeptis.*"

There is a more complicated shrine to America's values, where those who remain unmoved by the pieties of Middle America experience their own community: The Shrine of Enlightenment, wherever Americans read journals of opinion, speedread books, line up for the communal mysteries of cinema and theater, struggle valiantly to stay "in touch" and be "informed." For these, the words "New York" convey radiations of a sacred city: feelings of awe at pulsing energy and high intelligence, at the soaring, jeweled skyline in the night, at traffic congestion and subway confusions and municipal strikes, and seven times seven daily mortifications—the asceticism of modern believers. Out in the provinces, worshipers of modernity may be loyal and devout, but upon New Yorkers falls a special obligation of sophistication. And here, too, to an astonishing degree, the style-setters watch over attitudes with a shrewd canonical eye to ferret out the passé, the naïve, and the uninformed. Whole sets of words suddenly become unuseable. Some attitudes are inadmissible. Many sentiments are left unexpressed. Every national religion requires *illuminati,* and simultaneously resents them.

So vital is the American civil religion that many antipathetic groups within it mutually resist one another's states of soul. American politics involves competition over economic goods; but it is also, and sometimes more profoundly, a struggle between conflicting symbol-systems, conflicting forms of consciousness and perception and aspiration. Ironically, we discover here a theme that joins all of us together as Americans: we consider conflicts over money or power *rational,* but conflicts over fundamental symbols "irrational," matters of "prejudice." We do so notwithstanding our abiding tendency to structure every serious argument among us as though it were a moral argument. We think ourselves supremely practical about costs and benefits; yet we moralize one another (and the world) *ad nauseam.*

We have taken one of the greatest boy-liars and con men of history, Huck Finn, and made him a national hero, morally superior to all the "fools" he conned. Huck is hero to the Left because of his "authenticity" and his resistance to "civilization," to religion, and to bourgeois discipline. Huck is hero to the Right because of his unexampled entreprenurial skills. The face of "Huck honey" lurks behind the long-haired hedonists of the counterculture, behind every Horatio Alger, behind the bold pragmatism and rapidly shifting explanations of Richard Nixon.

Will Herberg cites a text from Herman Melville's *White Jacket* (1850) that precisely conveys the two-edged terror of our religion: "The rest of the nations will soon be in our rear. We are the pioneers of the world, the advance guard, sent on through the wilderness of untried things to break a new path in the New World. . . . Long enough have we debated whether, indeed, the political Messiah has come. But he has come in us." These are breathtaking claims. The nation as Messiah, the nation as governed by no former law, but called to try the untried, to break a new path, in a new moral world. No guide, then, but our own moral energy, our own self-confidence, our own moral authenticity: a Raskolnikov among the nations. America and Amerika: both possibilities coinhere. Our radicalism and our conservatism issue from a common root.

Over the disparate elements of American society, uniting all, is as it were a single arc of sky, a canopy, a limited symbolic horizon. The nation has sacred obligations—not to be merely selfish, not to be decadent, not to be wasteful, not to be vicious—sacred obligations to try to be a *good* nation. The nation has its holy calendar, its sacred cities and monuments and pilgrimages, its consecrated mounds and fields. It has in its president a priest, a prophet, and a king.

What, then, is the civil religion? *It is a public perception of our national experience, in the light of universal and transcendent claims upon human beings, but especially upon Americans; a set of values, symbols, and rituals institutionalized as the cohesive force and center of meaning uniting our many peoples.*

To understand this definition clearly, we must also state what the civil religion is *not* and list its manifest deficiencies.

The institutions of the civil religion are not the American churches. The American churches bend over backward in their respect for the civil religion. But *their* religion is not the civil religion of the country as a whole. All of them are, to some extent, at odds with the civil religion. The Protestant churches, naturally, feel this tension least and are only lately learning that the civil religion does not fulfill their purposes or meet their standards. But Catholics and Jews too cede much to it.

The civil religion is not some common core, some lowest common denominator, of all the beliefs of all our citizens. It is not discovered by taking an opinion poll. It is discovered by analyzing experiences, interpretations, and institutions of our national life.

The civil religion is not merely "the American way of life." Boosterism is an American habit, and "bad-mouthing" is a vice that our patriots dislike. But the civil religion includes rights no one may violate, lawful procedures for defending those rights, and ideals transcendent enough to stand in judgment over national practices at every historical moment. That is to say, the civil religion legitimizes, even necessitates, incessant criticism of "the Amercan way of life." The American way of life involves a dynamism of self-criticism and self-transcendence.

The civil religion does not command worship of the American nation. The civil religion makes explicit that America does not stand in the place of God. The tendency to make the nation God, of course, persists despite the prohibition.

The civil religion is not a naïve faith of "Middle Americans" only. Many of those in rebellion against the civil religion are often, on another level of consciousness, its most advanced exponents. New moral perceptions require in every decade a new *prise de conscience.* Television commentators, avant-garde writers, and scholars practice the civil religion as devoutly as Middle Americans do. Manhattan liberals often excel in piety, dedication, and saintliness.

In the American civil religion, as in any powerful religion, an elephant may drown, a mouse may wade: each seeks his level. There are cheap and vulgar understandings and complex, deep ones.

The civil religion does not include merely what is worst or mediocre in us, but also what is best and hopeful. Perceiving for the first time the extent of America's complicity in evil, many have grown faint of heart. This desire not to be evil is part of the civil religion.

Most of all, perhaps, we must note that there is more than one civil religion in America. There is, in a sense, *one* "American way of life" into which Americans of various backgrounds are constantly being drawn. But there are also inner contradictions and dissatisfactions *within* that "way of life." There is also a new urgency to explore America's neglected variety. Blacks, Indians, citizens of Spanish surname, white ethnics, Jews, Appalachians, and others are exploring their own self-consciousness, no longer intimidated by the dominant national style. If "the American way of life" is in fact pluralistic, then we must note the differences in America's many cultural worlds as well as their points of overlap. It may be more illuminating to identify the several civil religions in operation among us, rather than to emphasize the thin overarching unity that makes us all "Americans."

To speak in this way, of course, is to begin to use the phrase "civil religion" in two different senses. In the first sense, it points to the documents already written and the symbols already widely institutionalized. In the second sense, it points to cultural traditions and resources that have not yet been fully integrated into the national way of life. To employ these two senses is to view the civil religion of America as still in process and in tension, to view it as a national self-understanding not yet adequate to the nation's full experience.

The new civil religion must be broadened, but it must also be deepened. It must absorb and mirror the extensive variety of America—the spiritual, human strength of black endurance these many generations, the extraordinary model of pluralism furnished by Hawaii, the Hispanic sense of beauty and penetrating, personal speech. It must also become able to face conflict, evil, ambiguity, and tragedy.

Blacks and women will probably lead the way to both such expansions in our national awareness. The movie *Sounder* brings home to white audiences, perhaps for the first time, that the experience of the black family even under conditions of oppression is an untapped resource of national dignity and power. When blacks and women enter more fully into the iconography of the civil religion, they will inevitably bring into focus painful aspects of human existence which nothing in our present self-understanding draws upon. But Jewish resources and Catholic resources, Irish and Italian and Slav, also have much to teach the nation about patience, long suffering, and the subordination of moralizing to tolerance for human weakness. Atheists and agnostics offer symbols suggesting to all that human beings as they are, apart from reference to God, have dignity, beauty, and mysterious depths. The spiritual variety of our land has barely broken the surface of our public self-understanding.

The presidents we elect over the next twenty years will preside over these changes, or lack thereof. That is the deepest and most effective power we will place in their hands. It is a power less immediate than control over nuclear weapons, but more fundamental. For how we perceive our role in the world will go far toward determining how we dispose of our nuclear might. Power issues first from the barrels of symbols.

To grasp the resources our next presidents will have to work with, we must try to untangle several strands of our present self-understanding.

19

Five Protestant Civil Religions

Protestant cultural histories dominate America's public life, its vocabulary, its practices. But there are many forms of Protestantism. Five have political relevance, each with its own approach to the national civil religion.

First, there is the classic mainline Protestantism of New England, nourished today in churches like the Episcopal, the United Church, the northern Presbyterians and institutionalized in the élite prep schools and the Ivy League. This is the "high-church" tradition, in which much weight is placed upon institutional realities, on law and civil liberties, on a practical spirit of compromise and tolerance. Its political equivalent is liberal Republicanism, New York's Liberal party, and part of the left wing of the Democratic party. Political figures like Nelson Rockefeller, John Lindsay, Henry Cabot Lodge, John Chafee, and McGeorge Bundy suggest the style.

Second, there is the populist tradition of the lower classes, spread across the South, the Bible Belt, and the small towns and rural areas. The symbols of this "low-church" style are centered

in the individual; they encourage suspicion of formal authority.
The low-church tradition respects kindredship, tends often to
be xenophobic (regarding Catholics, Jews, blacks, Indians, La-
tins, Orientals), has a strong sense of its own organic health and
deep fears of the threat of "disease" from "outside." It is con-
vulsed regularly by the need to "clean house." It is a tradition
of much decency, order, kindliness. It values cleanliness. It is
troubled by strangeness. It has a strong sense of what is proper,
and it nourishes conformity to what is good, right, and approved.
Since its ideology is individualism and since it is highly informal
in its rituals and practices, its communal discipline and high
distaste for nonconformity are masked. The political expression
of this tradition is populism in the South, Americanism in the
small towns of the North and West. George Wallace, Lyndon
Johnson, Fred Harris, Lawton Chiles, Lester Maddox, Ralph
Yarborough, Albert Gore, and Estes Kefauver have been able
to tap the energy of its symbolic world.

Third, there is the denominational, commerce-instructed
moralism of the middle-class heartland churches. Reformist and
yet practical, determined to produce good individuals and to do
so by a kind of missionary salesmanship, this tradition is more
sober and decorous than its poorer cousin. Billy Graham works
within this tradition, but figures as diverse as Dwight Eisenhower and Hubert Humphrey also shape it. It has a slightly
Midwestern rather than a purely Southern flavor. It is Methodist rather than Baptist. It falls in between the "high" and "low"
traditions described above. It differs from the high-church tradition in its reliance on the experience, enthusiasm, and energy
of the individual; thus, it has a need for salesmanship and constant missionary activity. It differs from the low-church tradition
in its acceptance of structures, professionalism, bureaucracies,
expertise. The low-church tradition is essentially a band of the
many under a single leader, with as few trappings as possible,
priding itself on a certain amateurism. The denominational tradition prefers controlled emotions and energies and employs
middle-class skills for awakening and channeling them. The image behind the low-church style is the preacher on the side
of Light and against the impending forces of Darkness. The

image behind the denominational style is the smooth, sincere salesman, candidly offering a better product, putting his heart into his salesmanship. Most Protestant political leaders and movements outside the mainline tradition of the Northeast are distributed between the low-church and the denominational types.

It will surprise many, who think of him solely as a manipulator and pragmatist, to step outside their normal perceptions and recognize the extent to which Richard Nixon before Watergate pictured himself as reforming the American spirit, calling it back to traditions it had been slipping away from. It is easy enough to see Nixon in the same tradition as Billy Graham. Like Hubert Humphrey, he was the son of a small storeowner during the Depression and, as Eugene McCarthy once put it, "can't bear to see a customer leave the store without buying." But Nixon is much more ideological, has a much harder mind of his own, than his detractors expected. Except for Watergate, he might have gone down in history not solely as a pragmatist, but as a significant moralist, who dramatically altered the climate of the country and restored certain threatened symbols to positions of prestige. All the more powerfully, the Watergate scandal cast his moralism into bitter disrepute and poisoned his reputation with charges of hypocrisy. The symbols of "law and order" which he championed became the instruments of his disgrace.

Alongside these fundamental types, there is a fourth current in Protestantism, not permanent and dominant, but cyclical: an Awakening type, a leader who rises up out of Protestantism (often from the Midwest) and calls for general political reform. Such a leader often spurs a major political and moral realignment. Groups like the Quakers keep alive an underground of moral metaphor and practical moral activity. But from time to time the national situation causes some person or movement to leap into prominence around a burning moral issue: abolition, Wall Street, Prohibition, civil rights, antiwar protest (a college like Oberlin in Ohio is a weathervane institution for such Awakenings). William Jennings Bryan in 1896, McGovern in 1972—these are men who break outside the normal American traditions and yet walk a worn path in her history.

Fifth, there is the black Protestant experience, much more communal, much closer to emotion and raw experience, much more interpersonal and vibrant with living networks than that of most of the white Protestant stocks. Blacks, of course, have all the traditions mentioned above for whites; but they also have their own. A black man "tendin' to business" may be going to his friends to keep the lines of communal life alive, to keep his psychic network strong. "Brother" and "sister" have fuller resonance among blacks than among whites. Like white ethnics from southern and eastern Europe, blacks encountered individualism on these shores as a new and not wholly satisfying approach to life. Black politics radiates such body heat and lively sensitivity that a white politician at a black gathering sometimes seems as stiff and uncomfortable as an icicle in July. It was one of Hubert Humphrey's assets among blacks that he himself radiated a responsive heat and energy—he could swing. It was one of George McGovern's liabilities that he could not.

Each of these different traditions has its own view of America. Each has its own favorite metaphors and methods of proceeding. Each has its own fears. Each has its own aspirations and dreamlike images of fulfillment. Each has its own thought patterns about social decisions. Each has its own rituals and forms of celebration. Each has its own attitude toward tolerance, compromise, and practicality. Each has its own stereotypes of the others.

From his own religious tradition, each president tends to derive quite different conceptions of power and its exercise. Those of the high-church type benefit by a tradition of high-level casuistry regarding general principles, which enables them to act comfortably in positions of conflict and compromise. Those of the low-church type tend to claim a mandate from the people and to override debate and opposition; they also tend to hold moral principles in one compartment and practical expedience in another, and to alternate between compartments. Those of the denominational type tend to be highly moralistic, deeply "principled," and caught in frequent crises which their moral stiffness makes it difficult for them to negotiate.

In a little book called *So Help Me God,* Robert S. Alley sheds fascinating light on such variations. His categories are a little different from those we have employed here, but his approach to the civil religion is similar. Alley believes civil religion is "far more fluid a reality" than Bellah and others suggest. "The national mood, the international balance of power, and the strength of presidential personalities tend to construct a new civil religion in every generation." The civil religion is "affected in character and form by the quality of religion exemplified by the President."

Alley distinguishes three powerful religious traditions exemplified by our presidents: Congregational-Unitarian; Calvinist (including high-church and low-church variants); and Episcopalian. He calls these "Type A," "Type B," and "Type C," respectively.

Type A equates religion with morality and sees morality as essentially the product of human reason, an outgrowth of enlightenment. Presidents John Adams, Thomas Jefferson, John Quincy Adams, Abraham Lincoln, and Andrew Johnson were from this tradition. Deism rather than Christianity seems to have been more expressive of their symbolic world. Whatever their roots in historical Christianity, they were impatient with church restrictions and sought a more universal and reasoned field of symbols. The ethics of such presidents tended to be goal-oriented.

Type B assumes in Calvinist fashion that religion and politics are in tension until the latter is tamed by the former. The warding off of threatening evil with "the armor of righteousness" is one of its motifs; the advancement of God's cause by bold and active acceptance of America's destiny is another. Ancient Israel is its favorite archetype. It sees faithfulness to national mission as obedience to God. National success and national righteousness are intertwined. As the "mainstream" of English dissent in the New World, the several Calvinist traditions (Baptist and Presbyterian, Quaker and Methodist) have tended to generate a national righteousness, exemplified in diverse ways by Wilson and Nixon, Truman and Eisenhower. (Alley does not separate the high from the low Calvinist traditions, and so in this category he places his longest list. Apart from the four already named, he includes Andrew Jackson, U. S. Grant, Grover Cleveland, William McKinley, Theodore Roosevelt, Warren Harding, Calvin Coolidge, Herbert Hoover, and Lyndon Johnson.)

The Type B president tends to be legalistic, and closely links the symbols of religion and politics. After 1868, Alley notes, Type A has ceased to appear among our presidents, and the entire series of presidents, with three exceptions, were of Type B. With Andrew Jackson, the denominations of Middle America seized the symbols of the presidency from those of patrician, enlightened, Deist style and have held them almost constantly until today.

Type C, according to Alley's scheme, is the "via media" of Anglican and Catholic traditions. It prides itself on avoiding "enthusiasm" and "moralism" on the one hand, and immobility and legalism on the other. It favors doctrinal breadth and fluidity, a sense of harmony and proportion. It regards history as a school of methods for opening up narrow orthodoxies and making "unbending principles" pliable. It inculcates a sort of realism and long-range pragmatism. More than Type B, Type C measures the institutions and political claims of religion by practical criteria. More than Type A, it nourishes traditional symbols and rituals, often giving them new uses. Alley lists George Washington, Franklin Pierce, Chester A. Arthur, Franklin Roosevelt, and John F. Kennedy under Type C.

The United States has not had as president a Lutheran or a black or a Jew or a Pentecostal or an Italian-Catholic or a person of Spanish surname, or an atheist. The effects of such cultural traditions on the presidency are yet to be known.

Alley's scheme is imperfect, but it does bring to attention the symbolic traditions presidents have been shaped by. Certain possibilities obvious to one president may never show themselves to another, whose way of perceiving screens them out. Alley's scheme also has the virtue of suggesting that the religious traditions so far dominant among presidents are far from exhausting our people's resources.

20

High-Church America

The most remarkable model of American pluralism is probably to be found not in Boston but in Hawaii, where three distinct cultural traditions—Polynesian, Oriental, and Caucasian—live in relative equality and pride. The greatest influence upon the general American psyche, both in multitudes reached and in the transmission of daily attitudes and styles in ordinary life, is probably to be attributed not to New England Puritanism, but to the Southern and Midwestern evangelicals. Nonetheless, the self-understanding of America's Northeastern élites—classically expressed in Perry Miller's "New England mind"—may be the single most important force in several of the nation's basic institutions and in some of the nation's central intellectual traditions. To these élites from the private prep schools and colleges, among the financiers and the captains of industry, in high national leadership, in publishing and *belles lettres,* and now as well in the communications industry and the professions, the nation owes significant debts.

These élites have not been nearly so self-serving, vain, profligate or decadent as national élites elsewhere have been. Whatever their prodigies of spending and display, whatever their hardheadedness about power and wealth, they have been (as history goes) remarkably public-spirited, and on the whole relatively liberal. When one compares them to élites in other quarters of the world, their philanthropy, their defense of civil liberties, and their instinct for stewardship may perhaps be allowed to cover some of their sins. Their devotion to symphonies, art galleries, and universities significantly enhances our public life.

The nation's commitment to the Bill of Rights, particularly to civil liberties, is not constantly supported by the winds of popular sentiment. The steady devotion of the Northeastern élite to civil liberties has been an important factor in the preservation of such freedoms as we have.

The nation's favorite image of "blue-ribbon" integrity and granite morality is still centered among the scions of this élite. When, after Watergate, Richard Nixon sought to reestablish the nation's confidence in the Department of Justice, it was inevitable that he should turn to the single Brahmin in his cabinet, Elliot Richardson, and that in naming a special prosecutor Richardson should turn to another, Archibald Cox.

Thus, it is important to grasp clearly the shape of the civil religion of our Northeastern élites. It is, indeed, precisely this tradition that most nearly supports the portrait drawn by Robert Bellah in his essay "Civil Religion in America." Two streams feed this tradition: the high doctrines of public service nourished by New England Congregationalism and Anglicanism, and the enlightened rationalism of men like Benjamin Franklin, George Washington, and Thomas Jefferson. A powerful blend of secular practicality and religious conscientiousness was fused with a love of liberty. What Ralph Waldo Emerson wrote of the English in *English Traits* may with fairness be written also of this élite in America: "That which lures a solitary American in the woods with the wish to see England, is the moral peculiarity of the Saxon race—its commanding sense of right and wrong,—the love and devotion to that,—this is the imperial trait, which arms them with the sceptre of the globe."

Emerson adds as well, with loving ethnocentricity, a passage on traits of mind institutionalized still today in high-church America:

> The Teutonic tribes have a national singleness of heart, which contrasts with the Latin races. The German name has a proverbial significance of sincerity and honest meaning. The arts bear testimony to it. The faces of clergy and laity in old sculpture and illuminated missals are charged with earnest belief. Add to this hereditary rectitude, the punctuality and precise dealing which commerce creates and you have the English truth and credit. The government strictly performs its engagements. The subjects do not understand trifling on its part. When any breach of promise occurred, in the old days of prerogative, it was resented by the people as an intolerable grievance. And in modern times, any slipperiness in the government in political faith, or any repudiation or crookedness in matters of finance would bring the whole nation to a committee of inquiry and reform. Private men kept their promises.

The significance of Bellah's conception is partly a product of the historical moment when his essay appeared (1968). Racial unrest and the war in Vietnam were then calling into question the legitimacy of American institutions. The nation had shown that it could absorb into its symbol system (a fact earlier not to be taken for granted*) a Catholic president. Thus, Bellah was able to show that the civil religion was not identical to Protestantism nor to Catholicism either, and yet that it is, in an important sense, a set of public institutions of significant social meaning and effect. These public institutions, he argued, give the nation moral resources it otherwise might lack.

Barely a third of the nation today is of Anglo-Saxon stock and of that, only a small portion is of the high-church sensibility. Again and again at central points in the nation's history, perhaps particularly in the history of the courts, that sensibility has steadied the nation, kept its liberties more intact than might

---
* Clinton Rossiter in *The American Presidency* (1958) did not concede the immediate likelihood.

have been, supported the freedoms of the press and insisted on high standards of public accountability. These moral qualities are not without flaw. "The English," Emerson writes, "abhorring changes in all things . . . are dreadfully given to cant. The English (and I wish it were confined to them, but 'tis a taint in the Anglo-Saxon blood in both hemispheres), the English and the Americans cant beyond all other nations."

A kind of exclusiveness is another flaw. Dirt farmers in Alabama have been dismissed as "rednecks," Scotch-Irish Appalachians disregarded as "hillbillies," Midwesterners mocked as "hayseeds," Westerners disdained as "roughnecks," Catholics, Jews, blacks and others kept from important social worlds.

Until Kennedy, however, the national symbol systems, had been deceptively Protestant—high Protestant, in good measure—in their reach and range. W. Lloyd Warner describes in *The Family of God* a sacred ceremony at the Yankee City Tercentenary in Connecticut, a ceremony unwittingly designed so as to exclude over half its actual citizens:

> Since these groups, including Jew, Poles, Greeks, French Canadians, and others, were all of comparatively recent origin, none being older than about the fourth decade of the nineteenth century, when the Catholic Irish first appeared, to select appropriate symbols for sponsoring ethnic groups and to make assignment of them was a difficult problem for the central committee. Since the interest and main emphasis of those responsible for the subjects chosen was upon periods before the arrival of the new immigrant groups, the problem was even more thorny. The conception of the celebration and the pageant had to do with the Puritan ancestors and the flowering of New England culture; the themes of the great ethnic migrations and their assimilation—the melting pot, the Promised Land, and the goddess of Liberty welcoming them —democracy for all and every kind of race and creed—such themes were nowhere present. Indeed, those who conceived and presented the pageant saw themselves as teachers initiating the new peoples into the true significance of the nation.

The election of John F. Kennedy ruptured the strictly Protestant symbolism. Kennedy wore the top hat of a Harvard overseer jauntily and quoted from the Adams family with gusto. Still, Kennedy and "Camelot" (is it an accident the symbol is at the heart of the English kingly tradition, partly Celtic and from a Catholic era?) introduced new possibilities. Because Kennedy was suave, many have failed to note how utterly *Catholic* his imagination was—not Catholic as Joseph McCarthy was or as Eugene McCarthy is or Daniel Berrigan, but Catholic nonetheless. The cold eyes that had "looked into the abyss," his cry in Berlin that "life is not fair," the excitement in his mind about words like "burden" and "sacrifice," a hard political judgment wed to poetic moralism, a high sense of liturgy, a sense of rapidly passing time against an eternal backdrop ("not in the first one hundred days, nor in the first one thousand days, nor in our lifetime on this planet . . ."), a zest for battle, and an undisguised love of power and politics—all these were signs of a distinctly Catholic, even Irish Catholic, sensibility. Others too, felt liberated by these themes, so starkly absent in Protestant symbolism. The flavor was rougher, tougher, more naked, dangerous. (Henry Fairlie in *The Politics of Promise* takes a traditional British skepticism toward their Celtic flavor.)

Precisely for such reasons, Bellah was right to choose Kennedy as the chief figure for his study. Kennedy was a Catholic. But so far as the public office went, Kennedy could move comfortably within the symbols of the civil religion without either surrendering his Catholicism or making it offensively obtrusive. Bellah chooses key passages from Kennedy's Inaugural Address, which are easily paralleled by passages in other sacred scriptures of the land. For example, these, from the beginning:

> We observe today not a victory of party but a celebration of freedom—symbolizing an end as well as a beginning—signifying renewal as well as change. For I have sworn before you and Almighty God the same solemn oath our forebears prescribed nearly a century and three quarters ago. . . . And yet the same revolutionary beliefs for which our forebears fought are still at issue around the globe—the belief that the rights of man come not from the generosity of the state but from the hand of God.

And from the conclusion:

> Finally, whether you are citizens of America or of the world,
> ask of us the same high standards of strength and sacrifice
> that we shall ask of you. With a good conscience our only
> sure reward, with history the final judge of our deeds, let us
> go forth to lead the land we love, asking His blessing and
> His help, but knowing that here on earth God's work must
> truly be our own.

A critic might say that such invocations of God merely con-
firm the essentially irrelevant role of religion in a secular democracy, are ritualistic expressions which a president must use in
order to placate some voters or to dissemble a kind of ritual
piety, are echoes, even, of the traditional cant. Bellah answers:
"But we know enough about the function of ceremonial and
ritual in various societies to make us suspicious of dismissing
something as unimportant because it is 'only a ritual.' What
people say on solemn occasions need not be taken at face value,
but it is often indicative of deep-seated values and commitments
that are not made explicit in the course of everyday life." In
Brooklyn Bridge: Fact and Symbol, Alan Trachtenberg makes
a similar point: "Speeches might be dismissed as highly conven-
tional and insincere. Sincerity, however, is not a necessary quali-
fication for cultural significance; surely the conventions of language themselves suggest predispositions among Americans to
react in certain ways at certain times."

Kennedy's words arise from the substratum of American
experience. America has a mission to take up God's work against
"the common enemies of man":

> Now the trumpet summons us again—not as a call to bear
> arms, though arms we need—not as a call to battle, though
> embattled we are—but a call to bear the burden of a long
> twilight struggle, year in and year out, "rejoicing in hope,
> patient in tribulation"—a struggle against the common en-
> emies of man: tyranny, poverty, disease, and war itself.

These words are richly biblical, and they recapitulate America's self-understanding. As God led Israel out of bondage to Egypt, so did he lead his "second Israel" out of bondage to the king of England, for the sake of "mighty works" on behalf of all mankind. In this land it would not be enough—according to this high religion—to "get yours," to "get ahead," to enjoy *la dolce vita.* (By contrast, President Nixon, in his Inaugural Address of 1972, almost as if in answer to sentences of Kennedy, appealed to another of the nation's self-understandings: "Ask not what your government can do for you, but what you can do for yourself.") The American conscience does not rest at ease with the knowledge that 40 percent of the world's resources is devoured by a mere 6 percent of the world's people; many find America's consumer wealth a scandal against the national ideal. The national faith *might have been* wholly hedonistic, ruthlessly decadent. We have the power and the means. Instead, the call is to take up a higher destiny.

Not only exodus and destiny, also sacrifice and martyrdom. The Union endured "a time of testing." The most bloody civil war in history was fought here. Lincoln himself became an imitator of the Christ, yielding up his life for the nation. "Witness" and "sacrifice"—"a good conscience our only sure reward"— were added by high religion to the native pragmatism as much valued attributes.

Moreover, the nation itself plainly is not God. Whatever the basic need for civil organization—in order "to abolish poverty" and to attack the other "common enemies of man"—no state has absolute or total claim over human life: "the rights of man come not from the generosity of the state but from the hands of God." The classic formula of our national self-understanding, "This nation under God," does not, strictly, commit all citizens to a theistic position. Nevertheless, in the inaugural ritual, the president does not take his oath before the people only; "For I have sworn before you and almighty God the same solemn oath our forebears prescribed nearly a century and three-quarters ago."

Bellah comments:

Beyond the Constitution, then, the president's obligation ex-

tends not only to the people but to God. . . . The will of
the people is not itself the criterion of right and wrong. There
is a higher criterion in terms of which this will can be
judged; it is possible that the people may be wrong. The
president's obligation extends to the higher criterion.

Thus, the high civil religion keeps vacant in conscience the place
where God is properly honored, but it neither defines how one
ought to think of God nor obliges anyone actually to enshrine
God in conscience. It simply forbids the state to usurp his place;
it keeps that place empty. When Kennedy used the symbol
"God," many others could also accept that symbol without being
committed to his specifically Catholic traditions for interpreting
it. Nor did he have to borrow the Deism or Unitarianism of
some among the Founding Fathers or later presidents.

In the high civil religion, at least in classic *loci* like the Declaration of Independence and the series of Inaugural Addresses, the
symbol "god" functions as a sign that individual conscience
transcends the claims of the state. "This nation under God"
means that the nation is not the final arbiter of morality. That
in itself is a high achievement of political wisdom, of civilization, and of moral development. Bellah writes:

> Behind the civil religion at every point lie biblical archetypes:
> Exodus, Chosen People, Promised Land, new Jerusalem,
> Sacrificial Death, and Rebirth. But the civil religion is also
> genuinely new. It has its own prophets and its own martyrs,
> its own sacred events and sacred places, its own solemn
> rituals and symbols. It is concerned that America be a so-
> ciety as perfectly in accord with the will of God as men can
> make it and a light to all the nations.
>
> In times past the American civil religion has often been
> used and is being used today as a cloak for petty interests
> and ugly passions. It is in need—as is any living faith—of
> continual reformation, of being measured by universal
> standards. But it is not evident that our civil religion is in-
> capable of growth and new insight.

The high civil religion is not the same as glorification of the
status quo; it is not the absolutizing of "the American way of

life"; it is not a celebration of mediocrity. Quite to the contrary. It explicitly invokes conscience, transcendence, prophecy, and searing judgment. Lincoln, like some Moses of old, did not hesitate to hold the entire nation under as fearful a judgment as any leader has ever uttered upon his people:

> Neither party expected for the war the magnitude or the duration which it has already attained. . . . Each looked for an easier triumph, and a result less fundamental and astounding. Both read the same Bible, and pray to the same God; and each invokes His aid against the other. It may seem strange that any men should dare to ask a just God's assistance in wringing their bread from the sweat of other men's faces; but let us judge not, that we be not judged. The prayers of both could not be answered—that of neither has been answered fully.
>
> The Almighty has his own purposes. . . . If we shall suppose that American slavery is one of those offenses which, in the providence of God must needs come, but which, having continued through His appointed time, He now wills to remove, and that He gives to both North and South this terrible war, as the woe due to those by whom the offense came, shall we discern therein any departure from those divine attributes which the believers in a living God always ascribe to Him?
>
> Fondly do we hope—fervently do we pray—that this mighty scourge of war may speedily pass away. Yet, if God wills that it continue until all the wealth piled by the bondman's two hundred and fifty years of unrequited toil shall be sunk, and until every drop of blood drawn with the lash shall be paid by another drawn with the sword, as was said three thousand years ago, so still it must be said, "The judgments of the Lord are true and righteous altogether."

Carl Sandburg records that when President Lincoln finished the terse six hundred words of this Inaugural Address, witnesses saw many faces wet with tears. Perhaps at no time in the nation's history was the high civil religion called into such full and transcending power, utterly appropriate to the tragedy at hand. We do not have to imagine what would have happened had pettier and less profoundly American men than Lincoln given direction to the nation at that point; for in a few months Lincoln was no more, and such men nourished evils that plague us still.

21

The Second Great Tradition

The high civil religion, however, competes with a powerful rival in the Protestant world. This rival is not without its beauty —and its flaws. The custom is to speak disapprovingly of the evangelical Protestantism of the South and West. The great popular preachers—Billy Graham, Norman Vincent Peale, Carl MacIntyre, and dozens of other evangelists of radio and television —are an embarrassment to high-thinking Americans. Yet their social influence is enormous.

H. L. Mencken, in his usual debunking and entertaining fashion, wrote of Protestantism's decline. To one side, he wrote, the greater part of Protestant money is moving toward indifference. To the other, the greater part of Protestant libido is sliding into religious voodoo. In the middle is desiccation and decay. "Here," he writes, "is where Protestantism once was strongest. Here is the region of the plain and godly American, fond of devotion but distrustful of every hint of orgy—the honest fellow who suffers dutifully on Sunday, pays his tithes, and hopes for a few kind words from the pastor when his time comes to die."

In New England, Mencken asserts, Puritanism is overrated. "The fact is that the civilization in the region, such as it was, owed very little to the actual Puritans; it was mainly the product of anti-Puritans." At Harvard, he judges, real education began only with the rising minority of anti-Puritans, eventually to become a majority, who rose up and made Harvard secular. "Harvard delivered New England, and made civilization possible there. All the men who adorned that civilization in the days of its glory—Emerson, Hawthorne and all the rest of them—were essentially anti-Puritans." In modern times, Mencken avers, New England is not Puritan; every one of its clergymen would be found heretical if the Mathers could come back to life. "The old heat is gone. Where it lingers in America is in far places—on the Methodist prairies of the Middle West, in the Baptist backwaters of the South." This form of religion survives "not merely as a system of theology, but also as a way of life. It colors every activity; it is powerful in politics."

Imagine a religious map of the United States. Each county whose population exceeds 50 percent in one denomination is given a solid color representing that denomination. Each county in which one denomination has a plurality, but less than 50 percent, receives a shaded color. On such a map the original denominations of New England, Congregationalist and Episcopal, hold hardly a dozen counties on the entire map—one in Colorado, perhaps, another here or there. Roman Catholic colors dominate Northern urban areas. There are significant suburban concentrations of Presbyterians. Lutherans hold some counties in the Middle West. But almost the entire map—solid South, Midwest, West, and much of the East—is Baptist and Methodist.

Mencken praises the old civilization that prevailed in the South before the Civil War, "a civilization of manifold excellences—perhaps the best the Western Hemisphere had ever seen—undoubtedly the best These States had ever seen." The "main hatchery" of this nation's ideas, he writes, was south of the Potomac. "It was there that nearly all the political theories we still cherish and suffer under came to birth. It was there that the crude dogmatism of New England was refined and humanized. It was there above all, that some attention was given to the art of living—that life got beyond and above the state of mere infliction and became an exhilarating experience. A certain notable spaciousness was in the ancient Southern scheme of things. The *Ur*-Confederate had leisure. He liked to toy with ideas. He was hospitable and tolerant. He had the vague thing we call culture." Mencken bewailed the loss of this culture. "It is as if the Civil War stamped out every bearer of the torch, and left only a mob of peasants on the field."

That Billy Graham is today the South's most prominent and popular citizen would have driven Mencken's satiric fingers, itching, to the typewriter. That the president of the United States —four presidents in a row—should for twenty years have made Billy Graham the foremost representative of the American religion would have given him St. Vitus' dance.

Yet Billy Graham is not peripheral to the history of America. He draws upon a great symbolic tradition. Most Protestants in America accept a national self-understanding less self-transcending than that of high-church America. Their symbols and rituals closely link church and nation, Protestant Christianity and global politics. How mainline figures like Richard Nixon draw upon these symbols has been described by Lowell D. Streiker and Gerald S. Strober in *Religion and the New Majority* and by Charles P. Henderson in *Nixon's Theology*. In both these books, Billy Graham looms large. Billy Graham, John Connally has said, "is more than a preacher, more than an evangelist, more than a Christian leader. In a greater sense, he has become our conscience."

The peculiarly American form of religion is not "cool," like the high civil religion, but "hot." It is composed of five significant qualities: zeal, enthusiasm, messianism, individual conversion, and commitment equally to nation and to God. "To be an American," writes William G. McLoughlin, the foremost student of evangelical religion, "is to belong to a pietistic sect." The United States, he continues, "is unique among nations because it professes to a conscience as well as a mission." The most popular religious institution is the sect. Deeper than that, this peculiarly American form of Christianity makes the whole nation a sect. It makes belonging to America an act of "belief," a participation in a "conscience."

On Honor America Day in front of the Lincoln Memorial, July 4, 1970, Billy Graham applied religious language to civil institutions exactly as preachers have for many generations. We are here, he said, to honor the nation, "to renew *our dedication and allegiance* to the principles and institutions which made her great. Lately, our institutions have been under attack: the Supreme Court, the Congress, the Presidency, the flag, the home, the educational system, and even the church—but we are here to say with loud voices that in spite of their faults and failures we *believe* in these institutions!" [Emphasis added.] Graham spoke as though the nation were under a covenant with God: "God will judge any nation that turns its back on Him—especially a nation like America which has been given more privileges and opportunities than any nation in history." He asked "prayer and dedication to God and recommitment to the ideals and dreams upon which our country was founded."

Thus, America is not, in the minds of our thirty-one million fundamentalist Christians, and perhaps millions of others, a secular state. It is a sectarian state, founded on ideals and dreams intimately tied to Protestant commitments. These commitments are large enough to admit Catholics and Jews. But the history that binds them is preeminently evangelical Protestant and even Anglo-Saxon.

Exactly 144 years before Graham spoke, and 50 long years after the signing of the Declaration of Independence, on July 4, 1826, two founders of the Republic died. Both Thomas Jefferson and John Adams were "called by God" on exactly the same day, a sacred day. "In this most singular coincidence," wrote one divine as great crowds—thirty thousand in Baltimore alone—turned out, "the finger of God is plainly visible. It hallows the Declaration of Independence as the Word of God." In this double death Providence foretold that the principles of that Declaration would find "dissemination universal over the whole Earth." Most comforting to early Americans were two historic symbols: Teutonic Saxony and ancient Israel. By these coordinates Americans located themselves in history. A frequent phrase was "our British Israel," "our English Israel." Thomas Jefferson designed a national seal that would depict, on one side, an image of Israel, and, on the other, a symbol of Saxony: "The children of Israel in the wilderness led by a cloud by day and a pillar by night . . . and Hengist and Horsa, the Saxon chiefs, from whom we claim the honor of being descended and whose political principles and form of government we have assumed."

The following texts set forth one major theme of our tradition, nowadays seldom made explicit, but buried and active in the national imagination:

In 1836, two British Christians: "Blot out Britain and America from the map of the world, and you destroy all those great institutions which almost exclusively promise the world's renovation."

Philip Schaff, the historian: "The Anglo-Saxon and Anglo-American, of all modern races, possess the strongest national character and the one best fitted for universal dominion."

Robert Baird, 1844: The English and the German are "the chief supports of the laws and institutions of evangelical Christianity" and carry "in their hands the theoretical and practical mission of Protestantism for the world."

Horace Bushnell in 1865: "We are the grand experiment of Protestantism!"

Josiah Strong, an Ohio clergyman, whose *Our Country* (1885) sold hundreds of thousands of copies:

> It seems to me that God with infinite wisdom and skill is training the Anglo-Saxon race for an hour sure to come in the world's future . . . the final competition of races. . . . Then this race of unequaled energy, with all the majesty of numbers and the might of wealth behind it—the representative, let us hope, of the largest liberty, the purest Christianity, the highest civilization—having developed peculiarly aggressive traits calculated to impress its institutions upon

mankind will spread itself over the earth. . . . Can anyone
doubt that the result of this competition of races will be
the "survival of the fittest"? . . .
   Not only is [God] preparing in our civilization the die
with which to stamp the nations but. . . . He is preparing mankind to receive our impress . . . until in a very true
and important sense [our race] has Anglo-Saxonized mankind.

Albert J. Beveridge in 1899 believed it was the mission of
the United States to replace the British Empire in maintaining
world order: "It is ours to reinforce *that thin red line* which
constitutes the outposts of civilization all around the world."
(That image of "the thin red line"—my emphasis—recurs often in
American traditions.) Beveridge continues:

   The Republic never retreats. . . . Whatever its destiny it
   must proceed. For the American Republic is a part of the
   movement of a race, the most masterful race of history,
   and race movements are not to be stayed by the hand of
   man. . . .
   The sovereign tendencies of our race are organization and
   government. We govern so well that we govern ourselves.
   We organize by instinct. Under the flag of England our race
   builds an empire out of the ends of the earth. . . . Everywhere it obeys that Voice . . . which . . . makes of us our
   brothers' keeper and appoints us steward under God of the
   civilization of the world. . . God . . . has made us the
   lords of civilization that we may administer civilization. . . .
   The dominant notes in American life henceforth will
   be . . . administration and world improvement. It is the
   arduous but splendid mission of our race. It is ours to govern in the name of civilized liberty. It is ours to administer
   order and law in the name of human progress. It is ours to
   chasten that we may be kind . . . It is ours to build that
   free institutions may finally enter and abide. . . .
   American manhood today contains the master adminis-
   trators of the world, and they go forth for the healing of
   the nations. They go forth in the cause of civilization. They
   go forth for the betterment of man. . . . They go forth to

prepare the peoples, through decades and maybe centuries of patient effort, for the great gift of American institutions.

W. W. Rostow asks in *The Diffusion of Power: An Essay in Recent History* (1973) "Will the United States mobilize the strength, will and imagination to bring about the emergence of new nations in Asia, the Middle East, Africa and Latin America as congenial open societies?" There still exists a journal called by its founder *The Christian Century*.

People who would otherwise reject George Wallace—and many in this second Protestant tradition do—nevertheless hear in his speech recognizable themes from history:

America cries out for leadership. All of us, of all ages, races and colors yearn for the America we started out to build. The times beat against our happiness and our security like a hammer on an anvil. The times seem to overwhelm our leaders. . . .

America cries out for a turn of events. We want to be rid of the storm of doubt and the continuing crisis that begat new crises. We want victory in our lives and control of our times and real hope for our country in the battles for survival, security and greatness. . . . There are a lot of fancy philosophers and libertarian pundits whose books and pamphlets I haven't read and am not likely to read. But I believe that government governs best which governs least, and that whatever the people will have their government do is best done at that level closest to the people. I mean to defend my country against her enemies—foremost of which is the International Communist Conspiracy. I mean to labor at being the best Christian, and the best citizen, that I can be. And I mean to try to serve my country with an unashamed patriotism. If enough of us do that—if enough of us Stand Up for America—we can stop America's retreat from victory. But the stakes are high. We know that if we fail, liberty in all the world might flicker and die for a thousand years.

The radical and fundamental national metaphors are these: The Anglo-Saxon race is superior in its self-regulation, its ordered liberties, its administrative talents. The rest of the world is unfree, disordered, anarchic, threatening. Here there is order and light. We must never retreat. One surrender, and decadence may overtake us.

In 1898, for William McKinley, these national metaphors were potent:

> The truth is that I didn't want the Phillipines, and when they came to us as a gift from the gods I did not know what to do with them . . . I sought counsel . . . I walked the floor of the White House night after night until midnight, and I am not ashamed to tell you, gentlemen, that I went down on my knees and prayed Almighty God for light and guidance more than one night. And one night late it came to me this way—I don't know how it was but it came: (1) That we could not give them back to Spain—that would be cowardly and dishonorable. (2) That we could not turn them over to France or Germany . . . that would be bad business and discreditable. (3) That we could not leave them to themselves—they were unfit for self-government, and they would soon have anarchy and misrule over there worse than Spain's was. And (4) that there was nothing left for us to do but to take them all, and to educate the Filipinos, and uplift and civilize and Christianize them, and by God's grace do the very best we could by them as our fellowmen for whom Christ also died. And then I went to bed and went to sleep, and slept soundly, and the next morning I sent for the chief engineer of the War Department (our map-maker), and I told him to put the Philippines on the map of the United States.

This sense of destiny has serious uses. It continues to inform even enlightened views of the position of the United States in world affairs. It has both its good and its evil side. Thus, even Reinhold Niebuhr (1888-1971), the greatest theologian America has ever produced and the most incisive critic of our national chauvinism, expressed it in his 1943 essay "Anglo-Saxon Destiny and Responsibility":

> . . .
> only those who have no sense of the profundities of history

would deny that various nations and classes, various social groups and races are at various times placed in such a position that a special measure of the divine mission in history falls upon them. In that sense God has chosen us in this fateful period of world history. . . . It so happens that the combined power of the British Empire and the United States is at present greater than any other power. It is also true that the political ideals that are woven into the texture of their history are less incompatible with international justice than any other previous power of history. . . .

If Germany has been the particular bearer of the idea of destiny through power, the Anglo-Saxon world has been constantly tempted to express its sense of destiny pharisaically and to claim eminence by the right of its virtue. It is this element in Anglo-Saxon politics that has subjected it to the charge of "cant" from Continental nations. . . . The democratic traditions of the Anglo-Saxon world are actually the potential basis of a just world order. . . . The world community cannot be realized if the Anglo-Saxon world fails in its historic mission.

There is a tendency to view the chauvinism of Richard Nixon or the ethnocentrism of George Wallace as peculiar to them. They lie, rather, in the second major stream of American self-understanding. America has understood itself as a Protestant, evangelical, biblical nation. Much that is good flows from this understanding. Many of our internal and external misapprehensions arise from it as well. It guides domestic, as well as international, perception. Of Nixon's views we have made mention. A brief consideration of the uses to which Wallace puts this second great tradition may reveal some sources of his power.

In *The Politics of Unreason,* Seymour Martin Lipset and Earl Raab conclude that George Wallace in 1968 represented basically a "preservationist tendency." This was the main line of Wallace's spirit and his appeal. In its train, they adjudge, as part of its background but not its foreground, came institutional racism. Wallace wished to preserve the culture of Alabama and of other regions of the country, its symbols, its institutions. He pitted himself against the great powers of nationalization which had been called down upon the people, as he felt, from on high. He drew a parallel between these new powers and the bankers and plantation owners and mine operators who had plundered American localities in generations past. Riches were taken to faraway cities, while many on the land remained in poverty. Thus, the symbolic targets of preservationism were for a long time "the big boys" of Wall Street and the corporation executives of "the effete Northeast." Now for Wallace these symbolic targets have come to be replaced by the "snobs" of national government and their "allies" in the media. It is from such sources that the "guidelines" and the "superior morality" of the "experts" come. "You can't even walk across the street," Wallace shouted, "till they send you a guideline." The forces of modern liberalism have shifted from economic to cultural issues. "It used to be," Wallace told a crowd in Florida, "that liberalism meant letting the individual free but now it means coercion."

Thus Wallace—and other "populists"—point to a genuine dilemma in Anglo-American democracy. Liberalism as a tradition began by liberating individuals from a restrictive social order. "That government is best which governs least," encapsulates the older tradition. (This tradition survives in such decisions as that of the Supreme Court in 1973 regarding abortion.) Yet, as John Dewey noted in *Liberalism and Social Action* (1936), there has developed "an inner split" in liberalism. The emphasis on the individual promoted by Bentham and Mill can become a conservative defense of powerful interests.

Thus, Dewey wrote, new liberals of the 1930s expanded liberalism. "It is the business of the state," they held, "to promote all modes of human association in which the moral claims of the members of a society are embodied." The state does not remain neutral; it intervenes *for moral purposes*. The new liberals believe that the older liberal conception of the state "is in effect simply a justification of the brutalities and inequities of the existing order." They altered liberalism so that it came to mean not *laissez-faire* but moral intervention. Dewey concludes: "Because of this internal division within liberalism its later history is wavering and confused."

Practically all Americans are pulled between "do your own thing" and the need for law, controls, and order. Some want greater freedom in sexual matters and living styles, but stronger controls over industry and the environment. Some want "regional planning," and some want "community control."

"The political history of the United States is largely a record of domination by regional interests," wrote John Dewey in 1936. But George Wallace dislikes the countertrend which Dewey helped to establish: the trend of liberalism as a nationalizing force, pursuing national interests, under the banner of a superior national morality. "What did these so-called lib'rals bring us?" George Wallace asked huge crowds. "Drugs. Riots. Bureaucrats. Contempt for the average citizen, taxes that crush him and leave no freedom. Wars that can't be won. Aid to nations that spit on us in the United Nations. Thet's what they brung us."

Wallace attacks media liberalism for abandoning individualism in order to impose a new doctrine of national planning and national cultural standards. He attacks it for being "relativistic." He sees the struggle in America as a moral struggle. In a widely distributed pamphlet, *What I Believe,* he writes:

> For years Americans were the most admired people in the world because of their capacity for righteous indignation. Many Americans still rise to anger at evil, but our pseudo-intellectual leaders have used our colleges and mass media to preach moral and ethical relativism until many of our people have adopted a pretended sophistication and blasé attitude toward corruption, immorality, and even treason. America is in the midst of a full-scale retreat from greatness, and every honest American knows it. That retreat was begun by the treason of the intellectuals who, jaded and morally corrupt, lost their capacity for righteous indignation.

"Moral outrage," the radical-liberal writer Harvey Swados wrote the day after the election, "I had always thought, is what politics are about at bottom—at least when matters like war and peace are at stake, and sometimes even with questions of sewers, street lights and school crossings. Is it not precisely the moral element that has drawn poets and novelists into the political orbit?" Righteous indignation, a basic ingredient in the American approach to politics, but expressed in what conflicting directions, around what conflicting traditions?

Wallace is explicit about the *religious* nature of the struggle:

> As a result of the growing power of Washington, we have already become a government-fearing people instead of a God-fearing people. For decades now, politicians have encouraged us to look to government for strength instead of to our God. It is no accident that where the state becomes all-powerful, faith in Christ is no longer carried like a banner by Christian soldiers, workers, mothers, and businessmen. I have accepted Christ as my personal Savior, and that is one important reason why I have pledged my life to opposing tyranny wherever I find it.

The political dimensions are plain: What society in all the world is less "oppressive" than ours? Not one. And because we are so free, America's policemen are the thin blue line between anarchy and the survival of our Christian civilization.

Whose words are the following? Possibly Muskie's? Maybe Humphrey's? Those of McGovern?

> I am involved in America because I truly care. I care about this great land and these people and our freedoms. I am concerned about the present direction of America. We know it is the wrong direction. I want to help bring about the changes that will heal America and lead us to new victories. We can only reach this goal by being involved.

They belong to the same man who claims to understand best the pervading symbols of the American psyche. His brochure reads: "George Wallace's heart will always be with rank and file people. He listens to them. They trust him because he respects their thoughts. To him, the people's thoughts are what this election is all about." Mao Tse-George. Ho Chi Wallace returning to the "reactionary" villages to absorb the people's spirit, before turning it in a new direction.

It would be possible to draw out in detail other major civil religions in America besides those of high church America and the second great tradition.* But it is more revealing now to become concrete, and to recount some of the key symbolic moments of the presidential campaign of 1972.

---

* In *The Rise of the Unmeltable Ethnics* (Macmillan, 1972) I described an overlooked part of the Catholic experience in America and the understanding of America that flows from it. The importance of this Catholic "ethnic" civil religion is now widely recognized. Both Richard Nixon (early) and George McGovern (belatedly) identified the Catholic blue-collar worker as the pivotal constituency of 1972. Theodore H. White in *The Making of the President 1972* (Atheneum, 1973) described President Nixon's view of the nation as of 1970: "The President felt that there was a 'majority' growing in the country, and this new majority rested on reaching the blue-collar working people, above all on reaching Catholics. . . . The Nixon victory of 1968 had been won by the Southern strategy. . . ; the victory of 1972 would have to be won by a Northern strategy . . . the reach for the ethnic, blue-collar, Catholic vote." (pp. 49–51) For this constituency, Nixon's harsh speeches of 1970 backfired; by 1972, he had changed his approach to them. Even so, 47 percent of the Catholics voted for McGovern, 9 percent above his national average.

McGovern told White: "Our main problem is the blue-collar Catholic worker. . . . You just didn't know what would reach them." (p. 312) McGovern, according to one of his long-time aides, "came to resent the ethnics. The ethnics were the opposition, and his people shared his resentment—it became a campaign which couldn't understand its own vote." According to another aide: "Our people deluded themselves. . . .what the workingman resented was us." (pp. 317–18)

White, by the way, understates the Slavic Democratic vote in presidential races. In 1960, it was 82 percent, in 1964, 80 percent, in 1968, 64 percent. The Italian Democratic vote was 75 percent in 1960, 77 percent in 1964, 50 percent in 1968. (In 1968 Wallace won 12 percent of the Slavic vote and 10 percent of the Italian vote.) Nixon in 1972 was the first Republican in history to win a majority of the Catholic vote—53 percent. In 1968, by contrast, Nixon won an old-fashioned 33 percent (59 percent went for Humphrey, only 8 percent for Wallace). According to CBS, the Catholic Wallace voters of 1968 split almost evenly, 7–6, between Nixon and McGovern in 1972. Still, Nixon increased his vote among Catholics from about 7 million in 1968 to about 11 million in 1972. This gain of 4 million votes *also* represents a loss of 4 million to the Democrats; it would require 8 million new Democratic voters to make up for it. It is a potent swing vote.

Partly because of economic mismanagement and partly because of the Watergate scandals, the Catholic ethnic vote may again be bitterly contested in 1976. Nixon's "new majority" will not automatically remain intact. Cultural, symbolic issues remain in evidence.

Part Four

SYMBOLS

OF 1972

You must emerge, bright and *bubbling with wisdom and well-being,* every morning at 8 o'clock, just in time for a *charming and pro- found breakfast talk,* shake hands with hundreds, often literally thousands, of people, *make several inspiring, "newsworthy" speeches* during the day, confer with political leaders along the way and with your staff all the time, write at every chance, think if possible, read mail and newspapers, talk on the telephone, talk to everybody, dictate, receive delegations, eat, with decorum—and discretion!—and *ride through city after city on the back of an open car, smiling until your mouth is dehydrated by the wind, waving until the blood runs out of your arm, and then bounce gaily, confidently, masterfully into great howling halls, shaved and all made up for television with the right color shirt and tie—I always forgot—and a manuscript so defaced with chicken tracks and last-minute jottings that you couldn't follow it, even if the spotlights weren't blinding and even if the still photographers didn't shoot you in the eye every time you looked at them.* Then all you have to do is make a great, imperishable speech, get out through the pressing crowds with a few score autographs, your clothes intact, your hands bruised, and back to the hotel—in time to see a few important people.

—Adlai E. Stevenson, 1953

22

Traditional Symbols

Presidential candidates undergo rites of purification for the civil religion of which they will become high priest. Each must show himself worthy. Each must face ritual performances: press conferences, hand-shaking tours, speeches, carnival games, and solemn rites of government. But the key moments in a campaign are frequently those that shatter rituals. People probe their presidential candidates for "character," for some flash from the depths of a man that reveals his secret identity.

Nixon's campaigns are remarkable for their attempt to get around this requirement. In 1960, Nixon surrounded himself with Republican notables. (John Kennedy described this as the classic act of circus elephants, linked nose to tail, going around in circles.) In 1968, Nixon began with an incredible 18 percent lead in the opinion polls and a huge fund of discontent against the Democrats, tried to hide himself from the voters except in controlled circumstances, and nearly lost the election. Coming from very far back, Humphrey slowly, ebulliently, spontaneously, almost charmed the electorate out of its anger at the Democrats. In 1972, Nixon virtually did not campaign, leaving the empty field to the hapless George McGovern. RE-ELECT THE PRESIDENT, his campaign stickers said. His managers and he recognized quite coldly how little drawing power the man Nixon, even at the height of his success, held for the American spirit.

Most candidates for the presidency, even Nixon, must establish themselves in the public imagination. They must stand out from the other images presented daily to the public: *They* must stand out, not their image. Something of themselves must leap out of the television set, as it were, and make contact with the citizenry. For a president is not merely an actor toward whom the citizens are spectators. They participate in his actions; they identify with him. So far as his national actions go, they live in him. His acts are theirs. A president is not merely a mayor or a senator. He is their *persona*. He *is* the people, not in a sense that subsumes them under him (*"L'État, c'est moi!"*) but in the sense that he is their agent, their spokesman, their image of themselves. So long as he has their confidence, its actions have legitimacy and power. As their confidence in him deteriorates, so does his ability to act.

Virtually all a candidate's actions are public actions. All aspects of his life belong to the public: his relations with his family, his school record, his property arrangements, his past career, his deeds, his speeches, his capacity as an organizer and fund-raiser, his informal conversation, his friendships, his ability to manage his staff and to direct a far-flung campaign, his flair for dramatizing what he stands for, his self-control under pressure, his emotional accessibility, his capacity for dealing with pain or defeat or tragedy. The president becomes the vessel of the people's dreams. This does not mean he must pretend to be a god. It does mean he must actually be a leader.

The long political campaign of 1972 provided several memorable moments when ritual acts revealed the character of a candidate, or when the normal rituals were shattered. Not to calculate the power of such symbols is to be unrealistic.

Almost at random I have singled out several powerful symbolic moments in that campaign: two events in the New Hampshire primary; a Wallace speech and other events in Florida; the two-man struggle in Illinois; seven rallies in Wisconsin; a McGovern rally in New York City; and the making of a martyr. The events to be recalled are, in themselves, often minor. But they show something remarkable about power in America. Most of these symbolic moments I observed with my own eyes, travelling with the press for *Newsday*. Out of the library, into the press bus.

23

New Hampshire Snows

Just before darkness falls, Manchester, "The Queen City," looms off the highway. It is poorer, uglier, older, more industrial than I expected: towering red brick shoe plants and textile factories, Dickens-like and sad and cruel. Rickety-rackety, dark, odorous, town-prisons of New Bedford, Worcester, Lowell. . . . Where now are the people who became wealthy from such New England industries?

The twisting, narrow streets of Manchester are covered with unclean snow, silent and abandoned. Don't people know there is a primary? Don't they feel the windy tug of mystery and fate and power that swirls across the planet and now touches here? Where is their respect for magic and potency, for the secret voices of the gods? The heavens are parting and no one observes.

New Hampshire seems indifferent.

Sympathy for all the "Middle Americans" of this great land. The way the man at the parking lot looks at me as I drive in. Blue and orange New York license plates. The local people watch as eleven candidates, accompanied by assistants, staffs, experts, television crews, journalists, photographers, technicians soundmen, truckers, announcers, archivists and advance men, descend upon them—representatives of a foreign culture, creatures of another reality. In the hotel, they see David Brinkley checking in, and they *know* that in forty-eight hours he will know no more about New Hampshire than they, and yet there he will be on television seeming to know so much, not humble before the mystery of this people, but ironic and superior: the whole conception of television, anchor men, commentators—the assumption behind it—that someone *knows* so much, that people in New York and Washington think they know.

The look on the faces of the people when candidates, staff, and media descend upon a factory or cafeteria or shopping mall is the look upon the faces of the Vietnamese when American officials or soldiers came into their village. Taciturn. Polite. Shyly hospitable. Resentment shielded. Teeth firmly pressed together until the blight is lifted. "What do they care? What do they know or care about us? How long will they stay? They are here to use us, and they tell one another stories about how stupid, racist, backward, and inept we are." Middle Americans are the educated's gooks.

Out of prejudice and ignorance flow actions. Urban ethnic neighborhoods (in Detroit, Baltimore, Brooklyn, Cleveland, Pittsburgh, Toledo) are devastated, bulldozed, uprooted—not by bombs but by the callous cruelty of "city planning." Once vibrant communities of relatives and neighbors have been driven from their homes. Neighborhoods have been reduced to empty shells, as if by war. A visitor is appalled by broken windows; unpainted surfaces; piles of rubble; a solitary brick church alone in the midst of flattened acres; grass growing in the cracks of streets, window-high around abandoned homes. Survivors strive to carry on. Who among our experts, academics, planners, architects have given thought to *human* ecology—to living cultures, local ways, and family networks?

The great Muskie headquarters in the center of Manchester is respectably busy. There is something about the faces I do not like. Nothing infuses this campaign. "Beat Nixon," perhaps.

The signs everywhere say TRUST! . . . TRUST MUSKIE!
Long ago, I heard about a cigarette ad that said *their* cigarettes caused less cancer than other cigarettes. Sales dropped.
Priests in the confessional do not ask explicit questions about
certain sins, lest they suggest possibilities the innocent had not
imagined. Pleading trust raises questions.

Politics is not the realm for trust. Anyone who "trusts" a
political leader has misunderstood something fundamental. Politics is a field of compromise and conflicting interest and multi-
ple constituencies. Each political figure must necessarily hurt
each supporter some of the time. Imagine the cold Irish eyes of
Jack Kennedy telling voters to "trust" him. Never. Those eyes
said, "Come along with me. I'll have to hurt you. You'll have
to hurt me. What we'll do together is worth it."

With Muskie, there was no feeling of going anywhere. All the
good liberal sentiments. A better ADA rating than McGovern
or Humphrey. A judgment that the people wanted calm, stability,
no dramatic movement, only a steady incremental progress along
the liberal lines already laid down: end the war, protect the
environment, restore employment.

"Steady Ed" Muskie. Calming. Peaceful. "Trust me."

It is no age for trust. There is no possibility of trust. Trust
is not a sound political emotion. "Trust" is an educated liberal's
word, a word for people who believe in the lightsome ways of
brotherhood. "Trust" is the word of the children of light, not of
the children of darkness. It is a word for people who do not
understand that God "entrusted" his son to history, and history
slew him. Christianity is a dark religion. Its symbol is bloody
wood. "Trust" is a pagan sentiment, the kind of organ music
Kierkegaard mocks so correctly at the end of his *Concluding
Unscientific Postscript.*

Muskie sank on the hidden ice of "trust," the Muskie who
might, could, pull the two wings of the party together. He did
not seize the winning symbols.

In 1972, lower-middle class workers were angry and energetic, voter turnouts in the primaries set records. The status
quo is hard on workers. They wanted change, but *not* the same
changes the educated wanted. Their interests, needs, and aspira-

tions are not the same as those of the educated. But many of the changes recommended by the Left (health care, for instance) would ease the lot of the working class. There is no *necessary* conflict between the Center and the Left. It is a conflict of perception, language, approach, even taste. It is a profound *cultural* conflict. The spokesmen for the Right—men like Senator Jackson—gave the issues too negative a ring. Working people need to feel a burst of noble and good feeling about themselves; not self-congratulation, but a sense of moral value, the respect of their fellows. The Kennedy call "to get moving again" made many feel alive and confident and part of a great enterprise. When daily life is hard, that feeling is as indispensable as air.

Working people distrust the national culture of the educated. Muskie began to be perceived as slick. Part of the national culture. He lacked the edges, roughness, resistances: too smooth, too controlled, too much part of the world of the cool media. "I keep wondering when they will let him let go," a hardware store owner explained. "I kind of like Muskie. But on television he doesn't say what he's thinking. Why don't they let him get it off his chest?"

Locked inside Ed Muskie was an anger, "testiness," rage on which even the Republican National Committee tried to focus attention. Muskie's "instability," Senator Dole said in 1971, deserved to be watched. MUSKIE PIQUED TOO SOON read the Republican posters.

On television, Muskie played Super-Yankee, imperturbable New Englander. He tried to give himself a sense of place: man from a Maine village, skilled in the local ways. On the side of the locals against the nationals. But his sense of place was forced. He's *not* a reticent, carefully controlled, understated Yankee. He has a quick temper. He can be moody and ugly. His emotions follow patterns and go to ranges that Robert Frost never mapped. A credible citizen of Maine, he is not a credible Yankee. There was, on his part, a failure of self-knowledge which television suggested to millions: a faint distrust of Muskie, a willingness to drop him once given provocation.

And on a cold February day Muskie blew his cover. As a

"dirty trick," someone forged a letter from a nonexistent man in Florida. This single letter, published by Mr. Loeb's *Union Leader,* had a devastating effect. In it Muskie was accused of calling one of New Hampshire's minorities "canucks." Not only that, the *Union Leader* excerpted from *Newsweek* a story in *Women's Wear Daily* about Jane Muskie. It pictured her drinking with journalists, giggling, "Let's tell dirty stories." It made her look vulgar, tipsy, silly.

Looking for chances to be bold, angry at the embarrassment of his wife (a motherly, family woman, not one to enjoy the rigors of public stress), Muskie decided on one of his hurried days in New Hampshire to stride across town to the steps of the *Union Leader* and tell old man Loeb off. It could have been a great breakthrough—a bit of Muskie's honest rage out at last.

In 1960, under Loeb's provocations, Jack Kennedy did not show Irish temper; he showed Harvard cool. He ignored Loeb. *The New Republic* later chided Muskie for not imitating the classy manner of the Roosevelts. But Muskie was not Jack Kennedy, nor Franklin Roosevelt. In black sheepskin jacket and fur cap, he strode angrily through the streets of Manchester in a wet, thick snow; and television cameras on him, he dared Mr. Loeb to come out and face him like a man. Muskie stood on a flat-bottomed truck. Behind him were the white pillars of the *Union Leader* offices. The wet snow clung to Muskie's hair and face. Microphone in his left hand, without text, Muskie denied insulting French-Canadians. It was an important issue; 40 percent of New Hampshire's Democrats are French. "I remember as a boy being called a Polack," said Muskie. "I hated it. I'd never use that kind of term with respect to another ethnic group."

Then another charge of Mr. Loeb's tugged at his consciousness. Bad enough to malign a decent man. But to call his wife "Big Daddy's Jane" . . .

Muskie seemed possessed. "That man doesn't walk, he crawls," he said of Mr. Loeb. The months of travel, separation, hardship seemed to well up. He stopped. His face was contorted. He turned away. "Whether it was melted snow dripping off his long nose, or tears, I couldn't tell," wrote T. R. B. in *The New*

Republic, who was right below. "He couldn't speak for emotion." Finally—on television it seemed an eternity—Muskie was back in control and launched into a soft-spoken sermonette on fairness.

"The affair," T. R. B. commented, "has drawn unfavorable reaction. Men shouldn't be overcome in public." From his home in Massachusetts, editor Loeb accused Muskie of being "near hysterical." A man with such emotions should not "have his finger on the nuclear button."

Muskie's telephone canvassers in Manchester heard criticisms of Muskie again and again the next few days. A poll taken afterward showed slippage of seventeen points. All around the country, Muskie people reported a negative reaction.

Yet it wasn't simply that Muskie cried. Nixon had cried four times in public life—twice in connection with the Checkers speech. Muskie's pretense of calmness was shattered. Muskie later avoided the subject, suggesting that he wished it hadn't happened. From the beginning he might have presented himself as the kind of man who shows genuine emotion as he feels it—laughs, cries, is angry. The incident, in that case, might have been in character. Many would take pleasure in a man who with feeling defends his wife. Since in public up to this point Muskie had acted with slowness, caution, even prolonged indecision, his character now seemed to crack.

F.D.R., in similar circumstances, defended neither himself nor his wife nor his sons, but Fala. He even told an ethnic story: "You know, Fala is Scotch, and being a Scottie, as soon as he learned that the Republican fiction writers had concocted a story . . . his Scotch soul was furious. He has not been the same dog since." That would have been the Yankee way. People expect the candidate to be playing politics at every moment, and in a case like this politics means observing the liturgical character of the event. Not your spontaneous emotion but your device for making the telling point is what they watch.

Loeb had handed Muskie two great issues: ethnic discrimination and an insult to his wife. Muskie reacted like a person insecure about his good repute, not like a political leader about to score two impressive gains in one event. He had the kind of chance nearly every campaign brings in the heat of its last two weeks. The break you wait for.

But a faultline in Muskie was exposed. The *Union Leader* of March 6, one night before the election, carried a 2-inch high headline: MUSKIE'S LINCOLNESQUE MASK CRACKED IN N. H. SPEECH, and another, MUSKIE'S TEARFUL TIRADE REVIVES HISTORY OF INSTABILITY. The latter story read:

> Along the southern coast of Maine, there is a residential pattern of de facto segregation. Heavily French towns like Biddeford and Old Orchard Beach stand in marked contrast to rich Yankee enclaves like Kennebunkport, Falmouth and Cape Elizabeth. Ed Muskie, the Polish Catholic, lives in one of the Yankee enclaves Kennebunk Beach, just a few miles from the exclusive Colony Hotel where French were informally excluded before passage of the 1964 Civil Rights Act. . . .
> Anti-French jokes and asides are a staple of conversation in those towns. . . .
> Muskie has detached himself from the plight of upper New England's Catholic millworkers. His chosen Yankee environs of Kennebunkport and Cape Elizabeth are a far cry from the malodorous paper mill town of Rumford, where Muskie grew up and where his mother and four sisters still live. . . . Three of Muskie's sisters are married to French-Americans.
> Muskie rarely goes home to Rumford, nor does he spend much time in Waterville, where he once practiced law. . . .
> Muskie's career has taken him far away from Maine's Catholic milltowns. He is married to Jane Gray, a small-town Yankee ex-Baptist. Journeying to Wall Street to look for a job in 1939, he seemed Yankee enough to win several job offers, and he thinks of his appeal in these terms. Last year, he reflected: "I've always had a hunch that what impressed them was that I looked like Leverett Saltonstall."
> To win election in 1954 as Maine's first Catholic governor, Muskie eschewed identification with the Catholic cities and stressed his ties to smalltown Protestants. . . .
> John Sullivan, the 1934 Democratic candidate . . . opposed building a new bridge over the Merrimack River to link the French west side of Manchester to the rest of the city.

Sneered Irishman Sullivan: "Let the frogs jump across." On election day, Sullivan was massively defeated in the French wards and sank from political sight.

On the day he cried, Muskie passed over from being a suave politician to being Ed Muskie, and from being a Yankee to being himself. A campaign is a dramatic form with rules of its own.

Three other symbolic realities characterized New Hampshire in 1970: the symbol of rational debate; the argument over morality; and the symbolic interpretation of the votes cast.

On the Sunday before the election, 4 to 6 inches of fresh, soft snow greet churchgoers. Boots creak on sidewalks.

A ski parade for Muskie in Manchester's older working-class district moves past the McGovern headquarters. Quiet, chunky flakes gather on shoulders, seep between collars and necks. Arriving late, after five hours en route, three French-Canadian Alpine Clubs from Maine assemble in brilliant uniforms of purple and orange, blue and white, gray and maroon. The men line up laughing outside one silver bus and piss away the burden of a five-hour ride, a little yellow river cutting through the snow.

Muskie strides happily from side to side along the route, wav-to children held up behind steamed windows, shaking hands with older persons standing in the snow. Bands playing. Television cameras. Photographers. The ritual of connectedness: "Here I am among you. Drawing vitality from you. You make me godlike. My power flows from you." A certain sadness, because he will forget streets like these. Double- or triple-family three-story frame houses, "Irish apartments"—in Dorchester, Belmont, Arlington. In Slavic sections of Pennsylvania, one sees smaller, thinner houses, row after row. Have these people "made" it? Is this the affluent society? It is not poverty. But there is no money beyond a few amenities, television perhaps in color, a car. These people have no summer homes. College is not automatic for their children. A decent penury. Ninety percent of the population makes below $15,000 a year. It is hard to send five children to college on $15,000 a year. To make $15,000 most must hold two jobs or send their wives to work. It is hard for them to believe that others can't find jobs: they each find two or three.

Later that day, a bus ride to Durham for "the great television debate." The rush of the bus along the narrow strip of highway stirs the silent pines. Fingers of snow tumble, hit, bury themselves in the silent drifts.

Elections are imagined to be occasions for clarifying "the issues." The Jeffersonian model of democracy is fantasy: that independent men of judgment sit back and listen to an intelligent discussion of alternatives, then give rational assent to one side or the other. Human beings are not like that. The phrase, "the issues," is a code word. The same with the phrase, "the independent voter." These codes suggest that politics is rational. It is not rational to misconceive the nature of politics in a large democracy. Democratic politics on a scale like that of the United States is necessarily symbolic—not *merely* symbolic but *realistically* symbolic.

Consider the debate at the University of New Hampshire, carried by Educational Television. What could more adequately fulfill the rationalist myth than a public debate? Yet the first empirical generalization to be made about political debates is that they are sought by the underdog. Their purpose is not the rational enlightenment of a rational electorate. Their purpose is a gain in recognition.

McGovern had sought such debate when he stood below 20 percent in the polls.

On the stage at the end of a room in the student union sat the five participants in the ritual of rational democracy: George McGovern, Ed Muskie, Sam Yorty, Vance Hartke, and "Ned" Coll. The latter, an Irish-American admirer of the Kennedys and poverty worker in Hartford, proposed to "raise the level of seriousness" and "urgency" in our presidential politics. When his turn to speak arrived, he dangled a rubber rat in front of the camera. "Here's the problem," he said. "We're evading the problem." "We need leadership, not bullship," he concluded.

McGovern spoke to "the issues" of liberal-minded people nationally. Muskie kept in mind the local concerns of Maine and New Hampshire. Yorty spoke of World War II, including "Praise the Lord and Pass the Ammunition." Vance Hartke gave a folksy sermonette. Yorty to Hartke to Coll—a double-play combination to chill a rationalist's heart.

Afterward, a McGovern aide said all that needed to be said: "Well, we don't have to try that again."

Yet the debate had one effect. Muskie's record in Congress was at least as good as McGovern's, except on one issue—Vietnam. Muskie had blocked the Left's anti-Vietnam amendment at Chicago in 1968. In the greatest moral issue of this generation, Muskie had been "wrong" and slow to repent. Yet slowness of conversion was not a good political issue. So McGovern chose a new one.

According to law, all candidates had to reveal finances after April 7. McGovern set a higher standard of purity than that: voluntary revelation now. For weeks, McGovern had not been able to blow the issue into life. Ordinary citizens know that the wealthy give money and expect favors. They know that laws are seldom stronger than money, and that the ingenuity of the rich is boundless. It was a limp issue. At the debate, Muskie made the mistake of counterattacking. Charge and countercharge filled the air. Suddenly, campaign funding was a major battle. Radio and television had no news; they needed drama. Good versus Evil.

In 1968, George Romney had put up blue and white billboards all around the state, emblazoned: ROMNEY FIGHTS MORAL DECAY. Like a toothpaste. McGovern's billboards four years later suggested the same itch for moral purity: RIGHT FROM THE START.

A man who would be president of the United States, one would think, would be judged for his familiarity with the uses and the ways of power. He would be a man who had learned from his mistakes, attuned to imperfect solutions and calculated compromises: a man of wisdom. Morally pure? Always correct? On a par with "I will not be the first president to lose a war," or "America will never accept defeat."

Instinctively, especially in America, one's antennae buzz with fear when moral language enters politics. How many bodies have been mangled in the quest for moral purity? The deep Protestant longing for moral purity almost always has an anti-Catholic edge. Within Catholicism too, the worst evils come from moralism: Cardinal Spellman attacking Jane Russell in "The Outlaw," making Vietnam a "moral crusade."

McGovern's positions on almost everything were politically equivalent to those of many other Democrats. But McGovern added to them a righteousness and austerity that awakened in many profound antipathy. A man who speaks too much morality does not know himself. He misunderstands politics. He does not respect the density of human society. Implicit in McGovern's moralism was an unconscious contempt for ordinary Americans. After the election, he would give evidence of this contempt.

A gentler, more tender, more well-meaning person would have been hard to find. A great many Americans, nonetheless, came to loathe McGovern and to feel betrayed by him. The growth of hostility against him was implicit in his style from the beginning.

The last, and perhaps the most significant, symbol in New Hampshire was the interpretation of the vote. Riding once in an auto with Kirby Jones, McGovern's dour press officer, I asked him about the tactic of claiming a McGovern surge, even daring to predict an upswing. "What if McGovern gets less than 25 percent? If you hadn't said anything, that would look pretty good. Now it's going to look like a real fizzle." Kirby shrugged. Kirby always looked disconsolate.

McGovern's people kept the idea firmly planted: anything less than 50 percent for Ed Muskie would be a defeat. Someone on Muskie's staff, when Muskie was riding 65 percent in the polls, had said that if Muskie got "less than 50 percent, I'd die." Frank Mankiewicz, weather-faced former press secretary for Bobby Kennedy, kept the pressure on during an election-eve press conference in the Howard Johnson motel. He detected signs of "panic" in the Muskie camp. Of Muskie he later said, quoting Gertrude Stein on Oakland, California, "There's no there there."

Muskie was on the wrong side of the symbolism. The press took exactly the story line most favorable to McGovern: a distant underdog, surging, who in order to win could safely lose, so long as Muskie—with ten candidates in the field—was kept under 50 percent. Had the Muskie goal been 25 percent or just enough to finish on top, the drama would have been different. In 1960, Hubert Humphrey campaigned in his neighborhood state, Wisconsin, where he was known as "Wisconsin's third senator," and it would have done Jack Kennedy no good at all merely to keep Humphrey "under 50 percent." Kennedy had to win.

In 1968, Eugene McCarthy had caused a sensation by gaining a mere 23,000 votes. There are only 70,000 Democratic voters in the state.

The Muskie campaign was organized on a bandwagon principle. Its script was: Roll onwards, irresistibly. The Muskie staff worried about "losing" the nomination; they took for granted they would "win" it. It would have been better to work as if they were far behind.

On election eve the returns coming in on the CBS wires showed that the vote was heavier than in 1968. The democratic vote, in particular, was setting a record. Muskie won a solid victory against a large field: 47 percent of the vote to McGovern's 38 percent, with 15 percent scattered. If Nixon had beaten Humphrey by such a margin in 1968, it would have been a landslide. But McGovern's superior manipulation of the drama made the story come out as a great victory for him, a mortal defeat for Muskie. The myth of Muskie's invincibility was destroyed, even though he had won by a substantial 9 percentage points.

McGovern's organization got out 32,000 votes: a tiny reality behind a great symbol.

On election night, Nashua, where the *Union Leader* is not read, gave Muskie 57 percent of the vote. Manchester gave him 37 percent. Almost half the Democrats in the state vote in Manchester. Said Joseph Bartlett, the Senator's Nashua coordinator, "The two cities are 18 miles apart, ethnically the same, we did the same things organizationally. But they read different newspapers." As R. W. Apple, Jr., pointed out in *The New York*

Times, Muskie did poorly in the "French wards" of Manchester, but in French-Canadian areas outside the *Union Leader's* circulation like Berlin and Somersworth he did very well.

Sabotage on behalf of Nixon, in retrospect, occasioned the basic symbolic turning point in the campaign of 1972.

24

The Wallace Sun

The sun. Sun so white, brilliant, overpowering. A certain flatness and terror, all colors dissolving in shimmering blue air. Heat, lethargy, sensuous ease—what if the Pilgrims had landed in Florida instead of Plymouth? Yet it is astonishing how what people carry *inside* their heads can dominate their response to environment. There is a certain prudery in Florida, a certain discretion, that seems lacking in California . . . and so one gets over the shock of switching from snowy fields to sandy beaches, whiteness of two sorts torturing the eye, and begins to realize that many Floridians are emigrés from the North. The Mason-Dixon line cuts across people's hearts: the deep Southern imagination of the rural towns, the swamps, the older cities; the New York Jewish and Michigan Catholic imaginations of the developments and the resorts. Tamale stands, hamburgers, churches, drive-ins, driving ranges, baseball camps, and a hundred thousand picnic spots. One more America.

Walk to the Humphrey motel. Long blocks in the sultry heat. Jacket off. Sweaty. Luckily, I meet Gene Foley. He's just about

to pick up Muriel at the airport. A New York businessman full
of energy and enthusiasm and loyalty. He's rounded up a group
of wealthy Tampans to chat with Hubert at 11 P.M. Muriel is
backup. Silver-haired, sweet, determined. Off we go to a Latin
festival. A beauty contest. A dance. Picnic tables in a large
hall. Family dinners. Whiskey bottles in paper bags. The crowning of the chamber of commerce queen: Anglo-Saxon, Cuban,
Italian girls. Much cheering for favorites. A public ritual that is
for girls what football is for males. The family crowd enjoys
the brilliant dresses, the emotions of victory and rejection, the
choreography of events. By training, I am supposed to disdain
such things, to mock "The Miss America Pageant" on television,
to recognize its "sexism" and "commercialism." Yes. But I like
the people here, the families, the quarrels, the teasing. I love
the homemade pageantry. The girls seem happy, delighted even.
It would be nice to feel such delight.

Muriel gets to make a few "nonpolitical" remarks, including
a shouted word or two in Spanish. It is midnight and the businessmen, kept from their beds, may have disappeared in anger.
But no, they are waiting, and Muriel charms them. "Sometimes
you lose, sometimes you win. I remember 1960, in Wisconsin."
The heads of two couples who had moved to Tampa from South
Dakota and Minnesota nod sympathetically. "And this one, I'll
tell you, feels good. We have a good feeling about it. And how
wonderful it would be to win. And to invite all of you to the
White House and hold the same party there. There are so
many things we'd like to do for the country. One of my interests
is the retarded. . . ."

That night I read in the paper that one of Ed Muskie's talks
is interrupted when a naked woman walks slowly by carrying a
sign "Christ is the one!" I remember the Nixon slogan of 1968:
"Nixon's the one." Months later, I wonder if the naked girl was
hired by Republican saboteurs.

After mass on Sunday, a benefit picnic. Muskie was in short
sleeves, his pants hitched high over his sagging lower stomach.
He threw beanbags and won a back-scratcher. "A frontrunner,"

he said, "needs one." One young man, trying to keep a dark blue McGovern sign behind Muskie for every television shot, said quietly of Muskie: "He looks like a kind man. A Polish uncle!" Shirley MacLaine arrived, drawing fans, as the Senator was eating a picnic chicken, braless as the Senator was coatless, and stopped to talk a little politics. She refused the Senator's suggestion that she come to work for him, but for the cameras she and the Senator exchanged a polite, fleeting kiss.

In the backyard of Adrian Castro's modest home in Tampa, Muskie told a small group of neighbors that fifty-seven years ago, on the day of his birth, he could not have been a candidate for president. "I was a Catholic. I was the son of an immigrant living in considerable poverty. I was a Democrat in a highly Republican state. My father found prejudice and discrimination, but like millions of others in America he was able to fight his way through it." The Latin Americans in the audience were nodding. Muskie said all who succeeded had a "solemn obligation" to help the millions who do not now share these opportunities. He became vigorous and angry: "George Wallace will not be the Democratic nominee, will not become president, and will not be able to build the kind of America you want and love." He paused, fingering a glass of punch, towering over Frank Reynolds of ABC and everyone in the yard. "I know you won't agree with me on every position I take. You don't all agree with one another. You have every right to examine the values I hold, the kind of man I am, and then decide whether I am the man to build the kind of America you want."

It was as though his platform was basically himself. He treated issues as though they were secondary, divisive, not quite to the point, as though the nation wanted a kindly, decent, calm leader. He stressed how many states he had to run in, how hard it is to face down so many various opponents who were, in Indian style, saving their ammunition to ambush him at every stop. His shoulders seemed stooped. People noticed that he looked tired. "I never thought a politician could look so human," a Cuban lady in a pink dress said as the Senator was shaking hands. It was the kind of occasion Muskie—and George McGovern—enjoyed most: one-on-one.

At Orlando, the next day, George Wallace was speaking to the Jaycees at noon. Wallace fascinated me.

The dining room of the Park Plaza was not full. Wallace was not a hero here. The young lawyers who sat at a front table estimated that "maybe half" of those present might vote for Wallace. Most were native-born Southerners, successful men. Sentiment for more "dignified" candidates was strong.

Wallace was plainly nervous, too. His movements were jerky, his smile and self-assurance forced. Behind the podium was a screaming American eagle tapered off in corporal's stripes. The enlisted man. And on the wall was the Creed of the Junior Chamber of Commerce International:

WE BELIEVE:

that faith in God gives meaning and purpose to life.

that the brotherhood of man transcends his sovereignty of nations.

that economic justice can best be won by free men through free enterprise.

that government should be of laws rather than of men.

that earth's great treasure lies in human personality.

that service to humanity is the best work of life.

"Now I'm not gonna let out all the stops," Wallace teased nervously, not really looking at his audience, his eyes on the ceiling. His face was tanned and leathery. His feet kept up a little dance. He held both sides of the lectern. His fingers prodded the skin under his nose, brushed the side of his hair. He was a little like the schoolboy, brushed and dressed, squeezed into uncomfortable collar and shiny shoes, and declaiming in the school play. Wallace was conscious of being the son of a dirt farmer from Alabama—he mentioned his origins himself later, with a trace of deprecation and challenge. "Ah'm not gonna let out all the stops," he began again. "Otherwise ah'd knock these walls down." He then launched into the basic speech of his half-hour television special. He had six or seven main

points he wanted to make with a colorful anecdote and punch-
line for each. Wallace had the manner of a man saying forbid-
den things, opening up people's eyes to injustices and lies and
principalities and powers they already knew were plaguing them
but didn't talk about. As he spoke, heads would start nodding
vigorously—or, in this audience, look up briefly from their plates
and across at friends with a smile of recognition. Unquestion-
ably, the most successful part of the talk in this audience concerned Wallace's experiences with "the TV folks," the fellas
with the "button-down collars" and "the slick hair" who are put
behind a microphone and suddenly "become experts in jes'
about everything. You know what I mean." Wallace says some
of his key words in a way entirely his own: *"Experts,"* for example, is shot out with an ironic punctuation, spurt out, with a
lingering hard *x,* and a suggestion of diminishment in the *-purt*
at the end. He tends to throw some accents back to the first
syllable that are ordinarily thrown lightly forward to the second.
One of his favorite words is "recapitulatahs," over which
his tongue trips with the loving drawl at the end. His pro-
nunciation is part of his humor; it depends on an ear for status
and place, the unspoken realities of American inequality. He
plays skillfully off the stereotype of the Alabama sheriff and the
Southern demagogue. He knows that television commentators
are perceived as goody-goody preachers, the maiden aunts who
so terrorized the Huck Finns of the past. Television is civilization, and Huck Finn is a helluva lot smarter and more likable
than civilization.

Wallace tells how he was invited on one of those "talk shows"
in Portland, Oregon, and his interviewers questioned his facts.
"Now wait a minute!" Wallace told them. "Ah may not be the
smartest man in America. Ah may not be the smartest man in
Alabama. But ah'll tell you one thing. Ah sure am the smartest
man on this here program." The audience rocks with release.
They, too, are smarter.

Later that afternoon, at Cape Kennedy, at a shopping mall,
a small foursome is trying to keep together four hundred people
for Humphrey. An hour late. An hour and fifteen minutes. In-

side the new shopper's world, in a large open crossway, all air
conditioned and wet with a water fountain and green with plants,
the crowd holds. At last he comes. His head is up, chin chuck-
ing, pink and tan and smiling. Taller than one expects, not
short and round. His soft fingers flailing outward, beating the
air up and down as he shakes hands. An electric presence. Lov-
able, energetic Hubie: people know him. American effervescence,
American as a strawberry soda at the drugstore in a 1940 movie.
"I was there . . . ," he tells the crowd, reaching back in memory to every historic piece of legislation he has championed in
the last thirty years, a list approaching infinity, reaching back
(as the parody by Mark Shields of the Muskie staff has it) to
"1492, when I not only sponsored the legislation, I raised the
money for the ships," and it's all true and the crowd loves it.
Seeing a hesitant face, Humphrey strains out over the silver
microphone groping and pointing and tries another subject. He
talks so much not because he loses track but because he can't
bear not to have every single face loving him. He laughs, scoffs,
mocks himself (in America it is important not to take yourself
too seriously), directs his people to pass out the little card
with the recipe for "Muriel's stew" for "vim, vigor, and vitality"
and the colored picture of the two of them, healthy, alert, and
eager.

Humphrey will take the center from Ed Muskie in Florida,
Wisconsin, and Pennsylvania. No wonder Muskie resented
Humphrey's way of succeeding, and many on the Left despised
it. James Naughton of the *Times* described Muskie's frustrations:

> He was offended by the off-hand way in which Humphrey
> might say whatever came into his mind and hurt by the
> positive reaction such tactics could generate. In the space
> of one speech to the American Friends of Hebrew University
> in Philadelphia, Humphrey declared that he had enjoyed his
> visits to the campus in Israel, was on the board of Brandeis
> University and a fellow of the Weizmann Institute, had
> spoken at the University of Tel Aviv, had "worked with the
> ladies of Hadassah," had "just happened to be there for one
> of the services" at a temple in Minneapolis the night Presi-

dent Truman recognized the independence of Israel, had "known Golda Meir for years," had once been caught in "what they call a Hussein—well, anyway, one of those desert storms" in Israel, and planted "a couple of forests over there for Hubert and Muriel Humphrey" and had marveled at the spirit of nation-building in Israel. "I'm excited," Humphrey said. "I don't know if you get as excited as I do, but whenever I get a little discouraged I say to Muriel, 'Why don't we take a trip to Israel and get pumped up again?' "

Can any system be as corrupting as democracy? Entrusting oneself to the people seems such a noble thing until one sees all the varieties of all the people of this land, such an accumulation of envies, resentments, generosities, fears, aspirations, compassions, swindles, brutalities. One must offer oneself to all.

Take Florida itself. From the shimmering white waterfront of Miami to the dusty, dirt-poor gas stations of interior crossroads; from the bitter migrant camps of the southeast to the heavy orange-blossom scents of central Florida and the magnolia slowness of the Tallahassee Panhandle—what powerful vats of passion, struggling, turmoil, and hate. One felt the burst of racing tires against the speedway, smelled oil and dust, knew lonely death and riches. Almost a third of the voters are over sixty years of age. Several hundred thousand Cubans, a hundred thousand elderly Jews, mostly from New York. State troopers whose pistols seemed grafted on their thighs since birth, slow of speech, clear-eyed, and mean. Not a single culture, not a community, but an accident. And over all this a politician of vision is supposed to preside? The vote in 1968 was Nixon 886,000, Humphrey 676,000 and Wallace, 624,000.

Election eve, the Wallace faithful begin arriving slowly at the Park Plaza. Meek people. Mostly middle class. People who defer, who show respect. My experience with Wallace crowds continually surprised me: more gentle and courteous than any other.

A young rock group, with long hair and fringed white clothes. An electronics engineer. Doctors. Lawyers. Computer programmers. No blue-collar people. The Park Plaza is not a blue-collar place.

On the front of the hall: "American greatness can be pre-
served for future generations . . . but only if concerned citizens unite in effective political action. . . ."

John Gardner? Tom Hayden and the Port Huron statement?
Stokely Carmichael? Ah no, my friends, George Wallace.

"I have more of the people's issues on my one finger than
they got in all their issue books," he was wont to say. Joe Azbell, his newspaper editor turned propaganda chief, explained
to me that they had sent out seven million questionnaires asking
people what concerned them. "We know what the people think.
We got them. We got the issues." That's why they didn't need
the press or publicity. For a rally, all they did was take a small
ad in the local paper, a quarter-page perhaps, two days in a
row. You could feel the excitement. People would know. And
they would come. Azbell also explained to me that all their
work was done by their own staff. They didn't mind the amateurish look. Nothing slick. "We do it all ourselves." The TV
documentary that was so effective was made, he says, "for
$5,000."

They felt besieged. Wallace received an average of three
death threats a day. "I know the press'll put in the 'betchas,'
'gonnas,' 'gottas,' " Wallace would tease. But he was determined
to let the roughness through. "*They* change," he said of his
opponents. "Ah don't change." He was wearing colored shirts
and broad ties, longer and more artfully tailored suits, longer
hair dyed brown once a month. He kept tan and fit. And he had
the most beautiful wife American politics has seen in many a
generation. She kept a clanking, braceleted hand on his back
when he emerged from the elevator briefly as returns began to
come in. She was squeezing and pulling as he talked. Dark hair
and elegantly long, ivory throat, great soft eyes, and perfect
voice: a dream of the Old Confederacy. Ambition burned in
her. Scarlett O'Hara. *She* should be president. She *knew* he
would one day be. He seemed nervous before the cameras, shy,
vulnerable even. Her arm braced him. She whispered in his ear
at the first question. He mechanically smiled. "We're running
better than in 1969," he said to the camera. "What will you do
now, sir?" "I'm gonna watch TV returns and then think about

Wisconsin and Pennsylvania and other states. And if I win, this will be a significant victory." "By how much do you expect now to win?" "I'll be satisfied to win." He wore a fixed smile and let Cornelia guide him out the door.

At 8 P.M., ABC was projecting Wallace with 45 to 50 percent of the vote, Humphrey at 16 to 19 percent, and the rest divided. Billy Grammer, star of the Grand Ole Opry, warned the crowd to be ready to sing "On Wisconsin!" when the Governor entered. At 8:15, he tried to lead everyone in "Happy Days Are Here Again!" but no one knew the words. At 8:55, the handsome singer announced "Humphrey's theme song": "Born to Lose."

Charles Snyder, Governor Wallace's campaign manager, is a short, neat, carefully groomed young businessman; and Billy Joe Camp, his equally shining secretary, brought me over to him. Polite to a fault, they don't trust me. But they talk. "The Govnuh always worries more than the staff. He always thinks he's going to lose." Then Snyder wonders whether he should have said that. "Govnuh Wallace is a prophet. What he was talking about ten years ago, everybody is talking about now." Will you change the campaign in the North? Don't you sense a difference between the Protestant voters of the South and the Catholic voters of the North? "We won't change the campaign. We don't have to. We have the issues. We have—the Govnuh."

At 9:30, George Mangum, the fiery Baptist preacher with the tall coxcomb of gray hair and the booming voice read off the mounting totals, Wallace carrying every single district in the state with only Dade County too close to call, and sang out in happiness: "How sweet it is!"

Muskie was conceding. The three hundred Wallace supporters, sitting calmly in their chairs, as orderly as church people, listened in amazement as Muskie called Wallace a "demagogue who appeals to the worst in people." They guffawed. They were not even granted the grace of congratulations for a democratic victory, won in a democratic way. It stung, in a way that made them feel sorry for Muskie. It was what they'd come to expect from Northern "liberals."

"When the Govnuh comes in with his guests," George Mangum shouted later, "All you true-blue Wallace supporters will show the dignity you have." The people clapped righteously.

At 10:37, belting at last a series of rebel yells and whoops—instantly the cameras turned to the outbursts—the crowd welcomed the Governor, who had suddenly materialized in their midst. Security was heavy. Much clapping. Wallace cocky, waving arms. At the podium he wrinkled his nose. Hayseed to the end. His brown hair shone in the lights. A new red-striped tie cut the pale blue of his shirt. His brown eyes seemed strangely vacant, as if he weren't in the room at all. (It was a strange habit he had, leaving his eyes unoccupied and then suddenly returning and making them lustrous; it is perhaps the affliction of politicians who are spirited from environment to environment, suddenly here and then suddenly there, disoriented and required to save themselves by occasional retreats: like the zombielike trance of commuters, ceasing to live until required.)

"It is a vict'ry for the average citizen," he said in his own distinctive way. "People who have come from all over the United States to live here. An' it proves what I been sayin' all along. My candidacy is national, not regional." Then suddenly he was launched into his basic rally speech, or a version of it: "taxes . . . law and order . . . welfare . . . the elderly need to be helped; I want to help those that ought to be helped"—the U.N.: "we shud stop sendin money to countries that spit on us in the U.N."—"We're going to turn the Democratic party back to the party of the people, which it used to be." The issue is "the remoteness of the government from the citizenry. The people is fed up with buroc-racy. . . ." He thought it right to call his movement a form of "participatory democracy," because he "carried every district" and he did it without a great deal of help from a regular party or anyone. It was (he didn't have to say) his victory, he had done it alone, with in effect very little effort, except that for ten years he had been building a movement.

"This is a great country," he went on, after calling his state campaign chairman to take a bow. "But there are some kinks in it we want to iron out." Just the sort of sentence to raise a little fear in the hearts of his enemies. "I'm a serious candidate

in the Democratic party for the presidency of the United States."
He said that perhaps for his own ears as much as for any. He
didn't really believe it yet, as his prolonged delay in taking his
campaign to Wisconsin and then Pennsylvania would show. In-
excusably, he never had his name entered on ballots in states
like New York and California, down the line. He seemed to be
afraid of humiliation, hardly daring to believe his own power,
as if what his critics said had gotten to him. "I welcome the
support of persons of all colors and races. I'm not the demagogue they say I am. We need a change of direction in Washington, we will build a better life for all people in this country,
regardless of who they happen to be."

Then he trailed off again into taxes. "The income tax is regressive. . . . An' if it were lowered like it oughta be . . . it
would raise the morale of the average man . . . create more
demand for consumer goods . . . bring more employment. . . .
And we will have the American dream of a better life for all
our citizens."

Then he called Cornelia, and over she came like a woman
born for the stage, every motion fluid, and waving affection to
the audience while in full dignity, her green dress long and
sculptured and exquisite; and still talking and smiling, he leaned
over and up and bussed her, fleetingly, on the cheek and she
made as if a smile of pleasure, and his swift mind was calculating and he pointed, but she brought some of the young ones
around him first.

Billy Grammer's group was belting out the unknown and
forgotten "Happy Days Are Here Again" and the not-yet-
learned "On Wisconsin!" While down in Miami Beach, the
Muskie camp, on the heels of their sudden, unexpected rejection in Georgia over the weekend, finished behind Wallace's
42 percent, Humphrey's 18 percent and Jackson's 14 percent,
with a lowly 9 percent. Lindsay and McGovern were just under
7 percent each. McGovern did not claim it was a moral victory
to hold Wallace to under 50 percent.

25

McCarthy in Illinois

Eugene McCarthy ran his Illinois campaign as a toe-to-toe competition with Muskie. His buttons had a certain sly arrogance: "McCarthy vs. Muskie, March 21." The intelligent ones, it suggested, wouldn't need to be told whom to prefer.

Illinois had 170 delegates to elect. They were to be elected on slates in each congressional district. Mayor Daley organized uncommitted slates in Cook County, hoping to hold at least eighty votes at the convention. A group of reformers set up delegate slates nominally pledged to Muskie to challenge Daley's slates and to embarrass Muskie. Supererogatory Muskie delegates were packed into other districts too. Where there were, say, six places open, McGovern would have six candidates but Muskie ten, eleven, or twelve—thus confusing voters and weakening Muskie's chances.

The new McGovern rules for 1972 forbade Daley or any other elected leaders to endorse candidates. But they allowed organizations like the Independent Voters of Illinois (the state branch of the Americans for Democratic Action) to endorse candidates: the "ins" couldn't, but the "outs" could. At a meeting in Chicago on February 24 at the Sherman House, Daley told his workers he wanted his delegates to win. Reports vary. He said either: "The hell with the McGovern Commission," or "Up the McGovern Commission's. . . ." His slates contained mostly older male political leaders of his organization; they were selected from prearranged lists, which was against the rules. On March 21, Daley's slates were overwhelmingly elected.

Alderman William Singer, an ambitious young reform leader, immediately began the process of unseating Daley and his codelegates. This emotional contest as much as any other factor in 1972 cut the Democrats in two: a contest between people who believe in party loyalty and people who believe in party purity; between people who trust personal politics and people who trust rules; and between the new class of affluent liberals, in coalition with media blacks, and the old class of working-class Democrats, white and black. The blacks involved—Jesse Jackson was the most famous—were big neither on party purity nor on white man's rules nor on white liberals; they used and were used, for whatever power they could acquire. Who could blame them for that? Except that McGovern was not likely to be of much help to Chicago blacks, and Jesse Jackson was not likely to be of much help to McGovern even among blacks.

So you could say that in this comparatively simple election in Illinois McCarthy vs. Muskie the main attraction, hundreds of persons competing for the delegate slots in each district—the symbolic storm center of 1972 was concentrated. Daley's eighty-seven uncommitted delegates were elected, usually by large margins. In June, most of these would be banished from the Democratic convention, in favor of a "reform" slate rejected March 21 by the people of Illinois. The reform slate was more balanced in the ratio of blacks, women, and young people. It was deficient in traditional Democrats: Poles, Italians, Irish. Who is "us" and who is "them"? The Democratic party would find itself choosing between ethnic groups and classes, like Solomon confronted with a baby, but without his wisdom.

That March night, as the returns came in, the symbolic choice was made. McCarthy's literature announced: "We can stay with the old politics and Ed Muskie. Or we can take a step forward." McCarthy said: "Senator Muskie represents the real weakness of the Democratic party . . . namely, that it has become survivalist and protectionist and concerned, really, about winning elections." One of his campaign pieces said: "Only two candidates will be on the ballot. McCarthy the liberal and Muskie." And: "Gene McCarthy is more together than Ed Muskie will ever be." And: "Gene McCarthy feels the Democratic party has been mismanaged. . . . They must once again become the responsive party of the people." Then came the code words: "To offer alternatives." Nothing specific, but "change-oriented."

That night at the elegant Continental Plaza, McCarthy's young, affluent followers gathered in the well-appointed governor's suite for cocktails and folk songs. Paintings on the walls. Heavy furniture. Ties, expensive clothes, the smooth and intelligent faces of people who take care of themselves, travel, read, understand "the issues," "have principles." Nice people. They drink martinis, daiquiris, whiskey sours, gimlets. Good people. They sing a song beneath the balloons, some of them sitting on the soft carpet:

> *Weave, weave, weave me the sunshine out of the falling rain*
> *Weave me the hope of a new tomorrow and fill my cup*
> *again.**

Exuberant at the returns, the hero of 1968 returned. The room exploded in delight. McCarthy was taking the same percentage McGovern had in New Hampshire, 37 percent, and Muskie the other 63 percent. This was to prove both the relative high-water mark of the "new politics" across the nation and almost exactly the figure for the Nixon-McGovern outcome in November.

McCarthy was not humiliated in Illinois. With $250,000, com-

---

* "Weave Me the Sunshine" by Peter Yarrow © 1972 Mary Beth Music, 75 East 55th Street, New York, N.Y. 10022. All rights reserved. Used by permission.

pared with Muskie's $50,000, and in only three weeks of intensive campaigning (while Muskie was busy elsewhere), he had reduced his standing from 7 to 1 (a late February poll) to 2 to 1.

"I thank you," he said, "for what you did, almost as an act of faith." He recalled 1968. "I referred to us in Grant Park as the people in exile. We've begun a return."

"I haven't," he rubbed a finger over his lips and looked at the ceiling over everyone's head, "had a chance to study the returns. To see if Mayor Daley's support has affected the people's—I won't say 'judgment'—but their response." More cheers.

Ordinary people don't make judgments. They have Pavlovian responses.

Eugene McCarthy is quick to see through and to deflate the American civil religion, its rituals and its deficiencies. He is the only presidential candidate in recent memory to campaign to *give up* presidential powers, to *limit* presidential options, and to puncture presidential cults of personality. He is the nation's best known, highest-ranking agnostic regarding the national religion. He once rejected a vocation to the Catholic priesthood; he now rejected the presidency as priesthood. Even astute commentators have been unable to understand McCarthy's refusal to believe. *They* believe. His agnosticism affronts them. They called him lazy, moody, irreverent, unpredictable, irresponsible, not serious, a poet, a dreamer. Whereas in fact he is merely hardheaded, a skeptic, who refuses to accept the rituals, to confess the mysteries, to pretend to the powers. "I don't seek the presidency," he once said, "I am willing to accept it." Some thought he wanted, regally, to be wooed, coaxed, handed it on a platter. *He* meant: "Take the magic out of it. I'll take the issues before the people. That's all it takes." He was wrong, of course.

McCarthy's practical genius was that he recognized before anybody else the huge, growing numbers of educated, discriminating people. A whole new class of Democrats ready to come to power—intelligent people with latent political and organizational skills, high mobility, leisure, and political idealism. The billboards in Oregon in 1968 said: McCARTHY: THE MAN THE PEOPLE FOUND. But McCarthy had, instead, believed in the people before they believed in themselves. Not *all* the people, of course. That was his fatal flaw. He meant the *new class* of people, all those educated millions whose ranks had swollen since World War II, one new college springing up every two weeks. He had commented twice, between Nebraska and Oregon in 1968, that all the educated people were voting for him, the others for Bobby. Those sentences, and the voting patterns reflected by them, had led some to switch from support of McCarthy to support of Kennedy.

To them, Indiana had been Kennedy's finest hour. The very qualities that made liberal critics unhappy with Kennedy's campaign in Indiana—his tough, law-and-order outreach to the white working class, the confidence placed in him by both black and white workers in Gary and Hammond—assured them that he could do the most important job in American politics: heal the division between white and black workers by conceiving of politics as a coalition to help *both* simultaneously. Bobby Kennedy didn't ask them to love one another. He simply asked them to work for what both equally needed: jobs, houses, opportunity—and not at each other's expense.

McCarthy believed that once he held the educated Left (about one-third of the electorate) and penetrated even the liberal Republican vote (as polls in 1968 showed him doing), the working-class and black vote would naturally follow along. Where else would they go—to Nixon? The party professionals never gave him a chance to try. They too sold the workingman short. Even Kennedy was not sure in May, 1968, that he could persuade the convention to accept him rather than Humphrey, even if he beat McCarthy in California (as he did). "It will be tough," he once said, meditatively. "Very tough. The politics of a convention are not the same as the politics of the primaries. And not the same as November."

Robert Kennedy, I suppose, was the political ideal of many: tough, ruthless, unafraid of the dirt and power plays of politics, not surprised by the jungles of New Jersey or Massachusetts or Illinois or Texas, and genuinely appreciative of the differing needs of wide ranges of people. A power broker, you could say, to demean his vision. Or else, a man who grasped the evils, ambiguities and conflicts of interest involved in politics and was determined to give them the most moral shape he could—which might be little or much, depending as much on a wide range of people as on himself.

By contrast, although I loved the skepticism of McCarthy, and attended to his reservations about the mystique surrounding the Kennedys, McCarthy was too closely tied to the new class he had discovered and by his brave witness had empowered. In 1968, his people in Connecticut toppled John Bailey's machine, in New Hampshire knocked out Johnson, in Wisconsin won handily. They showed savvy and an enormous capacity for work. But they were—so I thought—unintentionally divisive. They sought too much morality, too much intelligence, too much class. They were trying to take over the party, to redefine it, according to *their* lights and *their* interests. They showed too little grasp of the needs and aspirations of the millions of constituents of the "old" party. Hating the bosses who blocked their way, often by corrupt methods, they also depreciated the ordinary, baffled, isolated traditional Democrats who had not gone to college or perhaps even to high school. "I will not say judgments but responses." They made politics a conflict between classes. Classes based on education.

In Illinois, on this happy evening, McCarthy carried only two counties, in both of which were large concentrations of university students. Muskie swept 66 percent of the vote downstate, and fell lower (60 percent) in the Chicago suburbs. McCarthy ignored the delegate races and won none. McGovern, who did not enter the "beauty contest" but worked hard for his delegate slates, won fourteen delegates, all in the northern and northwestern suburbs of Chicago and around the university town of Champaign. As R. W. Apple put it in the *Times,* McGovern "failed to accomplish what he set out to do: demonstrate that he could assemble a coalition including more than students and relatively affluent white liberals."

The vote in Illinois dramatized the uncertainties of ordinary voters. Edward V. Hanrahan had ordered the midnight raid in the course of which police killed Black Panthers. Dan Walker, authored the Walker Report that condemned "the police riot" of 1968. Both Hanrahan and Walker won in Cicero, a heavily Democratic town, and in their statewide victory shared many of the same voters in the same districts in Cook County.

Crossing town from the McCarthy celebration to the Muskie celebration drives home the cultural distance with shattering impact. The bright bronze rails and snappy uniforms at the Continental Plaza are fresh in mind as I enter the empty lobby of 8 South Michigan Avenue. No attendant. No sign. The rackety elevator to the ninth floor is occupied by the nighttime cleaning woman. The room for celebration looks like a room donated to Tuesday night meetings of the Boy Scouts in a public school built about 1888: the wooden floor is well worn, there are round pillars holding up the ceiling, the walls are institutional green. The young people serving free drinks are up to their soles in beer suds. These kids don't go to college. A very fat girl, boys with pimples, everyone in Sears Roebuck clothes. Limp crepe paper. No gas-filled balloons. And they are singing that haunting, lilting folk song:

> *What the hell do we care?*
> *Hail hail the gang's all here.*

Not exactly Stanford kids, I think, but they are the center of politics now. As the young workers go, so goes the future of the nation.

It is good, too, to see Muskie happy. In Stickney, Illinois, a few days before, he held a basketball at a playground and asked reporters: "What percentage do I have to get?" He shot and missed. "Who says I don't have balls?" Miss. There was something unutterably sad about Muskie.

So when he says, "I can't remember when anything has given me so much of a lift since I won my first race as governor in 1954," it makes one happy for him. He later adds for the press, "It hasn't been easy; it has a deteriorating effect on your spirits, when people don't perceive you as you do yourself."

On the third primary, Muskie rose again. But experienced correspondents were saying it was only fresh blood to keep the corpse alive another two weeks.

26

Sorting Out in Wisconsin

The character of a political rally is an index to the political religion of the audience and to the character of the presiding priest. The following rallies during the Wisconsin primary suggest the varieties of political religion in one state.

A McCarthy handout says: "The major differences between Senator McCarthy and other candidates come in attitudes toward American institutions. McCarthy has challenged institutions more openly and more often than any other candidate. He has done this not only in action but in speech." Shafter of institutions, Robin Hood letting fly at every escutcheon of officialdom: *Whirrr. Pfft.*

At the University of Wisconsin at Milwaukee, in the new student lounge, only about 200 of the 400 blue chairs were taken for the most brilliant talk of the campaign. McCarthy makes one recognize that other political speeches are the rearrangement of clichés, as if everybody is given the same twelve checkers and told to play them, but he turns the board over for backgammon.

McCarthy begins softly, runs the pads of his fingers past his nose, touches the edges of his silver sideburns lightly with his nails, shifts his left shoulder, rocks his weight from heels to toes. His tone of voice is comforting and quiet. Then irony slips out from sleepy branches. An arrow flies. The foliage falls quietly back in place.

Really, he begins, there are just two points to be made this evening. First, the rather careful traditions of the party. It's become, one might be inclined to say, merely survivalist. And that isn't the healthiest predicament. And, second, the issues that *should* be raised in a political campaign and often are not. Bad issues are driving good ones out of the field. In Florida. Here. Like busing. Are we to believe property taxes are the biggest issue facing Wisconsin?

A campaign creates a chance to select a *candidate*. Not twenty-three hundred issues in a telephone book. But a sort of incarnation of the issues. One person.

For example, *how* to settle the war. Not just announce you're against it. We've all been against it, you know. Except Muskie, who apparently was for it when it counted but now is against it. We'll offer him amnesty.

I will support a new government in Vietnam. I'd announce that and take the consequences thereof. You don't just choose a "date certain" for withdrawal, you must take responsibility for what happens before and after. I'd telephone the Pentagon and ask if by chance they have a general who knows how to disengage. Even one would do.

Then there is the problem of unemployment since 1945. Systemic. An expanding economy isn't enough, you know. Makes matters worse. What we need is legislation to absorb the unemployed into present production. A law that no one can work more than eleven months a year. We bring automation into industry, but still treat employment in the social terms of 1932.

The real problem, the heart of the matter, is corporate feudalism. It caused some concern, a year or so ago, whether Nixon should or should not send an ambassador to the Vatican. He should have sent one to the Pentagon, to GM, to ITT, to Dupont. Places that have more power than the Vatican. Corporations are independent of social control. What was ITT up to in Chile? Well, you know all about that. Corporations were not discovered here when Columbus arrived. They're not natural organisms, under laws that govern the moon and the stars. People invented them. We set them up by law. We can govern them by law. One might be inclined to do that if one stepped back and regarded a system which since 1932 hasn't figured out for itself how to halt a situation in which we have 25 million poor, 12 million on relief, and 5 million unemployed. That's not, exactly, my conception of efficiency.

Third, reduce the military. Cut back in space. Did you notice on television? The simulated shots were better than the real thing? We could simulate space probes more cheaply, one would think, and still satisfy television. And instead of sending three men to the moon, perhaps we could send them to pick up 80 pounds of East St. Louis and analyze that. No other candidate has this in mind. And perhaps there'd be an official report: "There once was a civilization in East St. Louis." Some indication, at least, of a Late Iron Age and an Early Plastic Age.

Fourth, the automobile culture. Americans love and cherish automobiles, so they can go from one polluted stream to another, check into the inadequate medical care along the way, and visit suburbs they haven't seen yet.

I'd have a national program for dealing with the auto. Again, probably the only candidate that would. The automobile is an antisocial force and should be so designated. Laws would regulate what kind, what size, power, cost. There's no word from God saying cars should be as big as they are or that their pollution and killing and overcharge of power must be borne by a civilized nation, as a kind of penance for its sins. No law that I know of in any case. Though these things seem to change nowadays.

Interesting fact: to offset the winding down of the war, Nixon expands auto production. Wars and automobiles have exactly the same function: to waste resources. If Marx had known about the auto, he'd have added another chapter. "To stimulate the economy, capitalism needs either war or the automobile." The automobile is a serious issue. More serious than the bus.

Fifth, I'd want to bring critical judgment to our system of justice. Hard drugs: We'd ban those. Marijuana? I'd insist on a warning on the package: "Smoking pot may be hazardous to your health." We need a *second* system of justice, for the poor and the young and political prisoners. Equal protection under the law. Trial by peers.

Sixth, doctors. Sickness was invented for doctors. Undertakers don't want to change the traditional relationship and from their point of view, of course, it's only a slowdown. Yes, I'd be inclined to judge the profession of medicine by rather high standards. To match their self-image.

Seventh, a presidential cabinet that is not a projection of the personality of the president, but, rather, of the party and its positions. Three or four members of minority races. Three or four women, like Golda Meir as Secretary of Defense, and Indira Gandhi as Secretary of Offense, since women may be the only leaders who know how to run a limited war and bring one to a swift close. Also, no former presidents of auto companies as Secretaries of Defense. A fairly strict rule against that. Barbara Tuchman would be my Secretary of State. State, you know, shouldn't have to go to the sons of Presbyterian ministers. We've had three of those. That should last us for a while. Why should State be the last established religion of the Western world?

Eighth, busing. My platform is the courts and the constitution on that one.

But the main thing is economic reconstruction. Not the distribution of wealth which this season's new populists are talking about. No. A distribution of production. In four stages: (1) An income floor of $6,000 for a family of four. (2) Employment distributed so that available work is shared with everyone. (3) Social control over what corporations produce and how they distribute it. (4) The prevention of wasted resources. Poverty doesn't arise from disparity of income, but from not directing properly either employment or what is produced.

In the question period, the audience having laughed again and again, McCarthy was alternately touchy and at ease, like a warm ocean current with sudden cold streams sliding through. His hair shone silver in the light. No American political figure has been more pleasant in voice, delicious in wit, delightful to observe. "Why are you so criticized by the press?" he is asked. The cold flash slides by before he speaks. There had been an article in *Life*. It takes him only a moment. "You may have noticed that the same editors believed in Clifford Irving." The McCarthy smile. One part self-deprecation, one part the sheer job of verbal murder. Not a better hit man in politics.

"Yes, well, if we have a third party, its symbol, you know, won't be an elephant or a donkey. But an Aardvark. Which didn't evolve out of or into anything but is a kind of absolute animal. Nothing else is as good as it is without becoming it. A donkey isn't quite like that. Donkeys are afflicted with sterility, I believe. An Aardvark. Any more questions? Very well, good. Thanks." A low-slung, casual peace sign, left behind as an afterthought, while he's already greeting the student committee on stage with a smile of delight, and the awestruck audience is still applauding erect. He had read some lines of his poems, including those on Vietnam: "We will take our corrugated steel out of your land of thatched huts."

Pete McCloskey, former marine corps officer and congressman from California, addresses a press conference on behalf of his former Republican colleague, John Lindsay. McCloskey's hair stands forward and out over his forehead like a tough kid from the winter of '43, his hand in his left pocket, his tone earnest and clipped, that powerful combination of Boy Scout and Hardened Veteran so effective in American life. Brevity. Controlled intensity. A man tutored to sights of blood and evil, but still an idealist.

Lindsay is casual, offhand. I had never seen him before except on television. In person, he lacked the moral intensity and passion I had always seen in him. He threw his lines away, seemed tired, dispirited. His gray suit was wrinkled across the legs. Once he desultorily fingered his gray-red-white tie. I thought he had given up caring. But on television later, the videotape of his remarks had the old intensity. In the flesh, there was the lack of passion. On the tube, there was as much passion as it was comfortable to absorb. His words too sounded harsher, more barbed, than when I had heard them with my own ears. His clear blue eyes, withdrawn and calm in the flesh, seemed on television to leap with fire.

The camera eye is not faithful. By what rules does one discount its effects in order to discern what appearance in the flesh is like? It picks up emotion below the surface of the skin. It gives clear eyes a special power. It flatters a soft, resonant voice. It prefers a calm demeanor under which it picks up the radiation of invisible emotion. The emotions John Lindsay does *not* reveal are his charisma.

Television is an equalizer. It disguises short men and tall. Lindsay was about 4 inches taller than I had imagined.

When George Wallace said "Send them a message!" John Lindsay may have been the first "them" on the postman's list. Lindsay had gone from being WASP scion establishment to being media establishment; guns of popular hostility had followed that very pattern. Lindsay reporting to Middle America in 1972 was like a report to the Vatican by the bishop of Sodom and Gomorrah. To the rest of America, New York symbolized all that was wrong with liberalism—including its wealth and power.

Later that afternoon, the anniversary of the Last Supper, Wallace is to speak at Serb Hall on Milwaukee's south side, barely a long walk from Arthur Bremer's apartment. Wallace had failed to arrive in Wisconsin just after his Florida victory. Perhaps he received intelligence that things were not going well in Wisconsin. In 1968, he received only 7 percent of the Wisconsin vote, about half his national average of 13 percent. Wisconsin had seen Wallace several times since 1964. Labor unions were now passing out "fact sheets": on crime in Alabama cities (murder up 56 percent in Montgomery in 1971, rape up 100 percent, aggravated assault up 43 percent); on "Right to work laws" there; on the maximum unemployment compensation, $60 (versus $85 in Wisconsin); on the $2,828 per capita an-

nual income of Alabama, sixth lowest in the nation; on the mere
$380 Alabama spends per pupil per year (versus $832 in Wisconsin); on the dropout rate of Alabama high schools, 31 percent; on the average wage of teachers, $5,825 (versus $10,016
in Wisconsin). "If Wallace can't control crime in one state, how
can he do it in fifty?" asked the mimeographed sheet of Region
10 UAW. "Use your VOTE wisely on Tuesday, April 4."

Perhaps Wallace's own fear of failure held him back. Every
available sign suggests that his staff and his wife praised, cajoled,
flattered, urged him to run, against his own fears, primary by
primary. Wallace often alluded to his reluctance to enter a
state, his surprise and pleasure at how well he did, his chagrin
that he hadn't started sooner and done more. Local personnel
seemed constantly in a state of uncertainty and ignorance
about the Governor's intentions. They had remarkable reverence for his judgment, though, even when big rallies were
scheduled in advance, then postponed, while the Governor
lingered mysteriously in Alabama. He didn't seem to believe
in himself.

The Wallace campaign arrived in Wisconsin with less than
a week to go. Outside Serb Hall, where he had drawn an over-
flow crowd of 1,800 in 1968, the white marquee announces FRI-
DAY FISH FRY. Inside, two hours before the scheduled talk,
only secret service men and two Wallace aides are in evidence,
setting up the heavy bulletproof lectern that was the object of
much quiet ridicule. A plastic vase of red, white, and blue
flowers is placed in front of the podium. Only 160 chairs are
set up, where there is room for 900. The Wallace people seem
worried about the turnout.

In the adjacent bar and bowling alleys, three Wallace women
rest before their duties start. They wear the red coats of the Alabama staff; their hair is blond and puffed. Dick the bartender asks
them why they bothered themselves with politics.

"Satisfaction." The prettiest of the three blinked her long
eyelashes. "Specially if George wins."

"Every time a politician says he'll do something"—Dick sets
his hands on his apron strings—"it costs me money."

The other bartender is Bob Lekfo. He told me he quit a job

in New Jersey for a lower paying one in Milwaukee ten years ago. "There are only four cities in the country set up for the workingman. I been to them all." He counts them out: "Denver, Houston, Minneapolis, Milwaukee." I ask him why.

"In New Jersey, a day at the beach—parking fees, beach fees, dressing room fees—before I even get some sun, eight-ten dollars for the family. Ridiculous. Here we get in the car, go to the beach, it doesn't cost a cent."

Other men are reading *Wallace Labor Action,* with its motto: "Smile, you're in Wallace country when you're with working people."

When it is time to get in the hall before Wallace arrives, the crowd cordoned back from entering parts and lets me through. When the rope is dropped only six hundred people file in, one hundred of those press, staff, and security. There are too few chairs. On television, it looks like standing room only.

In a maroon knit suit, Billy Grammer tries to warm the crowd with country music. He tells them about his "full-blooded Polack wife," but the Serbs and others in the crowd are not thereby made to feel at ease, not even when he smiles his full smile and says thoughtfully: "Y'know, ah learned that not all em Polish jokes are true." Serbs are not Poles. He tries to mention some specialties his mother-in-law had baked for him. A restrained crowd. He speeds up the music and urges everybody, "C'mon now, clap!" Catholics do not usually clap in church. The country music has a Southern, foreign edge to it. "Tell y'what! For th' first time ever, me'n' the boys'll play a polka. We been practicin'." At last smiles and feigned enthusiastic clapping; now people at least know what to do.

When the Governor comes in, the crowd bursts into adulatory applause, whistles, hoots. Some had been waiting years to see him again. Wallace gives the basic rally speech with fire and energy. He is careless now with statistics and figures. Between this talk and another later in the evening, the number of heroin addicts in New York fluctuated from 100,000 to 250,000. Wallace tells the crowd that people in Wisconsin are paying for welfare in New York. New Yorkers wish they were.

Suddenly a pretty black-haired girl in a yellow coat calls out.

She is waving a sign. I see the words "Bigots Are . . ." before someone begins tearing off the paper covering. Wallace stops. Underneath the top sign one can now read the original: it says LINDSAY. The girl's voice breaks the silence in deliciously moral words, "Why did they rip my sign? Why did they push me?"

The Governor quickly introduces once again a famous local Medal of Honor winner, Gregory Wetzel, who is on the stage. Wetzel lost his left hand in Vietnam. The crowd applauds.

A bulky young worker, shy and blushing but determined, like a member of a college wrestling team, steps in front of the girl in the yellow coat and folds his arms. Wallace moves on from the middle of his interrupted sentence.

Later, on the way out, three young veterans tease the girl in the yellow coat. "Let's go get some pizza. We can talk about how great George is."

"You won't have much to say!" she taunts, as girls have always taunted.

"You're being facetious," the other boy says, not quite handling the word.

One boy has a sparse black moustache. "You hear what he said about the courts? They'll get him for that."

"He's got protection."

"I'm telling you, they have to stop him. Whatta guy."

An hour later, at Racine, the rally is on again, this time in Memorial Hall, well after working hours and publicized through radio spots. The crowd assembles early; some are turned away at the door. 1,200 sit inside, 330 in the balcony, standing room for 250. Excitement crackles. The loudspeakers are tuned just right, then turned up louder, like a rock festival. "I've laid around and played around this ole town too long," Billy Grammer is singing, his blue eyes flashing. And: "Horseshoe diamond ring."

Mr. Karl Prussian, twelve years a counterspy, is introduced by George Mangum in the latter's high nasal best: "If you've been followin the Conservative movement in the U.S., you'll *know* the man ah'm about to intr'duce to you." "George Wallace," Karl Prussian says, "is a man of God." "God bless you!"

George Mangum says. We're in Protestant territory in Wisconsin now and the symbols are colliding, and sparks are shooting. It's meetin' time, and everyone's at ease.

George Wallace, Jr., his hair as long as John Lennon's, swings out gently, his red and gold tie against a white patterned suit whose alternating weave the shifting light brings out, like some upholstered chair in gramma's living room of long ago. He flourishes his dark electric guitar, tenderly, with restraint. No wild vulgar rock, no Mick Jagger here, but son of a man misunderstood, a young, patient, and determined Alabaman. "Gentle on my mind . . ." is his first number, and his second is: "I shot a man in Reno just to watch him die," sad and haunting, guilt-stricken and wondering, perhaps like a premonition.

Then the Governor, half-reluctant, half-jubilant, explodes across the stage. Pandemonium. He likes the crowd. His eyes begin to shine. Nervousness falls away and his movements become fluid, confident. Each gesture draws a response. He throws away lines, bantering with Mangum who is pumping his fist from his shoulder into the air lifting the applause, the whistles, the loyal cheers. The Governor now has his fist in hand, right in left, squeezing a little, makes a bow and sweeps hand from forehead in suggestion of a salute, with a crisp little cut on the end. He takes a deep breath.

"I tell you," he punches out into the super-loud speakers, "we're gonna give St. Vitus dance to the leadership of the Democratic party." Wallace from one side, McCarthy from the other, both disdain the leadership of the party. Each, of course, has a different image of *who* the leadership is. McCarthy means the Humphreys, Daleys, Muskies, Baileys. Wallace means them, too, but mostly he means the leaders of the left wing— Lindsay, McGovern, Kennedy, and perhaps McCarthy, too. In view of who won the nomination in 1972, Wallace seemed to name the powers more precisely.

"Ah'm sick of permissiveness in this society," Wallace spits out through the booming speakers. "Ah'm tired of false liberals!"

Here, an aside is necessary. For years, Wallace has claimed that *he* is the true liberal, the one candidate for the working-

man and for individual rights. Lipset and Raab (1969) cite
testimony from Alabama political leaders: "His economic programs surpassed the fondest dreams of every liberal in the
state. He did what all the populists have always dreamed of
doing." "He is more liberal than Johnson, I tell you—more liberal than Folsom and Kennedy ever were." Even Julian Bond:
"He confuses me because he's liberal on a great many questions,
except race."

Wallace himself rejects Ultra-conservatism because "those Ul-
tra-conservatives are conservative just about one thing—money."
Wallace noted that Goldwater in 1964 "did not have the support and confidence of the working people in this country." He
made an implicit distinction between cultural conservatism and
economic conservatism; he called himself a conservative "who
has a record of . . . support for the workingman." He saw the
need for a "marriage between classes." But Wallace said in
1964, "I think there is a backlash against the theoreticians and
bureaucrats in national government who are trying to solve problems that ought to be solved at the local level."

In Wallace's campaign strategy of 1968, Lipset and Raab
say, "anti-Negro sentiment was a secondary bond, of varying
saliency, rather than a primary bond." Wallace did not build
his 1968 campaign on *attitudinal* racism (his feelings or anyone else's) nor on *ideological* racism (negative affects and images
about a group as a whole); but on a general resistance to cultural change, whose (important) side effect was *institutional*
racism. This would have been sufficient reason for genuinely liberal people to reject him. But other factors complicate the picture. The 1968 platform of the American Independent Party
included welfare liberalism to so explicit a degree that John
Ashbrook told the American Conservative Union: "True conservatism cannot be served by George Wallace. At heart he is
a Populist with strong tendencies in the direction of a collectivist
welfare state. . . . We find George Wallace's candidacy repugnant to the ideals of American conservatism." The overwhelming
majority of a hundred leading conservatives, polled by *Human
Events,* opposed Wallace.

It is easy to understand why some Southerners respond to

symbolic attacks on "theoreticians" and "bureaucrats" from Washington and how symbols of "national government" merge with the "national networks." Government and media are perceived as cultural forces imposing a new morality, a new social order, a new personal identity on unwilling citizens. In this resistance, Southerners are not alone. Farmers and city folk in Wisconsin—and in every other state—feel that their own cultural morality is undercut in the livingrooms of their own homes. They do not feel that their own cultural morality is accurately reflected on television. TV is not *their* icon.

Outrage at "a bunch of welfare loafers sittin' in the sun"; outrage at stories in the paper about one man in New York on five different welfare lists, another in Los Angeles collecting ten different checks; outrage at nonelected federal judges; outrage at foundations whose "$200 billion property and income are tax free"; outrage at busin'—which, along with "work" became in 1972 the two great symbols of cultural morality in conflict. Wallace tells of Nixon asking Mao Tse-tung in Peking for advice on dealing with busing. "I don't ask about busin'," Mao tells him. "When I want to bus 'em, I just bus 'em." And Nixon slaps his knee: "We jes do the same thing! We've got more in common than I thought." "Thet's why they got along so well," Wallace arches an eyebrow. The crowd howls with laughter till it hurts.

"Ah'm sick n' tired of giving up 50 percent of my income to the United States, to waste half of it overseas on nations that spit on us and half of it on welfare."

"An' now they tell us Vietnam was a mistake. A mistake that cost the average citizen 50,000 lives, 300,000 wounded, 120 billion dollars down the drain. Ah don' call that a mistake. It's a tragedy." Like David Halberstam, he puts the blame upon the best and brightest—"them." *This* is how *they* run our lives.

Wallace reads the papers to cite "proof" for his positions. Everything confirms his vision. "Puttin' money into schools doesn't mean that schools are good." New York City schools, he says, pay more per capita for pupils than almost any other schools in the nation. The audience knows *those* schools are a blackboard jungle.

But *the* issue is saved till last: Property taxes. "In Alabama, here's what we pay in Alabama. Listen, now. For a $10,000 home, $40 every year. For a $15,000 home, $67 every year." The crowd is gasping. He goes on. "For $25,000, $105. For a $30,000 home, $130 every year." They buzz and shake their heads, then break into sustained applause. "Mark my words, by November 7, even President *Nixon* is going to call for a reduction in property taxes in America. They always come aroun' to what Ah'm sayin. Sometimes it takes a little while. You jes mark my words."

I leave the auditorium with my wife, exhausted and excited as if it had been a championship basketball game. The crowd spills happily through the municipal parking lot, abuzz. A man so loose with truth, so only half-right, yet so on target compared with all the others. He lacks the seriousness, the class, Americans like to see in their president. The nation dreams of upward mobility. It is a snobbish nation. Many will penalize him for mispronouncing words and making fun of people of status. In that sense, the nation is safe from Wallace, because of snob appeal. Even at the bar at Serb Hall, one man had said: "If I wanted a dictator, I'd move to Spain or Greece." And the bartender: "Maybe for two years. He'd clean things out." Then a shrug. "More than that, he'd be dangerous." But did they vote for him?

Imagine the nation this way, I tell myself: the nativism and traditional extremism of the Right is maybe 10 percent; the New Politics is maybe 10 percent. Another 20 percent on the Left and 20 on the Right understand politics through symbols closer to its own extreme than to the other. The future of America depends on who takes the middle 40 percent. Most of these lean toward the Democratic party; that's why it's the majority party. What ties them to the Democrats? Not economics only, although the pocketbook is powerful. Rather, the symbols and loyalties of "our kind" against the "others," our culture, our identity, against theirs. It isn't only because the Democratic party offered economic rewards to workers that, in the twentieth century, it replaced the Republican party as the party of the majority. It's because it *saw the world through the eyes of the worker, identified with his style, his ways, his morality* and championed him against those who were his "betters."

Morality is the highest kind of status. The "best people" don't believe their being best is due merely to their having money. The Democratic party once made the workingman's culture the criterion of healthy morality; it denounced Republican morality as cant. Now certain key Republicans and affluent suburbanites are becoming liberal Democrat; and the old cant appears in new form, on the Left.

A truck-driver's son in a community college, for example, is told in class that after World War II many veterans from the working class went into teaching merely for a job; "obviously," the professor asserts, "they lacked high ideals and dedication." Now, the professor patiently explains, many upper-class kids, instead of taking higher pay elsewhere, are turning to teaching "with high ideals and dedication." Morality is here defined by social class. The lower classes can't have higher sentiments; the upper class can't have vulgar ones. The truck-driver's son is furious, but the professor doesn't understand. Cant.

Hatred for the middle class is intense in the "adversary culture." Resentment against TV repairmen, football coaches, truck drivers, barbers, construction workers, and auto mechanics is common in our higher literature. Norman Mailer calls the people "the wad." Some on the Left seem to feel besieged, surrounded, outnumbered. Defeat seems to be a symbol some require.

What if the middle is far healthier than the fearful Left supposes? In any case the middle feels abandoned. Why is a man with as many deficiencies as Wallace has—and knows he has—given time to persuade more and more people that no one else will hear their pain?

In the dark night chill of Wisconsin, I am sad that the "hidden injuries of class" to which Wallace speaks so grossly and mendaciously have not found a more high-minded voice: a Lincoln, a Roosevelt. Not a single credible voice underneath the whole dark sky.

Hubert Humphrey's schedule is unbelievable. Up before 6
A.M., last event not finished until past midnight. Sixteen appearances one day, eighteen another. He *wants* the White House,
the groan of desire is audible. His energy is astonishing. Unlike
Muskie, he likes people, needs them, grows strong from them.
My father-in-law in Iowa tells me on the telephone: "Hubert
is going to win. He's coming up."

I accompany the Humphrey press to one of Hubert's stops, a
school for handicapped children, for the deaf and the retarded.
He shakes hands with every single Sister. Every one. And every
child he can reach. Schedule allows for twenty minutes. Thirteen used for shaking hands. The talk goes on for twenty minutes, *on* for twenty-five, *on* for thirty. The hands of the poor
priest who is trying to translate into sign language are wearing
out . . . thirty-five minutes . . . another man takes over as
translator . . . "And some of the greatest men in history had
handicaps"—he tries to think of one, his eyes flash, cheeks acquire that familiar beaming, knowing look. (Press thought I
didn't have anyone in mind!)—"Thomas Edison. We *all* have
handicaps. . . ." [Press starts thinking of Hubert's.] "What's
the most important word in the English language?" [The restless, indifferent, perhaps retarded children can hardly wait.]
"Service!" [Then he remembers the Catholic nuns.] "And
the other most important word is 'love!' " [Two minutes on
service, three on love—it's a larger theme.] "And what are the
last four letters in the word American? I CAN. Look at them.
Spell it. I can. You *can*. You're great. You're wonderful. God
bless you." The tears are in the corner of his eye, the tears
that cause him such grief on television. His head chucks up and
down happily as he wades back through the crowd of distracted,
uncertain, uncomprehending kids. Their indifference drove him
wild. He had to reach them. Had to. Or wanted to. A combination of generosity, sentiment, need to love, need to win love.

It is remarkable, isn't it? No pragmatic justification for what
Hubert did for those deaf children. Americans love professionals, killers especially, ruthless investigators, determined secret
agents, anybody who absolutely concentrates on proficiency, un-

distracted by human involvement. But in fact people are amazingly distractable, shamelessly seduced into their own humanity. Calculation may be a political ideal, one to which politicians often fail to measure up.

At a press conference, Hubert is asked the meaning of "viable." The press is really hostile. Is his candidacy viable? The press pretends that politics is a matter of being consistent on certain issues. Journalists worry about Hubert's waffling and rapid heedlessness. Don't they understand that politics is a matter of meeting decisions as they come, not what you said a week ago but what the facts today demand? There is a conflict between the myth of the committed politician, clear on the issues, and the job of persuasion the politician must actually do on every single audience. Many in the nation value issues and consistency; politicians, by contrast, value their own capacity to get various groups to *go along* on concrete legislation. Commentators value consistency; politicians value persuasion. Talking issues isn't the whole of politics. So there's a tennis match at every press conference. Humphrey's head snaps back, his lips form a strained smile: "Take a look at me! Alive, active, with it! I've been a trailblazer! How are we going to reduce *arms* in the future? How are we going to find 22 million *jobs* before 1980? That's what *I'm* thinking about. Is that viable?" His small round jaw juts forward out of his cheeks. Eyes flash. He slapped that one back just inside the line.

It is not the politicians' *positions* the press tries to understand. It is their tennis game. Why is skill at fielding questions, especially hostile ones, valued so highly? "He's a pro," newsmen sometimes shrug. The profession of placing answers to questions where they can no longer be returned. Match point.

The press story on Hubert is that he represents the "old" politics. Good "old" Hubert, doing all the "old" things. The cult of the fresh and the new is journalism's cult. It has little to do with real life on earth or good politics. The vaunted business of "informing" the public is, in fact, the business of selling novelty. Hubert suffers. The limitation of the press is not that it isn't free; it's that its goal is news.

In a hotel room, Jackson has a press conference. Members of "Common Cause" somehow elude the Secret Service and raise a challenge about campaign finances until an irate newsman asks them what paper they represent and tells them this is a *press* conference, and to shut up or leave.

In another room, Lindsay is holding a press conference. He says his victory will "surprise" everyone. He calls the voters of Wisconsin "wise, tough, and independent." This is not a string of Wisconsin adjectives, not quite the way people here think of themselves. These are words New Yorkers find attractive. Better, that Wisconsinites have common sense, maybe, and shrewdness, perhaps; that they are *good* people, with distinctive progressive traditions—these things *could* have been said in flattery. "Wise"—it is too high and toney a word; "tough"—no, people here prefer to mask their strength under goodness; "independent"—well, Wisconsinites have experienced the virtues of solidarity, cooperation, and concerted organizing. Wrong approach.

Muskie at the A. O. Smith plant gate. Snow falls on the iron rail. An inch of wet slush underfoot. Workers would rather hurry past. Earlier, at the Capitol Court Shopping center, high school kids shout over the crowd standing in the rain (before it turned to snow): "Ask him if he brought his crying towel." Two women, uncertain who was who, cup their hands: "Boo McGovern!" One girl pushes another: "I shook his hand!" holding it aloft for inspection and wonderment.

At a Polish ballroom that night, the last event of the campaign, surrounded by Congressman Pucinski and Rostenkowski from Chicago and introduced in Polish by Mayor Gribbs from Detroit, after a pounding drum-led chant of "We want Muskie! We want Muskie!" amid signs reading POLISH POWER, HE BELONGS TO US, and MOVE NIXON OUT, Muskie talks about growing up in Maine, in a town of only three Polish families, seeing his father's Polish newspaper from Stevens Point, Wisconsin, and how only after his election as governor in 1954 did he make contact with Polish communities in the country, at a meeting in Wilmington, Delaware. An old lady beside me raps my arm and whispers loudly: "Is Muskie a Polish name?" I nod. "Oh, I didn't know," she says, and listens. His family, Muskie said, lived in the Russian-occupied sector of Poland, knew the tyranny of the Czars and the poverty of large families with no inheritance or land to pass on. His grandfather decided to send one son—a whole family line. Immigrants brought more than selves, he says. A whole family line.

But none of the preparatory political work had been done for a speech like this. Muskie didn't recognize that Poles in Milwaukee (and elsewhere) have special problems in this society in combination with other groups of low status and that the rise of black consciousness found no effective parallel among third- or fourth-generation Poles. People lack political awareness *as* Poles, few think of themselves as "ethnic." They've been taught it's wrong to think that way. Little in Muskie's perception made contact with them. He did not speak of the cultural and moral pressure they felt, of their feeling of unfairness in the way liberals regarded them, of a politics that might restore families and neighborhoods, of a new pride and self-consciousness that might guide them in the future. All he offered was nostalgia—romantic, inaccurate nostalgia at that—about an America that never was, "when what made America great were our differences." America was as cruel as it was generous to immigrants. It is still a cruel and violent place for urban dwellers. One out of four in the old days went back to Europe. Muskie understood nothing of the hard edges of their daily lives. All he had to offer was an Americanized Polish name.

On television later that night, surrounded by law books, his left eye a little baggy with weariness, in a reading voice rather than a speaking voice, Muskie presented himself in a last-ditch videotape. Alone with the law books, trying to be reasonable, calm, unruffled, he reached for the eloquence that had won him so much praise in 1970. He added the argument—more impressive in retrospect—that *he* could beat Nixon. But such an argument sways political professionals, seldom the people. Muskie needed to be seen *with* people, *doing* something about their grievances. He needed to share their anger. 1972 was not 1970. Muskie worried about winning and holding the Left; it was the Center that was angry. The Left wanted trust, belief, moral concern, commitment to changes dear to "the young," the poor, the blacks—or at least to the media that so identified "the constituency of change." The Center—at least the urban, ethnic, working-class Center—wanted tax relief, attention, status, moral equality with blacks, a new system of law and order (*not* mere "cracking down," but real relief from real disorder), defense against urban "renewal" and highways. Besides that, it wanted integration in a way that did not punish those who accepted it. It wanted long-range security and stability in neighborhoods and families, a share in the new opportunities for higher education, and representation in judgeships and higher offices. It wanted to be seen and heard.

Something new was beginning to happen and it wasn't antiblack (although there was conflict over limited supplies of real goods like jobs, homes, places in college.) The new mood wasn't exactly the alienation George Wallace aimed at (Slavs in Milwaukee voted for Wallace at less than his statewide average). It wasn't the alienation George McGovern was speaking of.

After Florida, while Muskie called Wallace a demagogue, McGovern pointed to the legitimate frustrations of many Americans. He was conciliatory to the Wallaceites; and his young Harvard pollster, Pat Caddell, was advancing the thesis that "alienation" cut across all ranks and classes of Americans. The fallacy was that alienation is not one, any more than the American culture is one. Each of our many tangled cultures has its own pathologies and beauties. McGovern strode into Wisconsin with the best organization he had anywhere in the country, with the state's long tradition of progressive politics, and with the precedent of Eugene McCarthy's brilliant showing there in 1968. McGovern had a clean Midwestern face and manner, the moral intensity so important to the Left, and the social-evangelical Protestantism so familiar to Wisconsin and Minnesota.

Late on the last night, (it was nearly midnight) he entered Ratzsch's German restaurant with his wife. He seemed to be encouraging her, telling her he would win: "I've always said that Wisconsin is the most progressive state in the nation." Perhaps Eleanor McGovern was discouraged or weary or both and he was trying to tell her it was worth it, it would end well.

Moral reform in politics periodically sweeps across America, almost always eastward. McGovern's was a fresh face. The name seemed Irish. The professional strength of the Kennedys was known to guide his staff: Mankiewicz, Salinger, Dutton. He seemed honest, quiet, dependable. He did not seem Eastern and slick. He was hitting some new notes: not simply the war but tax reform. There was an edge of outrage and anger in his voice. Arresting. The media at last had a dramatic story.

When the vote rolled in on April 4, McGovern, Wallace, Humphrey, and Muskie split the field:

McGovern 30 percent; Wallace 22 percent; Humphrey 21 percent; Muskie 10 percent. It was victory without a majority, but it put McGovern on the main track. Muskie was fatally wounded and growing weaker. McGovern's basic early plan had succeeded brilliantly. The flaw in his campaign was not yet visible to the nation; he had not yet faced the spotlight of public examination.

27

Together with McGovern at the Garden

The stark political contrast between George McGovern and Richard Nixon was obvious to the White House staff even in the days when Nixon's standing in the polls was barely even with, and sometimes lower than, Senator Muskie's. Ordinarily an incumbent president runs far ahead of his lesser-known competitors, especially before one of them is singled out by nomination. But throughout his career attachment to Nixon has seldom been broad and never deep. Against the Democrats in 1972, therefore, he wanted to face the candidate most narrow in appeal. His campaign's "dirty tricks" contributed, especially in New Hampshire, to McGovern's win.

The President sought to clutch three central symbols to himself: that of the embattled, fearless activist; that of planetary peace-maker; and that of bold initiator and architect of world order. In the spring of 1972, Nixon ordered the renewed bombing of Hanoi and the mining of Haiphong harbor in reprisal for a major North Vietnamese offensive in the south, and in the teeth of his imminent visit to Moscow. These were risks, closely calculated, but dangerous. They undergirded his voyages to Peking and Moscow with decisiveness and power. His accomplishments on these trips set in motion great tides in world affairs. They assured him of deserved esteem on the part of his countrymen and a lasting place in history. They gave substance to his desire to present himself as a *presidential* man, a man of accomplishment and solid know-how against an untried man of narrow gauge.

Nixon's strong suit has always been world affairs (where—one is obliged to ponder—his lack of scruples and gift for cold analysis are better respected than within the United States). On his return from Moscow, Nixon was careful to stop for tumultuous crowds in Poland, televised scenes that for urban ethnic peoples more deeply stirred personal emotions (irrationally but effectively) than the vastly more important visits to Peking and Moscow. (I recall watching the Slavic faces in the happy crowds and, against the surging joy that an American president was there, sadly shaking my head: "That's it. This election's over.")

In this context, there are rival interpretations of the disposition of forces in the election of 1972. Some observers held that through antiwar "organizing" the new politics had gained millions of new adherents since 1968; that the new millions of young voters enfranchised for the first time would swing massively to the support of the new politics; that millions more blacks, Chicanos, and Indians than ever before would be registered and vote; that women would contribute new votes to a candidate favorable to women's liberation; that, in short, the Left was not only the cause of true morality but also the cause of a new majority.

By contrast, other observers discerned that the new politics was increasingly isolated in American life. The excesses of the Weathermen, of Dr. Spock, and the Berrigans had made the war in Vietnam too irksome to continue, but had not built up an effective electoral coalition. Quite the opposite. A majority now hated the war, but hated the public dissenters even more. From a moral point of view, the dissenters had done the nation

a high service; from a political point of view, their moral righteousness and their civil disobedience rendered the Left suspect
as a guardian of the nation's laws and institutions. In this view,
the propagandists of the new politics made a decisive mistake.
Joseph Duffey, assessing his own losing senate campaign against
Lowell Weicker in Connecticut in 1970, described that mistake:

> It is always tempting to blame our defeat on those people
> who never understood what we were trying to say or who re
> jected our efforts to lead them. But the fact is the search for
> a "new politics" in America is still at a very primitive
> stage.
>
> For a decade now most liberals and reformers have acted
> as if there were only two major problems in America—race
> and poverty. Many of our policies have been formulated as
> if the nation were composed of only two major groups—the
> affluent and the welfare poor. But somewhere between af
> fluence and grinding poverty stand the majority of American
> families.
>
> The "new politics" has thus far not spoken to the needs
> and interests of these Americans. We have forgotten that
> they, too, feel the victims of decisions in which they have
> no voice.
>
> There is a real sense in which our liberal proposals for
> meeting the crises of race and poverty have failed. First,
> these programs have done little to solve these social prob
> lems. Second, these policies and the way they have been
> most often presented have served to further divide the
> peoples who must stand together if ever there is to be a
> majority constituency for change in America!

At four points leaders of the new politics were vulnerable
in the eyes of many Middle Americans: their professional power,
status, and affluence; their ignorance of the economics of working
people's lives; their sense of moral superiority; their way of
violating the moral sensibilities of others.

A candidate of the new politics who wanted to avoid these
sources of criticism would have had to devise a fourfold strategy.
First of all, he would have had to identify himself with the concerns and dilemmas of traditional Democrats who were of lower

educational status, grinding economic circumstance, and insecure ethnic or regional feeling—people who felt left behind by the worlds of power, education, and affluence. He would have had to think through his political rhetoric, programs, and actions to see where these were excluding such voters.

Second, he would have had to lead the way to policies that *united* the races, instead of taking sides, that brought a new perspective to public efforts to make life better for working people of all races.

Third, he would have had to mediate between the new morality of the educated "swingers" and the old morality of working people—teaching each how to respect the other.

Finally, he would have had to propose a strategy for urban areas to heal the conflicts inherent in integration—real and imagined; areas where competition is bitter over homes, over jobs, and over places in unions, in colleges, and in other positions of power and where crime and drugs are decimating communities of all kinds.

The partisans of the new politics tried to avoid the manifest difficulties of such a strategy. It was easier to speak rhetorically of "coalitions" and to hope that "pocketbook issues" would make traditional Democrats swallow their "prejudices" and vote along with the new politics—easier than to face the cultural conflicts in urban areas with clear eyes and solid political skills. A deadly mixture of disdain for the morality of Middle America and hopeful sentiment about the willingness of Middle Americans to be led by their moral superiors was hard to overcome. Activists who began to sympathize with the grievances and dilemmas of Middle Americans—and in the McGovern campaign there were many—were uncertain what political shape to give the anger and aspiration they encountered.

Years of neglect had taken their toll. The vehicles of the old politics—unions, ward leaders, traditional politicians—no longer carried conviction; but the new politics did not fill the vacuum.

The Nixon forces, mightily abetted by McGovern's lapses, labored in systematic fashion to fill this vacuum. By election day they had cut into the traditional Democratic vote in almost every constituency, taking away 10 percent here, 20 percent there, 5 percent in another place. (They did not do so well among workers in Northern cities who voted for Wallace in 1968; these split almost evenly, six out of thirteen for McGovern, seven for Nixon.)

With brazen skill, the Nixon organizers kept hidden from the public through the five long months of the campaign the full dimensions of the internal spying, burglary, and financial abuse whose tip surfaced on June 17 when the Watergate spies were discovered by a black security guard. Nixon offered traditional Democrats the reassurance of an able, bold, tough leader—but, most of all, opposition to what George McGovern had come to symbolize. Unbelievably, McGovern not Nixon was made the central issue of 1972. McGovern had not adequately defended himself against this possibility. He was exceedingly vulnerable.

It is difficult to define all the elements that enter symbolically into one's own mind as one votes, let alone into the minds of millions of others. Nevertheless, a symbolic interpretation of McGovern's campaign may be useful. His strengths, as we have earlier recounted, were many. Weaknesses for which he should early have compensated were also many. He lacked urban experience; he lacked contacts in cities, lacked a feel for cities, lacked the language and the style of urban life. Similarly, he lacked contact with traditional party figures. Late in the campaign, when his staff looked through photo files for pictures of McGovern with Jewish, Italian, Polish, and other symbolic leaders, few if any were available. McGovern should have made quiet efforts to identify himself with broader constituencies far earlier in his campaign than he did.

This is all the more true because, in order to overcome Senator Muskie's long lead in the polls and in the preference of party leaders, Senator McGovern had first of all to mobilize the constituency most favorable to himself—college-based, rooted in the antiwar movement. Some ex-Kennedy staffers like Pierre Salinger and Arthur Schlesinger, Jr., somewhat tarnished as "realists" because of their service with John Kennedy and their record on Vietnam, moved back to the left wing of the party by support for McGovern. They were not sufficient ballast against McGovern's identification with the new culture, in which antiwar sentiment was vocal and passionate. Far more than his actual voting record—his career was not very different from that of other candidates—this identification singled McGovern out from the other candidates. The constituency he came to stand for, his chairmanship of the commission on party reform, the funds he raised, the names he collected in the congressional struggle to end the war, and his "moral purity" became his greatest political assets. They were also severe liabilities.

McGovern later protested that he was as square, old-fashioned and staid in his morality as any Middle American, and that both his enemies and the media unfairly caricatured him as a creature of the counterculture, imprinting him with the three scarlet A's: abortion, amnesty, and acid. Early, however, perhaps out of short-term necessity, his campaign identified itself with the college youth culture, with the music and appearance and speech of "the movement," with the vocabulary and symbols that, not always unwittingly, excluded many traditional Democrats. The trauma and hard-edged desperation of urban working people, black as well as white, never reached the center of his campaign. McGovern appeared as "the man with the white hat," a relative innocent from the prairies, whose style was "tender." These images did not touch the harsh conflicts people actually felt.

Economic realities are life and death to working-class families with four or five children to put through school; the loose talk around the McGovern campaign of thousand-dollar grants seemed careless to the point of contempt. For weeks and weeks, McGovern had no clear figures about costs. People came to feel McGovern's campaign was toying with them. Suburban professionals who have hopes of career advancement and steady upward progression of earning power seemed not to comprehend that half of all American families earn less than $11,000 per year, with infinitesimal chance of later advancement; and that only 10 percent of all families earn more than $15,000 per year. To toss around thousand-dollar figures casually was insulting.

In California, after his rather narrow primary victory, McGovern had a private party for major donors. Newsmen sat outside the door, excluded, but taking down names of movie stars, money-makers like Hugh Hefner and industrial heirs like Stewart Mott—names, as one of them put it, "that will go down real good in Dorchester."

McGovern used the symbol of being "different" from other politicians. He made unnecessarily high moral commitments, Political realities again and again made him back down. He was then subject to charges of hypocrisy. A political leader can generate passionate moral energy without any appeal to his own moral purity. John and Robert Kennedy, for example, did not campaign under the banners of purity, honesty, and superior moral character. Means in politics are inevitably mixed and less than pure.

Even in the primaries, in March, reporters began taking notes of the occasions on which McGovern went back on prior pledges. They nodded when he held closed-door meetings with politicians like Mayor Daley, when he was less than candid with the press, when he not only visited Lyndon Johnson and Mayor Daley, but lavished excessive praise on both. It was not that McGovern's practice was lower than that of other politicians, but that he had constructed so simon-pure an image for himself he left himself no room for maneuver. He did not establish early enough the degree to which "dirty hands"—a need to do things one considers immoral or improper (telling a half-truth to the press, for example)—are a normal feature of everyday life, including politics. He made "morality" a central symbol in an area in which the benefits of that symbol could be turned against him (or anyone else) in devastating fashion. According to his own later admission, he could scarcely comprehend the ferocity of resentment he aroused and especially the fact that so many considered him "immoral."

Perhaps the main public event of his virtually uncontested primary campaign in New York State serves as well as any other symbol to illuminate how he unwittingly separated himself from millions of traditional Democrats. Foreshadowed in it is the exclusion of the Daley slate from the convention in Miami, which clinched McGovern's character in the public mind. If Mayor Daley isn't a good enough Democrat for George Mc-

Govern, then who of us is? If purity tests are to be established, many wanted to be counted out. If McGovern had wanted Daley in the convention, he could have kept him; McGovern refused to intervene.

The pledge of "one-thousand percent" support for Eagleton and then his long-delayed dismissal from the ticket was, in the eyes of many, merely a repetition of the basic McGovern pattern. First comes the overstated ideal and high moral enthusiasm. Then comes a hard political choice between the image of his own purity (oddly identified with his will to win) and loyalty to persons. Moments of weakness and delay follow, and then McGovern chooses. Daley is sacrificed, and so is Eagleton. Both are Catholics, both are the "regular" type of Democrat. The signals are far more clear to "regulars" than McGovern realizes.

Even the defeat of the abortion resolution at Miami Beach followed this pattern, except that in that case McGovern chose to offend *both* halves of the party. He offended the anti-abortionists by letting this divisive issue come up at all. He offended the pro-abortionists by rigging votes so the other side would win. He boasted of an "open" convention and, when it suited him, ran a "professional" convention. McGovern wished to seem both "pure" and "realistic."

In politics, only the latter is possible; a person who tries to be both is certain to end by being neither. The reason for this is not that politics is less moral than, say, journalism or publishing or academic life; but because—to paraphrase Eliot—social life does not support too much morality.

In Madison Square Garden, then, on June 14, a celebration of moral purity is held. "Together with McGovern at the Garden," it is called. Its purpose is to raise funds. Mike Nichols and Elaine May come back together just for the event; so do Peter, Paul, and Mary; and Simon and Garfunkel. The contrast between such a rally and a Wallace rally—or, say, a gathering of Bob Hope and Billy Graham for Richard Nixon—explodes the circuits of the mind. Comparative liturgies!

June 14 is Flag Day. But there are no flags on stage. No

flags surround the Garden. High up, forlorn, the huge Garden flag sighs in the smoke lazing in the lights.

The evening celebrates the resurrection of the youth culture. It is a meeting of "the little girls in tennis shoes" (Richard Reeves); of grandmother's ankle dresses, gingham and satin and lace; of boys with grandpa's mutton chops and John L. Sullivan mustaches. The liturgy of a new class is performed: evangelical sentiment, teardrop for teardrop, parallel to a Wallace rally.

Trying to tune his guitar, Garfunkel teasingly demands that the crowd be silent: "Can't you see we're *sensitive!*" (It is the key word of "the movement.") Peter, Paul, and Mary, Dionne Warwick, Simon and Garfunkel in every song celebrate the mobile, lonely, vulnerable, middle-class life. Of how many private hurts they sing! "If only we have love!" Dionne Warwick warbles in blue-flowered, cottony, innocent, white gown: "Imagine! No heaven—no hell—no countries—no religions! When the world will live as one." Universal, homogenized, educated, lovely, when the world will live as one!

> *You may say I'm a dreamer. But I'm not the only one.*
> *Someday I hope you will join us and the world will be as one.*
> *If only we have love. If only we have love.**

The crowd whistles, claps. One girl near us (not enough love yet) pulls another down so she can see.

Like medieval jesters, fuzzy blond hair and threadbare jeans shining in the light, Simon and Garfunkel offer "Jesus loves you, Mrs. Robinson!" and the most revealing line: "I'd rather be a hammer than a nail." The songs of wanderers: "To Look for America" (in Saginaw, Michigan); "Feeling Groovy"; and, down and out, sharing a last cigarette, "Good-bye, love, hello, loneliness!" Songs of the vulnerable, the compassionate, the

---

* "Imagine" by John Lennon © 1971 Northern Songs Ltd. All rights for the United States of America, Canada, Mexico and The Philippines controlled by Maclen Music, Inc. c/o ATV Music Group. All rights reserved. Used by permission. International copyright secured.

idealistic, without edges and toughness or the bite of economic reality. (Seats in the Garden sold for $100 and $8). Songs of those who scarcely recognize that they are middle class, love wine with dinner, love a place to go in summer, love cheese and fruits, love stereo, and do not love blast furnaces and mines and assembly lines.

No Lawrence Welk. No Johnny Cash. No Benny Goodman. The music, as at most McGovern rallies, is single-mindedly sectarian. The most public campaign event in New York State is not chosen with the *Daily News* in view, but *Variety* and *Rolling Stone*.

Nostalgia. A last gathering of the decade that had been. "After changes," a striking line went, "we are more or less the same."

But also bravado. Bald-headed Peter, aging, tells the crowd that the campaign picture of McGovern, shirt sleeves up, "is the best picture since, you know, Kennedy." And he boasts: "I'm not going to move toward the center. The center is moving toward us!"

It was Bob Dylan night, his songs coming back like redis-covered Reformation hymns. Peter, Paul, and Mary voice a threat. It foreshadows Miami Beach:

> *Get out of the way if you can't lend a hand*
> *Because the times they are a-changin'*
> *The first ones now, they will be last*
> *For the times they are a-changin'.*

With bursting applause the crowd comes to its feet for over a minute.

The answers are known, they are "blowing in the wind," and if your politics is different from those of this crowd, you feel the certainties, the nostalgias, and the impatience of Wallace crowds. Two raw hungers in America, demanding to be fed.

Elaine May and Mike Nichols hit the tone exactly. "After

---

* "The Times They Are A-Changin'" by Bob Dylan © 1963 M. Witmark & Sons. All rights reserved. Used by permission of Warner Bros. Music.

so many years of being a liberal, after so many years of losing,"
Elaine begins, "It's nice to know we're about to break a perfect
record." After the laughter: "At first I was skeptical. But now,
more and more, I'm beginning to have the feeling he could do
it. Yet as a liberal, and as a Jew, it seems to me wrong just
to coast. I need to keep alive a tiny, burning flame of doubt."

Elaine and Mike, playing liberals, "don't understand, exactly, McGovern's economic policy." But they do know it is
motivated by "idealism and harsh, pragmatic realism." That it
is "tough but tender." "Now what is it again?" It's so hard to
keep the right thoughts straight.

Hubert Humphrey, Elaine confessed, was "great in '48." Mike
was dry: "I don't think Hubert Humphrey ever was what he
was."

"Part of the Democratic party," Elaine pieced out, "is the
Democratic party machine. The other part is the Democratic
party." Cheers.

At 11:05, the entire cast gathers on the stage, flashing peace
signs, for a three-minute ovation. Then a great chant goes up:
WE WANT McGOVERN!

George and tiny Eleanor, radiant with the success of their
first evening at the Garden, finally appear. McGovern's Midwestern twang is touchingly attractive, makes people feel ecumenical and large, as though through him they have a tie with
that dark, sprawling beast they know as "Middle America,"
that dragon, or friendly dinosaur, whichever it might prove to
be, slumbering, necessary to their design.

"It is a wonderful night of coming together," McGovern says.
"Not only for so many of you." The performers, reconciling
painful separations for tonight's show of unity, duck and nod
while applause gathers. "But also, after many weeks of separation, tonight will be a wonderful coming together for Eleanor
and me." The crowd cheers, a growing naughty edge upon bil-
lowing laughter. In his hayseed voice, McGovern replies: "I'm
just not used to this New York sophistication."

He tells them how he "loves this country, enough to hold it
to a higher standard, away from the killing, death, and destruction now going on in Southeast Asia." "I love this land and

cherish its future. I want to set about making this country a great, decent, and good land . . . to be a bridge from war to peace . . . a bridge across the generation gap . . . a bridge across the gaps in justice in this country. . . . As the prophet wrote: 'Therefore, choose life . . . be on the side of blessing, not cursing' . . . on the side of hope, health, life. And peace for ourselves and peoples all around the globe."

"Each of us," he concluded, in a message to be heard again at Miami Beach and throughout the autumn, "is a child of a great and free people. We must match our decisions and performance to this nation's ideals. So that future generations will love the great and good land you and I have made it . . . a people who truly care about each other." Delicate and sensitive, these words conclude the worship service of the evening.

Three days later the burglars at the Watergate were trapped by police in Washington, D.C. Six weeks later on a triumphal night in Miami Beach, at 3 A.M., before a throng as deeply moved by the miracle as this one by the hope, George McGovern was nominated by the Democratic party as its candidate for the presidency. No Democratic party officials were with him on the stage in New York. Many were absent or disgruntled in Miami Beach. Yet against impossibly high odds, this decent, tender man as the culmination of years of effort and organization had seized the presidential nomination. He would spend the autumn trying bleakly to create an ecumenical movement that would bring back together all the political religions of the party into union with its suddenly victorious sect. Religious animosities, once allowed to open, are very hard to heal.

"Come home, America!" McGovern would proclaim. But his vision didn't look like home to a majority of Americans. It would be blind to blame them for deciding that he—like the movement of which he was a symbol—failed to represent them, blind to hold that the new sect represented what is right in America, and they alone what is wrong.

28

The Shooting
of Governor Wallace

A leader whose blood flows wantonly upon the earth has tapped the mystic bond between him and his fellows. The fragility of the common life erupts in him. The sight of a bold, energetic man—bleeding, prone, pale, his crimson blood in widening circles on the ground—attacks the stomach, awakens sympathies the mind may not admit, molecules of our blood crying out to his.

When George Wallace fell beneath the fierce, rapid shots of the idiotically smiling Arthur Bremer, blond-haired and eye-shaded, sweaty and muscled and triumphant, the Governor of Alabama was on the threshold of a major double victory in Michigan and Maryland. To that point, George Wallace had accumulated more popular votes than any other Democratic candidate. He had spent less than some others; he appeared less; he had only a phantomlike organization. His name had not been properly entered in the California primary; he neglected New York entirely; he spent barely a day in each of Pennsylvania and Massachusetts; unaccountably, he failed to test Ohio. He waited a week before entering Wisconsin; he was half-hearted in West Virginia and Indiana. The only state in which he seriously campaigned was Florida.

Governor Wallace was of too low a class, of too little education, to represent the United States with the status and prestige the better type of people would prefer. (Not that he didn't receive a slice of the better people's votes—his gains in the suburbs of the established was one of the startling phenomena of 1972. He won some wealthy suburbs of northwest Milwaukee, for example, but not the south side.) His past suggested racism and more than a touch of demagoguery, yielded too many hints of fat highway contracts and uncertain accounting methods, exuded the sultry breath of slow, steady corruption in the Southern style, as different from Northern urban corruption as mint julep from Irish whiskey, Huey Long from Boss Pendergast.

National prejudices against Southerners, moreover, are very strong. Clinton Rossiter in 1959, listing the requirements for prospective presidents of the United States, expressly excluded Southerners, along with Poles, Italians, and Greeks. The nation would experience, he thought, too great a symbolic shock.

Just to be certain, Richard Nixon, one leg sinking in the quicksand of his own "Southern strategy," sent financial help to Wallace's Democratic opponent in the gubernatorial primary of 1970. Wallace was already, on Monday, May 15, 1972, a potent symbol. He struck fear into many hearts. He won outpourings of remarkable affection. He stirred bitter militance among many who are normally content merely to obey their betters. What he lacked most was moral stature.

And then on May 15, at the start of a hot afternoon, at a shopping center in suburban Maryland, Arthur Bremer called out his name and Governor Wallace, coatless and excited, turned to find what he had long waited for, dreamed about, dreaded. Gun-flash, bullets that could not be held away. He seemed to see a face that had often, so often, haunted his glance as he stood behind his bulletproof podium. A face that had haunted his bodyguards—heavy, shirt-sleeved, faithful men, whose set faces accepted the world's hostility, who more than once felt hearts leap against their ribs as they reached to prevent missiles —eggs, oranges, rocks—from striking their sworn hero, their reason for existence. Not the face of Arthur Bremer, but the face of that evil which surrounds the circle of light an Alabama Baptist daily inhabits, the face a possum sees just as the dogs surround him, the face of a cat before the bag is tied in which the boys will drown him, a familiar face in Alabama —death.

Cornelia was over him, giving love-to-love panicky resuscitation, kneeling over him in yellow dress, offering her back to America, his crimson blood upon her dress as John Kennedy's had once splattered Jacqueline's, Cornelia and Jacqueline merged now in the mists of memory like two fated sisters, dark and beautiful, of presidential politics.

And, days later, after President Nixon had flown to Baltimore to be with the Governor in his hospital room, *they* came —the symbols of the class, the education, the moral prestige he had always reached for in his dreams but self-doubtingly knew he would always lack—Senator Kennedy and Ethel Kennedy. Their coming, it was later said, thawed some inner cold within him, carried comfort to a spot never reached before. "The Governor showed certain qualities," Senator Kennedy said, "in a way I have a unique understanding for."

So to all Governor Wallace's other accomplishments was added the symbol of his own blood: by it he was now purified, now consecrated. On his moral record, now, are the courage and stubborn will of a long recovery, of paralysis and humiliation and insistent pain from poisoned and infected intestines. He is known to have descended more than once into the valley of the shadow of death, down into despondency and a sense of bitter failure and the silent honeysuckle wish for death. Then, like Richard Nixon, he seemed to resolve to fight his way back, and the resolve—future uncertain, fate undeclared—seemed to quicken his powers of will. Health allowing, he will be a formidable figure in the nation's future.

Death, failure, torment on the wheels of fate—these, too, the American presidency offers those who seek it. The drama of the office knows no parallel.

29

Eight Major
Presidential Symbols

Even a brief survey of these few moments of the campaign of 1972 yields a maxim: *symbolic materials course through the humblest events of national life.* It is probably not useful to isolate every kind of symbol. Symbols are effective precisely by being concrete, woven into the texture of events, not quite able to stand on their own. Abstracted, no longer incarnate, they lose their power over us. Stated as propositions, they are all too easy to reject. It does not follow that anyone does, can, or should live without symbols—only that it is helpful to learn to recognize them as they are.

Everything we read in the newspapers, see on television, or witness in the flesh incarnates historical and cultural symbolic forms. We are so close to American daily life, it is so much a part of what we take for granted, that we fail to see how deeply it has limited our perception, character, and outlook. We are a strange and unusual people. We are not universal beings. We are a peculiar human culture on this planet.

Rather than attempt to summarize what the election of 1972 revealed about the strange shapes of our several self-understandings, I have decided to list here several of the symbols whose power in our lives has been remarkable throughout our history. Each revealed its power in 1972. For illustrative purposes, I have added material from other years.

The American people have seemed to love eight qualities in presidents, at least until the present. This does not mean they cannot learn to love new qualities, nor does it mean this list exhausts what is required of a candidate.

1. *Action.* A reporter once asked President Johnson about his low standing in the polls. President Johnson replied that polls were, just then, the least of his worries. "Hell, I could either bomb Hanoi or fly Air Force One all the way to Peking to beg for peace. Either way the polls would shoot up twenty points." The people don't like uncertainty. Action rallies them.

2. *Honesty.* Perhaps the best tribute to this quality is paid by Richard Nixon's lifelong efforts to master the forms of sincerity, even when quite patently he hides his thoughts. Since at least the time of Franklin Roosevelt, the people have come to expect intimate discussions (on television or radio) with their presidents. Even on occasions when presidents have told only a partial truth or even plainly lied, they have affected candor, for their hold upon the popular mind depends upon a bond of frankness. "Honesty" is perhaps too weak a word; the presidents depend upon the confidence—the latitude and energy—the people make available to them. Against the tides of fortune, the complexities of government, and the conflicts of competing institutions, the president is the people's voice. The bond of confidence between him and the people measures precisely his power over Congress and events.

Such confidence is based on the president's political competence and on his identification with the people; it is different from trust in his morality. People sometimes have confidence in a politician they don't "trust"; he may be a proven operator, but if he serves them well, they tend to forgive his moral faults.

Regarding his service to them, however, they insist on straight talk, straight action. This is why people could forgive Nixon the Watergate scandals easier than they could forgive him the expenditures for San Clemente and Key Biscayne. Many never trusted Nixon, but had confidence in his leadership.

People understand the necessities of a certain measure of "bureaucratic truth" and "diplomatic truth," a margin within which less than the full truth is acceptable. They have to believe that the context within which untruth is excusable is a context of integrity. In auto repair shops, in daily news accounts, in advertising, in university catalogs, in the noble sentiments voiced by wealthy élites, in every portion of society, citizens grow accustomed to distortions, pomposities, and outright lies. But to be called, and to be proven to be, a public liar is a devastating loss. The mayoralty of New York in his grasp, Mario Biaggi was instantly destroyed on this account. Public fascination during the Watergate scandals did not center on Nixon's responsibilities for the actions of his entire staff, but rather on the far more narrow symbol: Did he lie? And, concerning the vacation White Houses: Did he cheat?

3. *Goodness.* "President Eisenhower is such a *good* man!" it was said. He had a habit of plain speech, common sense, an attitude of goodwill toward others. He was a model of the virtues of smalltown America. Perhaps he used the appearances of simplicity to mask political astuteness; even in international affairs, he may have been deceptively successful. The fairness, integrity, decency, generosity, and incorruptibility he manifested have come to be much treasured. Americans like to think they are "a good people." So their alter ego must be "a good person."

4. *Self-control.* The president is often baited by carping opponents, hostile segments of the press, angry constituencies, hecklers, irreverent questioners. His ability to respond coolly and, if possible, with wit is much prized. Thus, Kennedy's performance in the first Great Debate of 1960, Nixon's exchange with Khrushchev at the kitchen display in Moscow, Muskie's reply to students who seized the microphones in Uniontown in 1968, and other similar events have been high points in their careers. In every campaign, a moment of confrontation

unexpectedly arrives. Such moments are eagerly anticipated. The American imagination loves the ordeal of "High Noon," and cherishes the opportunity to watch its leaders under fire.

5. *Genuine emotion.* By contrast, the public also seems to want to "get behind" public images and catch a glimpse of its leaders' unplanned, unstructured emotional responses. On this point alone, Humphrey set out upon the seemingly hopeless task of 1968 to charm the electorate by his ebullience, spontaneity, genuineness, and emotional risks, in contrast to the strictly controlled presentations offered by the Nixon campaign. John Kennedy was much helped by statements attributed to his father or his mother which, at first glance, might have seemed damaging. "We all have fathers," he would smile. "Give 'em hell, Harry!" people would encourage President Truman's lack of restraint. People seem to like a leader who can give rein to his emotions because he knows his emotions are trustworthy.

6. *Administrative control.* The way a leader organizes and disciplines his own staff is also a major public symbol. Are they all "yes men"? Are they unified, so that the people know who is in charge? Administrative skill was one of Eisenhower's strong points in the public mind, if not behind the scenes. John Kennedy created a new model of administration—bright, young, lively, creative, yet intensely in control. Even Nixon's disturbing centralization of control within the hands of three or four of his most intimate staff won tentative support from many. The fact that after the primaries McGovern seemed so little in control of his own central staff, let alone of his field staff, made him seem "dangerous," dangerous not because of his ideas or programs but because he might become the tool of forces larger than himself. The chaotic debates of the Miami convention, allowed to go on in the name of "openness" but closely controlled on critical votes, were signs of McGovern's ambivalence. The freewheeling style of the new politics—enamored both of "do your thing" and highly systematic organizing—stirs up a central symbolic conflict that must one day be resolved.

7. *Decisiveness.* A leader is expected to lead—and to lead instantaneously, without generating uncertainties in others. Timing is a fundamental ingredient in decisiveness. In emergencies,

"What thou dost, do quickly!" is a maxim of critical importance. When McGovern delayed a week before asking Eagleton to leave his ticket and another week before appointing a successor, he stretched trust in his mastery of situations beyond endurance. The dilemma McGovern faced was extremely cruel; there was, perhaps, no way to walk away from it unwounded. But while personal decency and sobriety might have bidden him to make haste slowly, he put the nation through an agony of indecisiveness it could scarcely forgive him. Imagine, by contrast, a decision taken within twenty-four hours both to replace Eagleton and simultaneously to name his successor. (In the face of international calamity, a president would be expected to be that decisive). McGovern would, then, at least, have shown a talent for cold and penetrating power.

8. *An instinct for ends and means that are "characteristically American."* There is what Clinton Rossiter calls "a grand and durable pattern of private liberty and public morality" within which an American president must operate. Even where there are no laws or well-charted seas, where precedents are lacking and unparalleled perplexities arise, the president must choose ways of proceeding that awaken in the public echos of recognition. What Harold Laski calls the "inarticulate major premises" of the presidency limit the ways a president is free to move. Nixon, seemingly, has violated these premises—break-ins, burglaries, and buggings invaded private liberties. The style through which he operated—cordoned off from the Congress and the people by his two key assistants, H. R. Haldeman and John D. Erlichman—violated traditions of public morality. It was not so much specific immoral deeds that bred outrage, but untraditional tendencies of centralization, dictatorship, and arrogance.

The choices the nation has made since World War II are two: to become the foremost world power and to build a complex social order based on high technology. Both of these choices require centralization and fairly ruthless presidential leadership. The office of the presidency today demands a strong executive, swift to act in international affairs and vigorous in domestic policy. The nation's defense against dictatorship rests, to this point, less on restrictions under law than on internal restraints upon the presidents themselves. It is these restraints that have proven to be weak. The public expectations that these restraints must remain in force have proven to be strong.

Thus, around Richard Nixon in August, 1973, swirled two major symbolic currents. On the one side was the Scylla of seeming to allow his administration's serious violations of personal liberties and public morality to go unpunished. On the other side was the Charybdis of unattractive and uncertain alternatives. One set of symbols demands strong, continuous, unhampered executive power; accordingly, many citizens will no doubt prefer no change of command in the middle of a voyage, even if a scoundrel is at the helm. Another set of symbols demands effective restraints upon an office that might otherwise transmogrify into dictatorship; accordingly, impeachment, resignation, or at least solemn public censure seem in order.

How these conflicting symbolic needs will be reconciled is impossible to predict. Much depends upon accumulating public evidence, upon the slowly clarifying power of the people's judgment, and upon the political wisdom of the Congress. Characteristically, Richard Nixon does not accept blame; usually, even when he seems to be confessing fault, he fiercely justifies himself. Should he do nothing whatever to ease the situation— neither humbly censuring himself nor observing new respect for personal liberties nor discovering new sensivitity to traditional restraints—the symbolic dissonance of the next few years could be unbearable. But no one should underestimate Richard Nixon's ability to turn symbols around: to make himself an object of sympathy and to make his accusers seem immoral. Nor should one underestimate the power of future presidential actions to make today's events recede into memory.

Still, whatever happens in the last term of Richard Nixon's presidency, we have again encountered the edges of symbols still alive and powerful. The instinct of a president for ends and means "characteristically American" remains subject to searching judgment and trampling retribution. "Mine eyes," the most American of anthems warns, "have seen the glory of the coming of the Lord!" That glory, ablaze with vengeance, gives power to the national conviction:

Glory, glory, hallelujah!
His Truth goes marching on.

Nixon will attain his just deserts. Whatever the immediate verdict, the age of innocence departs.

Part Five

A NEW AND
DARK FAITH

Lincoln is the supreme myth, the richest symbol in the American experience. He is, as someone has remarked neither irreverently nor sacrilegiously, the martyred Christ of democracy's passion play. And who, then, can measure the strength that is given to the President because he holds Lincoln's office, lives in Lincoln's house, and walks in Lincoln's way? The final greatness of the Presidency lies in the truth that it is not just an office of incredible power but a breeding ground of indestructible myth.
　　　　　　　　　　　　　　—Clinton Rossiter, *The American Presidency*

30

America as a Business

Jeb Stuart Magruder, John Dean, John Mitchell, Ronald Zeigler, John Ehrlichman, H. R. Haldeman, and others in the Nixon administration and the Committee to Re-elect the President shared a special world, had a different sense of reality from that of many of their antagonists in politics and in the press, saw the unfolding story of American politics in their own way. They prided themselves on their special form of pragmatism. They used the word "power" frequently, as if power were reality's fundamental ingredient. Their language sprang from the gravelly soil of management and public relations. For the personal "said" they preferred the machinelike "indicated." They liked "process" and "interface" and "inoperative" and "viable." They hesitated to commit themselves beyond either side of a "time frame," and dated their assertions with "not at this time." They spoke of "making a determination" and "discussing the public relations aspects" and "zero-defect" systems. They spoke as though their perception, memory, and responsibility were neatly bounded by administrative charts, outside of which they wished neither to see nor to hear. It seldom occurred to them to go to the President or other superiors, man-to-man, to talk about situations in wholes. They lived in a world, apparently, in which no one was expected to be a rounded, twenty-four-hour, flesh-and-blood human being, but only a "professional" with his own defined "competence."

The pre-arranged script for the Republican convention at Miami allowed for spontaneous demonstrations of specified length, which the chairman would (according to the script) gavel to order. The convention was the most complete metaphor for the Nixonian conception of politics: a well-managed, carefully staged business. "The business of America is business," Calvin Coolidge once said, but the Nixon administration tried to install a more penetrating perception: "Run America like a business." They applied management techniques to politics. They adapted to the era of technology by seeking concentration, control, remote and high-level centralization. They tried to "discipline" subjective human qualities so as to keep them out of professional relationships, no one fully exposed to the President, the President never fully exposed, each person showing only those facets of himself required by "the game plan." Thus, wholly normal human questions were repressed or simply never arose; they were not "called for" in the script. Since many corporate officers live this way, many professional men—lawyers, brokers, managers—found White House attitudes fairly "realistic."

The President himself received a full "news digest" every day, but not a finger-smudging, inefficient, noisy newspaper to thumb through, having to jump from page 1 to "page 8, column 5"—near the girdle ads. Questions raised for nine months by two reporters in his hometown newspaper, available at 10 cents a day, never occurred to him until March 21, 1973; so he publicly testified in May. That testimony was released through others; he kept himself suitably remote.

No wonder the President called H. R. Haldeman and John Ehrlichman, as he accepted their resignations, two of the most selfless and dedicated public servants he had ever met. No wonder words like "discipline," "selflessness," "hard work," and "loyalty" meant so much to the White House staff. They were required to bend their humanity to the abstract, impersonal needs of efficient management. They were exhibiting in their lives part of the collective, collaborative, managerial American dream: monolithic mastery of command and control. Politics was to be driven out. Administrative expertise was to become the new American form of government.

What was at stake in the early months of the second Nixon administration, therefore, was not merely the dangerous expansion of executive power at the expense of the Congress, the courts, and the press. These were only the instrumental struggle. What was at stake was the supplanting of the nation's fundamental symbolic form, embedded in the Constitutional "system," by a new symbolic form, that of the high-technology corporation. It was not exactly a totalitarian dictatorship the nation was moving toward, not monarchical or imperial rule in the manner of a Caesar or a Mussolini, a Stalin or a Hitler. It was rather the controlled efficiency of the Chase Manhattan Bank, IBM, Exxon, and General Motors. The energizing motive was not greed (although the Nixon estate grew from 1968 to 1973 by hundreds of thousands of dollars), nor autocracy nor romantic will-to-power. It was impersonal efficiency, remote control, government by self-effacement. In part, Nixon's personality was satisfying its own needs by the kind of men he permitted around him and the style he encouraged them to adopt. In part, the whole enterprise filled the nation's growing self-conception as Technopolis, where the national language is Technopolese. It is a fate more seductive than Fascism. It is more rational than Fascism. It is similarly centripetal, similarly faceless, similarly banal.

Professional football is the most accessible public liturgy of the nation's new self-consciousness. It was not merely the popularity of football that led the President to identify with coaches, game plans, and quarterbacking. The underlying social metaphor of the game served his psyche superbly. Professional football is a collective enterprise built upon high specialization, a brief but intense performance of precisely defined tasks, a competition between rival conceptions of organization and deployment. The moves, possibilities, elements of surprise, squad "cuts," and internally defined objectives of the game celebrate exactly the world of America's technological élites. Football is "big business" not because large sums of money are involved, but because it exhibits in clean ritual lines the underlying social drama of corporate business. The goal of a football team is not to change the shape of the world but to "win," and to do so weekend after weekend in the satisfying ritual circles of the myth of eternal return: yet another heroic play, yet another victorious moment, in repetition after repetition. The *agon* of football slakes the hunger of the soul for an ancient immortality: identification with the highest, most beautiful achievement of concentrated energies.

We hear today that business, like technology or even science, is "going nowhere," is "neutral" or "objective," and that it is enough to play by the rules of "the free market," the imperatives of "efficiency," and the "dynamics" of "growth." There is some disparity: football is static and the economy is dynamic. But professionalization, specialization, and teamwork shape the individual psyche equally in football and in the corporation. A coach is in charge; the others follow orders with all the skill and inventiveness they can. "Desire" makes the dead administrative charts and the chalk diagrams leap to well-oiled and hard-hitting life. The basic problem for management is to "inspire" and to "motivate"; the game plan does the rest.

For a season, then, President Nixon was drawing on the most powerful underlying symbol of our actual social life: that selfless, disciplined specialization demanded of professionals today. It was against *this* system—the system of dehumanization—and not against the Constitutional "system" that the unconscious protests of the "counterculture" were truly aimed. The loose clothing, the casual manners, the forced and eccentric hedonism, the resistance to precision and organization and discipline—these were not expressions of contempt for "the Protestant ethic" or for classic American individualism. The counterculture retained a high Protestant moralism of its own, an intense romantic individualism ("do your thing"), and even the piety of past Protestant "awakenings." (In *The Making of a Counter-culture* Theodore Roszak, who is not a Protestant, overlooked important ingredients of pentecostalism and piety.) H. R. Haldeman, crewcut, humorless, working sixteen-hour days, taking home movies of the President, yellow pad and organization chart in hand, counting out the President's day by minutes—here was the system the counterculture was resisting. The men around the President merged the corporate system with the Constitutional system.

The young professionals of the Left—of the McGovern organization, for example—*also* believed in teamwork, in expertise, in careful planning, long-range game plans, and precise tactical execution (as in beating back challenges at the Democratic convention). They represented a romantic style of corporate professionalism; the Nixon men, a scientific style. The McGovern professionals wanted more room for the ego, imagination, feelings. When they exalted "the individual," they did not mean precisely the individual that the Nixon team was praising, but something wilder and less tamed. The Left tended to value authenticity, those elusive inner feelings in which true personal identity is believed to be locked. The Right, less introspective, less soft, tended to value "will" and "control." More realistic, the Nixon professionals cherished a precise grasp of power realities; with a firm grasp on these, a superior individual exercises dominion, it is thought, over events. The Democratic campaign flew apart; the Nixon campaign was relentless in pursuing levers of power.

Each group has its own form of contempt for law. The Left tends so to value the "authentic" voice of conscience that it holds institutions and laws to be lower-order instrumentalities. It often points to "higher laws," in the face of which the laws of federal or local institutions do not hold. The Right tends so to value the individual's superior "realism" that it holds institutions and laws to be slightly outmoded instrumentalities. It often points to "hard facts" which oblige "intelligent men" to strike boldly outside the law. It is as though the Left has absorbed the freedom-seeking romanticism of the frontier, the Right its hardheaded and rapacious boldness—a frontier being exactly the realm where law has not yet established its restraints. Americans of all persuasions, loving frontier situations, defend their own forms of lawlessness.

Old-fashioned liberals, both of the Right and of the Left, are our most consistent defenders of obedience to laws, despite the laws' inadequacies. Liberals symbolize—to romantics of Left and Right—both civilization and its pale constraints.

The Watergate scandal for a time brought together conservatives, radicals, and liberals. The symbols of the high civil religion—honesty, integrity—were marched back with honor. Barry Goldwater denounced the White House, as did many other Republicans whose loyalty is formed by ideals older than those of contemporary professionalism. Radicals began, sometimes grudgingly, celebrating the successful functioning of the eighteenth-century "system." Liberals began praising a Bible-quoting Southern senator, a conservative law-and-order judge, and the rule of law. Nixon, at last, had "brought us together."

Yet it was not exactly the Constitutional system that rescued the nation from a slide toward Technopolis. It is true that when several key individuals wanted to resist executive power, the "system" was there for them to use. But the number of heroes who made the system work was not legion: barely four—two young reporters for *The Washington Post,* a federal judge, and Senator Sam Ervin. Two lucky flukes and elaborate veils of secrecy, almost flawlessly maintained for nine months, began unravelling and flailing in the winds: a piece of tape on a lock while the burglars were in the Watergate and a sudden confession by a conspirator facing heavy sentence. The truth had come within inches of being concealed forever. "For want of a nail . . . a kingdom was lost." By slender threads, by trivial accidents, overnight, a seemingly irresistible juggernaut was reduced from triumph to humiliation.

There were three elements in Nixon's fall. Nixon tended to reduce politics to power and technique. Second, he trusted public relations images more than genuine symbols. Third, he sponsored luxuriant growths of "official truth." In order to see how to reform the presidency, we need to study the weaknesses in the office that permitted these faults to mushroom.

31

Three Corruptions

In 1962, after his losing campaign for the governorship of California, Nixon was linked by a judgment of law to fraudulent statements about Governor Brown. On that occasion, according to the decision of the court, Nixon himself approved—and improved—the fraudulent text. H. R. Haldeman and Maurice Stans were on his staff in 1962, and Haldeman signed checks for $70,-000 to pay for the fraudulent postcards. James Reston wrote of Nixon's career until 1962: "He mastered the techniques of politics before he mastered the principles, and ironically it was this preoccupation with techniques that both brought him forward and cast him down."

Nixon came back from defeat in 1962 just as earlier, in 1952, through the "Checkers Speech," he overcame rejection by most of the powers of the Republican party. It is as though in each decade Nixon is "cast down," only to rise again. No wonder he attributes nearly magical powers to his devotion to technique.

Before the Watergate scandals became public, Attorney General Richard G. Kleindienst told a joint session of three Senate subcommittees that President Nixon believed that "executive privilege" extended to all two and a half million employees of the executive branch. If the senators objected, he said, they could impeach the President. Senator Ervin asked how evidence for impeachment could be gathered if no witnesses could testify. No evidence is needed, Kleindienst replied, only the vote of the Senate and the House. The Attorney General's turn of mind was breathtaking. He dismissed *evidence* and spoke of *power*. What if the Chief Justice presiding over impeachment proceedings insists on evidence, Kleindenset was asked. You can impeach *him* too, Kleindienst told the senators. He added that they could also impeach the Attorney General. His speech was brazen. But like a dagger intended for someone else, barely ten days later it was sprung into its owner's stomach. News of Watergate erupted, Kleindienst was obliged to resign, and the word "impeachment" echoed differently in the White House.

Even the Constitution came to be discussed among Nixon's men in the language of power. Donald E. Santarelli, Associate Deputy Attorney General, talked to a writer from *The New Yorker*: "The executive branch has gained power. It was inevitable. Its basic design is geared for efficiency; it has adopted management tools—computers, executive techniques. Congress fell behind, and now it is fussing in a stew of its own making. . . . Executive privilege isn't a legal question; it's a political question. That's the key thing. Don't be fooled. These battles are basically political. . . . If you're on the side that's gaining power, you praise the changes. If the changes mean you lose power, you bitch about them. . . . The Constitution is flexible. Period. Your point of view depends on whether you're winning: 'My side won! I'm happy!' . . . The Constitution isn't the real issue on this; its how you want to *run the country.*"

Lest we become too moralistic about Santarelli's views, I. F. Stone's observation in *The New York Review of Books* should be recalled:

> To be honest about it, how one feels about the "inherent" powers of the Presidency has been generally determined

throughout our history by how one feels about the use to which they are put and the pressing needs of the time. The Presidency is a great office precisely because of its flexibility in emergency. People on the Left like myself applauded when Truman and Eisenhower invoked executive privilege to shield government officials against the witch hunt, as waged first by Nixon on the House Un-American Activities Committee in the late forties and then by McCarthy in the fifties. We applauded when, in conflicts with the military-industrial complex, Truman, Eisenhower, and Kennedy in turn impounded, i. e., refused to spend, money voted for arms race purposes, including such projects as the 70-group air force and the Nike-Zeus antimissile.

These are but a few of many examples of a double standard which must be faced before one can reasonably decide that abuse of "inherent" powers has grown so serious that it is a clear violation of the Constitution and a danger to the Republic.

The Left in America does apply a double-standard, especially in regard to its despised enemies. Yet it is not merely the Left's double standard that conservatives find so irksome, it is the capacity of the Left to direct the moral judgments of opinion-setters in the media. The Left wraps itself in moral superiority as an instrument of political gain.

To some extent, the Nixon team believed it had finally mastered the secrets that had kept the Left in power for so many years since 1932. The Left, they divined, used moral language but acted with naked pragmatism. The Right, by contrast, was handicapped by the stiff ideology of men like Taft. The important thing was for the Right not to be trapped by ideology. Reduce issues to questions of power and technique. Set goals, and bulldoze obstacles out of the path.

Again and again, Watergate conspirators would use the example of actions of the Left as warrant for their own actions. They seemed to resent the cloak of morality thrown around those on the Left who acted in "civil disobedience," while *they* were expected to remain wholly within the law. They pointed to breaking and entering, the destruction of files, the leaking of secrets, "trashings," the fourteen hundred bombings of 1969, the widespread writings on "revolution." Instead of estimating that the federal government was infinitely stronger than the tiny radical fringe, they felt threatened and besieged—remembering, perhaps, their surprise and panic at the huge demonstrations after the shootings at Kent State and the invasion of Cambodia. To those who believe in management and control, the nation must have sometimes seemed unmanageable. If the nation itself was not threatened, the Nixon administration's vision of how to control it was. The Nixon men identified their vision with the best that is in America. A threat against their kind of system was in their eyes a threat against America.

Nixon's second flaw was the confusion of public relations imagery with genuine symbols. Plainly, Nixon is in touch with a number of powerful symbols from the American past. Many highly educated people despise the "trickery" of his speeches, yet Nixon consistently rings changes on moral values many Americans historically respect. He speaks of "taking the hard way" rather than "the easy way." He praises certain economic values ("We must avoid the permanent strait-jacket of controls"). He enjoys traditional jingoism (America must remain "number one"). He relishes the American instinct for the superlative ("the most productive system in history"). He delights in the nation's naïve conception of historical "firsts" and "greatests." Nixon employs motifs with a well-established popular history; the symbols he uses are authentic enough.

Ordinarily, however, Nixon abuses these symbols. He manipulates them in predictable and hackneyed fashion; they are old standbys, old routines, used to deaden perception rather than to awaken it. He seldom uses the nation's symbolic resources to shed new light, to illuminate present dilemmas, or to break new ground. He uses his technical skill to promote his policies of the moment. He can change directions at will. That is why his speeches give no sense of *leading* people on to new terrain. They quiet, calm, reassure. Their chief inducement is to make partisans exclaim: "My side's winning! I'm happy!" His speeches have an *administrative* function. They are intended to make people docile, not to inspire them to question, to open their eyes, to act. The point of his speeches is not to unleash energy; the point is to control energy.

But besides this misuse of genuine symbols, the White House under Nixon preferred to manufacture public relations images. The thinking in the White House was schematic: "We're weak *here;* we need to project a more human side; what's the best device?" First came diagnosis, then projection. Nixon is not a very warm or sportsy person, so special efforts were made to associate him with athletes and coaches; a bowling alley was installed in the White House and a picture of Nixon bowling was sent on the wires. One does not start with a personality and then let that person cast a national image as widely as possible. It is not even as though one merely avoids his weak spots and unflattering angles, and favors his strengths. It is, rather, that one starts with an abstract scheme—*this* is what we want to project—and then begins to manufacture it with the available material.

There is a critical difference between public relations image-making and genuine symbolic engagement. The one is manipulation from outside-in; the other is expression from inside-out. The one tries to execute a prior construct or design; the other tries to allow what is inside to manifest itself. The one tries to guide the reactions of observers; the other tries to make contact with them, so as to liberate energies within them. The one tries to channel the reaction of observers for the use of the political figure; the other tries to invite observers to begin perceiving and then acting for themselves. The one flatters or reassures observers with prearranged forms; the other tries to awaken in others powers that go beyond the uses of the politician. The one regards image-making as a technique of the politician's power; the other regards symbols as social resources in whose light the politician falls under a judgment greater than himself. The one regards images as instruments; the other regards symbols as transcendent energies calling all to be better than they are.

It is true, of course, that even genuine symbol-making can be demagogic. George Wallace, for example, calls upon energies that are volatile, that induce hero-worship, and that threaten to run roughshod over laws, traditions and rights. These are genuine symbols, well-established in America's cultural traditions, and yet ambivalent in their power: they may reinforce participatory government or they may abolish it in favor of allegiance to a charismatic leader. Even unsophisticated people sense the danger in Wallace's appeal—as a protest candidate in a primary he receives votes which in a serious final election have so far been denied him.

Eisenhower, too, was able to call upon genuine historical symbols, to give them a "conservative," stablizing cast. John Kennedy called upon them to give them a romantic cast. Genuine symbols are capable of many uses.

Often in this respect John and Robert Kennedy have been accused of arousing untoward expectations, of superficially spreading the excitement of "style" and "charisma," of lacking a solid grasp of institutional complexity. The excitement they generated, it is said, exceeded substance; "style" exceeded performance. Such charges do not take account of distortions inherent in the television era. What television made of the Kennedys goes beyond what John (or Robert) actually said or did. (As television, for its own purposes, later magnified the "youth culture," so it earlier magnified "Camelot." The Kennedys did not object.) Yet thousands of persons who were first politically "awakened" by the Peace Corps, VISTA, and other Kennedy programs that are now said to have "failed" are still creatively at work. There was a long-range realism in JFK's "romantic" attacks on bureaucrats.

JFK was (it is said) a rhetorical radical, an ideological liberal, a fiscal conservative, and an institutional tory. It is, indeed, a tory conception of institutions to try to inspire persons, knowing that one cannot mold institutions suddenly to one's will. ("Popes come and go, the Curia remains forever"—it is an old Catholic saying.) The Kennedy "politics of expectation" was in fact an invitation to expect very little from established institutions, a pledge to work within a time-frame not bounded by "the first one hundred days, nor . . . the first one thousand days, nor . . . our lifetime on this planet," but to begin with a tiny but growing "band of brothers." The creative energies inspired by this quite Irish vision are still unfolding. Legal practice and public health medicine and citizen advocacy have been significantly altered by Kennedy realism. It is a realism different from those America has known before, a moral style quite different from that of our Protestant past. The accounts on its debits and its credits are not yet closed.

There are, then, many ways to invoke genuine symbols. There are many ways by which to be measured inadequate in the light of those symbols. Yet there is a difference between the power inherent in genuine symbols and the power of mere image-making. There is no simple and clean way to distinguish them. But as a rule of thumb, one may gauge the difference by a candidate's willingness over a period of time to trust himself to give-and-take in unstructured and unpredictable circumstances. On election eve in 1968, for example, back-to-back telethons were conducted by Richard Nixon and Hubert Humphrey. The Nixon show was carefully managed and controlled, so as to show Nixon in a favorable light. The Humphrey show allowed Humphrey room to err, to make mistakes, to be himself even with his loquacity and watery eyes and superficial glibness. It is true that the latter framework suited Humphrey, and the former Nixon and that in a sense each was seeking to present his strongest side. Still the weakness of Nixon was his need to think out what he ought to project and to control himself accordingly. The strength of Humphrey was his willingness to trust his own spontaneities, faults and all.

John Kennedy prepared himself thoroughly for television appearances; in this sense he was also, like Nixon, less than purely spontaneous. Once on camera, however, he had confidence in his own poise. Nixon too gained a great deal of confidence during his first term in office; his television appearances were vastly improved. He learned to be more humorous, relaxed, at ease with the presidency. Nevertheless, with Kennedy one had the sense of genuine engagement; with Nixon one still senses his effort to present himself according to some plan, his struggle to hold back those dark sides that, from time to time, nevertheless succeed in breaking through: his bitter comments about Manson's guilt, his comment about student "bums," his recriminations after the defeats of Carswell and Haynsworth. These are not flaws due to temperament alone. They spring from Nixon's determination to project himself as he is not. He would not *need* to falsify. Many politicians who are shy or not photogenic, who lack "charisma," gain strength from being what they are and presenting themselves accordingly.

Nixon has proved that a person with a difficult temperament can, by hard work, master the art of television. But the extension throughout his administration of a mammoth effort to manufacture the exact impressions he wishes to create introduced a new dimension into the politics of image-making. He gave the virtual monopoly of the media exercised by the President in recent administrations—by Kennedy and Johnson as well as by himself—a new twist. Kennedy had a flair for capturing the imagination of the media. Johnson, exposing the scar on his belly or lifting his dog by its ears, exhibited a news-hungry personality. But Nixon set out not only to control his own image, but also to alter the practices of the media themselves. Kennedy and Johnson, as it were, wanted favorable exposure. Nixon desired control.

The third flaw in Nixon is his need to structure reality his way. In totalitarian regimes, vast efforts have been undertaken to revise history. Nixon's efforts, by contrast, were to revise present perceptions of reality. Nixon believed that the national media (as distinct from the local media) were his political opponents. He felt he could not obtain a fair presentation of himself so long as media executives, editors, and reporters presented him as *they* saw him, rather than as he saw himself. Since the national media, by and large, represent a national culture not fully acceptable according to the values, mores, and perceptions of the many local cultures of the land, Nixon calculated that he would have political support for an attack upon them. He objected to the "instant analysis," which after each of his speeches established a new context congenial to national commentators. He wished to control the context in which his appearances reached the people. Thus, through Spiro Agnew, he launched his famous assault on the networks, the national papers like *The New York Times* and *The Washington Post,* and the national news magazines.

But the Nixon administration also set out to manage the daily
realities which the people would see. In the election campaign
of 1970, bearded "students" were deliberately and carefully admitted into audiences addressed by Agnew and Nixon, as foils
for their contrast between "the silent majority" and the unkempt,
vociferous "few." A rock-throwing incident was, apparently,
staged at San Jose. In 1972, acts of sabotage and manipulation
were practiced by the President's men. Fake letters and tele-
grams by the thousands poured into the White House. Fake polls
were released. New rules were promulgated for government press
releases; "poverty" was semantically abolished. False ads with
false signatures were published. The prisoners of war disem-
barked after careful conferences with "briefing officers" and made
"spontaneous" remarks praising the President in phrases later
set carefully in presidential speeches. College campuses, peace
groups, and the campaigns of Democratic candidates were in-
filtrated, crimes were provoked by government agents, dissenters
were spied upon and betrayed by federal agents and their homes
and offices burglarized by White House spy squads. Plans for
domestic surveillance which FBI Director J. Edgar Hoover rejected as illegal were ordered into operation by the President
(and, he insists, rescinded five days later). Perjury and public
lies characterized some of the President's associates.

What is real and what is fake? Nixon created a category of
"official facts," which from time to time had to be revised. Earlier
versions were called "inoperative." What the President actually
said was subject to official doctoring, with the explanation that
the President had "misspoken himself'—that is, had not said
what he really did say, please correct the transcript. The President telephoned John Dean on Easter; then did not. The President did not see John Dean thirty-five times from January to
April; then he did. The logs of what was discussed could not
be released because of "executive privilege"; then they were.
The tapes of these meetings were in the President's personal
keeping; then H. R. Haldeman had some at home.

Every president has enormous power over the nation's sense
of reality. The definition a president gives to events becomes a
reality all citizens must thereafter contend with. What the presi-

dent says has a *prima facie* truth until it is disproven. In the Nixon world, the attempt to contrive a self-contained reality went to unprecedented lengths. Congress was weak. The courts were steadily falling under the appointive power of the President. The national media—which alone had the resources to track down presidential assertions to their untruth or their truth —were being pressured to "give both sides." That is, the President gave *his* side, then the media could publish, in roughly equal doses, criticism of the President and support for the President. Increasingly, the administration was in the grip of "presidential truth." Peace in Southeast Asia was proclaimed, while American bombs rained down and battles raged. One wonders whether Katherine Graham, owner of *The Washington Post,* ever awakened at night, fearing that perhaps the White House was planting false information for the two younger reporters of the *Post,* who almost single-handedly were pursuing the strange trail of the Watergate conspiracy, and that the White House would eventually reveal the ruse and the *Post* would be discredited.

In early 1973, the President was at a peak of popularity, power, and virtually unchallenged control. Senator Muskie began to speak angrily of "one-man rule." Protests mounted, but so did impotence. Flagrantly, the President impounded funds the Congress authorized and vetoed bills he did not like. No means of limiting presidential power was in sight. The Nixon game plan for managing the entire nation was on track and rolling with gathering momentum. Such moments, in politics, are the most dangerous of all.

Reality is not kind to private worlds. When they meet success, illusions swell. The humblest reality—a piece of adhesive on a door, a single person venturing beyond the circle of official truth —can explode them with astonishing abruptness.

Symbolic realism is an effort to make one's own symbolic world open to the complexity of humble realities. Presidents are in times like ours easily isolated from the lowly, ordinary messiness of daily life. What good is an elaborate system of information if a president's sense of reality, his judgment, is far removed from actualities? Attempts to reform the presidency must reach these roots.

Our danger is not that our president is treated like a king. Our danger is not that the office has a sacred quality, that people invest in it too many of their hopes and fears and too much trust. Our danger is that one man, kept from humbling contact with humble things, is not a sufficient guide to the politics of daily reality. The *metaphysical* function of the president—his sovereignty over what we may take to be real—has been inflated beyond human capacity.

How can we reform the presidency, for the president's protection and for ours? Political scientists, historians, and political leaders may have more practical suggestions. But perhaps a theologian may be permitted one or two reflections.

32

Reforming the Presidency

The presidency has in recent decades acquired symbolic power far beyond that of Congress. Television, above all, places at his disposal a highly personal medium. It magnifies individuals, picking them out from crowds, lifting out a single face for intense and gripping presentation. Television cannot do equal justice to the Congress. Humans participate easily in the drama of persons; we have only a pale comprehension of social forces and institutional processes. To this fundamental human imbalance, television adds the harsh individualism of the camera.

The camera is metaphysically biased. It cannot reveal everything about human life. It selects only those features that suit its nature: personal drama rather than abstract, underlying causes; facial surfaces rather than movements of the spirit and the mind. It is a powerful instrument, often unsparing and ruthless in its revelations, suggestive, quick to capture certain quicksilver movements of emotion behind the texture of a face or the radiance of an eye. But it is not a good instrument for rendering those kinds of complexity that require many words. Television fixes on the president and makes him the main symbolic representative of government. Symbolically, it dwarfs the Congress and the courts. There may be a balance of powers in the government; but no such balance exists on television.

Thus, television places in the president's hands enormous metaphysical powers not provided for in the Constitution—powers over reality, powers over appearances, powers over perception, powers over the imaginative matrix within which issues are presented. The Constitution did not intend for the president to have powers of speech and presence beyond that of other citizens. It envisaged that he would argue as a man among men. Now television takes his face, as it takes no other face in politics, into every living room. Not merely his *words*—in a speech barely audible to a distant audience or on the cold printed page—but his *presence* dominates the attention of citizens who sit in silence and only listen.

For nine months after June, 1972, the vast majority of newsmen assigned to Washington merely reported what the White House told them regarding Watergate, with little further inquiry. One reason they were comfortable in doing so is that television lets the president establish the underlying sense of reality within which all citizens live and move. The medium is insidious. It is a holistic medium, a purveyor of "wholes." It sets "facts" in "contexts." It provides images which block necessary insights and prompt misleading ones. It deflects attention. It sets up appearances as persuasive as reality itself. Television is not a good instrument for complicated, remote investigative reporting. It requires the "big story." It lacks the patience available to a daily newspaper, and it cannot accommodate the mass of tiny details by which a lengthy investigation proceeds. Most profoundly of all, it silently suggests what is the "reasonable," "calm," "moderate" attitude to assume. Television is a *total* guide. That is why watching it is effortless.

If we are to reform the presidency, the heart of the matter is the president's power over reality, his symbolic power. The social reality of the United States cannot be left to definition by one man alone. Whoever names a problem gains power over it; to set the terms of debate is to narrow possible resolutions. There are at least four reforms that might be taken, by Constitutional amendment if necessary, in order to restore a balance of powers in symbolic realities.

First, Congress, and in particular the opposition party in the Congress, must have a single spokesman who can personify the Congress of the United States, just as the president personifies the executive branch. In 1972, the Democrats in Congress worked out a plan for selecting members from their midst, on a rotating basis, to respond to speeches by the President. Far better would be the selection of a single permanent member as "Opposition Spokesman" ("Spokeswoman"). He (or she) need not be the *leader* of the opposition, although obviously the public prominence he or she would gain would yield considerable power. He or she need not supplant the majority leaders of the Senate or the House, for example. It would not necessarily follow, either, that the Opposition Spokesman would be the next presidential nominee of his party. He might be selected, indeed, precisely because he could not or would not be the nominee. His utterances would then be uniquely free of the taint of personal ambition.

Unless a single voice is found, the Congress will not have a unified presence in the minds of the people. On a rotating basis, each participant lacks the opportunity for a cumulative strategy and the public wastes valuable reaction time becoming adjusted to the idiosyncrasies of each new personality. Familiarity with a single person humanizes and dramatizes the nuances of issues. Without a single face, a group like the Congress seems diffuse and ineffectual. Congress must recognize that television is a reality not foreseen by the Constitution. We must banish it or adjust to it, capitulate to it or make it serve us.

The Opposition Spokesman might be elected by the members of the opposition party on a biennial basis, or annually. He could be subject to recall, and even obliged on certain points to represent exactly a majority view, rather than his own opinions. His power would derive from the collective of which he is part. His would not be a personal office, but a voice of collective wisdom.

It goes without saying that presidential access to television should as a rule be followed, on an equal basis, by access for the Opposition Spokesman. The objection against television commentators, that they give instant analysis without having been elected by anybody, would thereby be circumvented. After every presidential speech, the duly elected Opposition Spokesman should comment, *immediately* afterward, not on a subsequent day. At times, the Opposition Spokesman may reinforce the pleas of the president, as perhaps in time of national emergency. At times, he would set forth the particulars of his disagreements.

In no case should one branch of government have sole power over the terms of perception and action.

Second, the range of executive power has such enormous sweep that the president should be obliged on a biweekly basis to come before leaders of the opposition for a public, hour-long accounting of his policies. These conferences would be in addition to press conferences. Their purpose would be to allow opposition leaders to bring questions of fact, goals, priorities, and procedures into public view. Without such power, how will the Congress and the people learn in what entanglements the 2 million 500 thousand employees of the executive branch are involving them? Agents of the executive branch have often implicated the United States in unexamined military and commercial practices. Executive policies, out of public view, mired the nation in Vietnam long before the people knew how deeply. Executive impenetrability encased President Nixon in the scandals of his election campaign more foolishly and for a longer time than the public should have endured.

The executive branch does not come *under* the Congress. But it is accountable to the people. As representatives of the people, the leaders of the opposition party in Congress would function as public interrogators of the president. In such a forum, the separation of powers would not be impugned. The obligatory question periods would not be "hearings." They would not be official functions of the Congress, *qua* Congress. They would be modeled on press conferences, except that elected officials of the opposition rather than newsmen would raise the questions. The site could be alternated between the White House and the Senate caucus room. Congressmen would here be functioning as surrogates of the people's right to facts and information. The president might bring with him various cabinet officers, to help him with precise replies. It would not be permissible for him to absent himself. The president is at present accountable to the people almost solely on election day. He would now become so on a regular basis, in respect to truthfulness and fact, under questioning, at such biweekly conferences.

Symbolically, these conferences would equalize the presidency and Congress. As the congressmen would question him, so the president might use these sessions to voice his criticisms of the Congress. The citizenry would be privileged to see both branches of government in direct debate.

It will probably prove wise in such encounters for congressmen and president to be respectful of each other. Drama there will be. New forms of civility between the branches of government will have to be arrived at, especially in times of high emotion.

Third, the president's cabinet should always, perhaps by force of law, include a proportion of members of the opposition party. A paramount need of the president is a unified executive branch. But a second, indispensable need is for counselors close at hand who have a political base outside his own party. Better that he should know in his own councils the questions troubling the opposition than face them only *ex post facto* and across Capitol Hill. Telling the truth to the president is difficult for persons around him, even in the best of times. In the worst of times, an institutional device for providing the president with a built-in opposition may well be his salvation, as it might have been at several junctures in the last three administrations.

Fourth, we must begin to think of a step we have for two centuries avoided—the separation of the presidency into two functions: the head of state and the chief executive. I realize that this suggestion is not immediately practical; it is too radical, too shocking to our tradition. But thinking about it illuminates our present dilemma. And perhaps one day it will seem obvious and practical. For our present arrangement flies in the face of human nature. Human beings are symbolic animals. We are not "rational," in the sense that we respond, or should respond, solely to pragmatic calculation.

Sophisticated persons often speak as though our need for symbols were a weakness, infantile or adolescent. The truth is more humbling than we like to admit, enthralled as we are by symbols of skeptical practicality and superior penetration. The truth is that when we are attracted (or repelled) by symbols we are simply being ourselves, creatures of flesh and blood, of sensibility and imagination as well as of intelligence and judgment. We cannot help responding to a chief executive with all the extra affect of an appropriate response to a head of state. We do not really have a choice between having such symbols or not having them. Our only choice is *which* symbols we shall cherish, and how we shall interpret and criticize them.

Human beings *will* make the president into a symbol of the nation, *will* be preoccupied with his personality, *will* treat him as a sacred figure. The reasons for doing so are too close to reality to be successfully resisted. Even Eugene McCarthy, our most eloquent presidential candidate on the dangers of the "personality cult" and the "sacralizing" of the presidency, became himself the figure of a cult. He broke the hearts of many when, at the end, he abandoned the role.

Until we recognize the psychological realities of citizenship —the almost mystical fascination even our professors and our students sometimes feel toward politics—we will continue to talk wistfully of some other world than this one.

At the height of the Watergate revelations, on the eve of dramatic testimony by former White House counsel John Dean, Leonid Brezhnev arrived in Washington. President Nixon's presidential activities resumed first place in the headlines, and the Dean hearings were delayed. Brezhnev did not come to visit the Congress. The Congress does not personify the United States to the world. Our fate in foreign relations is tied first of all to the president. It is idle to believe that the symbolic power of that role can be wished away.

What we can do, perhaps, is establish a head of state to greet foreign dignitaries and to visit them abroad, to officiate on

occasions when a personification of the nation is required, to become the central figure even at the inauguration of the chief
executives, and to live at the White House. The chief executive,
who would be elected every four years as at present, would live
as cabinet officers live.

In *The Federalist* (LXX), Alexander Hamilton marshaled
arguments against any but a one-man executive. He opposed
"vesting the power in two or more magistrates of equal dignity
and authority; or—vesting it ostensibly in one man, subject, in
whole or in part, to the control and co-operation of others in
the capacity of counsellors to him." Hamilton wanted energy
in government. He wanted a unified executive power, able to
act, even with secrecy if necessary, but in the end clearly accountable. "Energy in the Executive is a leading character in
the definition of good government," he wrote. "A feeble Executive implies a feeble execution of the government. A feeble execution is but another phrase for a bad execution; and a government ill executed, whatever it may be in theory, must be,
in practice, a bad government."

Hamilton did not want the chief magistrate to be able to
evade responsibility. Thus, he opposed a multiplication of executives or executive counselors:

> the plurality of the Executive tends to deprive the people of
> the two greatest securities they can have for the faithful ex-
> ercise of any delegated power: *first,* the restraints of public
> opinion, which lose their efficacy, as well on account of the
> division of the censure attendant on bad measures among
> a number as on account of the uncertainty on whom it ought
> to fall; and, *secondly,* the opportunity of discovering with
> facility and clearness the misconduct of the persons they
> trust, in order either to their removal from office, or to their
> actual punishment in cases which admit of it.

Councils to the president, Hamilton fears, "are generally nothing but a clog upon his good intentions, are often the instruments and accomplices of his bad, and are almost always a cloak
to his faults." It is easier to confine executive power when it is
held by one person—easier to locate it, easier to discipline it.

These objections do not tell against the division of executive power into chief executive and head of state. In *The Federalist* (LXIX), such a division is foreshadowed in a distinction between "dignity" and "authority." "The President," Hamilton writes, "is also to be authorized to receive ambassadors and other public ministers. This, though it has been a rich theme of declaration, is more a matter of dignity than of authority." The Founding Fathers were rationalists. In their eagerness to demythologize hereditary kingship, they underestimated the power and authority hidden in "dignity" and "ceremony." The separation of this hidden power from practical executive power is a form of "the separation of powers" the Founding Fathers neglected. Television has now made such separation imperative.

Imagine for a moment that Leonid Brezhnev on his visit to the United States in June, 1973 was the guest primarily not of Richard Nixon but of the here-proposed chief of state. It is true that Mr. Brezhnev's practical accomplishments would depend almost entirely upon the authoritative, executive accomplishments of Richard Nixon. But the ceremonial pictures of the event would always have shown Brezhnev with the chief of state, and Nixon only in the background, like the dutiful manager of a bank when the chairman of the board presides. In that case, Nixon could not have basked, as he did, in the reflected glory of the United States of America in negotiation with the Union of Soviet Socialist Republics. *He* would not be the symbol of the United States, only its faithful administrative servant.

Similarly, if the president of the United States could not ceremonially receive the heads of industrial corporations or the leaders of labor unions, could not play host to the Girl Scouts or the returning prisoners of war, was barred from conferring Medals of Honor or Orders of Merit, could not appoint honorary panels or preside on honorary occasions—then a powerful wedge would be introduced between the president's ability to *personify* the public and his need to *persuade* the public of a political course of action.

A president may hold all the powers and responsibilities for foreign affairs and domestic management now in his possession, while being stripped of his role as personifier of the national

identity, and be greatly liberated, not impeded, in his performance of his daily duties. It is true that he would lose some of
the magic and mysticism surrounding his present office. It is true
that, living outside the White House and working in closer
proximity to the working offices of the Senate and the House, he
would not be held in quite the awe his present eminence now
affords him. But his actual administrative authority would remain
clear and untrammeled; his access to radio, television, and the
press would be uninhibited; his capacity to conduct foreign affairs—even his authority over nuclear weapons—would remain
intact.

There would be one change in the presidency, and one only;
but it would be a substantive one. No longer would the president be the personification of the nation and no longer could
he derive from that personification a cloak for his administrative
failings, a moral stature to which his deeds did not entitle him.
His stewardship of government, naked and undisguised, would
be easier to measure. His pretenses would necessarily be fewer.

"Moral leadership" would still be open to him. For on him
would still fall the task of defining what in each season is significant for the nation's attention, and what commands its capacity for action. He would define the goals, priorities, and practices of political administration. He would take to the people
the courses of action he felt they should embrace. He would
wrestle with the Congress even as he does now.

He would lose, it is true, that power to tame men and to
awe them by the honors he can bestow; for he would no longer
bestow such honors. But he would not lose his capacity to telephone private persons for advice or to invite them to his offices
or to be photographed with them—so that some sense of central importance and proximity to power might be shared with
them.

A chief of state, meanwhile, would be elected at the beginning
of each decade. By his prior career and his personality he would
furnish to that decade part of its symbolic character. He would
be charged with reinforcing ceremonially all those qualities
among citizens that make a nation civilized, accomplished, and
creative. He would be the organizer of scientific academies and

prizes, of artistic performances and certificates of honor, of such studies and commissions—on violence or urban needs or pornography or education—as national perplexities might make appropriate. A sizable budget would be available to him for these activities. Although he had no powers of military command, the chief of state would be the Ceremonial Marshal of the Armed Forces, charged with review of their fitness and their readiness. He would preside at launchings and reentries of ventures into outer space, and other scientific-technical initiatives. His intellectual creativity and personal enthusiasms would become a major source of public dialogue about national priorities.

Chief of state and president would, indeed, compete in the public mind as symbols of prestige, as establishers of trends, and as directors of opinion. A chief of state of one political party and a president of the other might, quite subtly, wage war for the support of public opinion, not so much over individual policies (over which the chief of state would have no jurisdiction) but rather over the "tone" and "style" and "direction" of the government. Each would no doubt find it to his advantage not openly to bait the other; for each would need the other's support, a divided public not being of assistance to either. The longer term of office of the chief of state would yield him some independence from the president; the actual Constitutional powers of the presidency would yield the president more than sufficient independence of the chief of state. Yet for symbolic reasons it would be to the interests of both to work in significant harmony. By conferring honors, by speeches, by establishing official commissions, the chief of state could strengthen—or weaken—the authority of the president. By opposing in the Congress the budget requests (beyond a fixed base) the chief of state would annually present to pay for his cultural activities, the president would have a weapon in reply.

Suppose, for example, that from 1960 to 1970, Averell Harriman or Adlai Stevenson or Dwight D. Eisenhower or Margaret Mead or Loren Eisely or Kingman Brewster or John D. Rockefeller III had been chief of state. In electing a chief of state, the people would be electing a person to represent them to the world and to preside over their cultural life. The election could be held after a national primary. The two candidates who finished highest in the primary would then oppose one another in the general election, such election being held in the odd-numbered year before a new decade opens (an anniversary year of the Constitutional convention of 1789).

It is not likely, of course, that so bold a revision of our Constitution as I am here proposing will be undertaken in the next ten or twenty years. A practical people like our own will be unwilling to take so long a step too quickly. The presidents themselves will resist this loss of power, understanding quite well, despite their protestations against "mere ceremony," the irresistible prestige they now acquire through being prime minister as well as king; through living in the White House where Lincoln lived and Washington and Wilson; through bargaining with a senator or giving warning to a general; through drawing on the symbols of continuity and grandeur in the role of chief of state.

The main point of this proposal is not to suggest that the roles of chief of state and head of government can in fact be separated with maximum practical gain both for the presidency and for the nation. The main point is to emphasize the unforeseen aggrandizement of the office of the president, when television and the course of world affairs exalted his symbolic power without providing any safeguards for the people's liberty and free perception of reality. If this proposal does not provide a way to restrain the president's swollen symbolic power, while keeping intact an energetic executive power, some other proposal will have to be better designed to meet the same two purposes.

The path of dictatorship lies through symbolic power—through propaganda. If once a president gains monistic power over the nation's symbols, his ability to override and circumvent and dominate the Congress seems now quite evident. If a president is restrained by symbolic pluralism, the danger of dictatorship is largely overcome. For a president not supported by the citizenry can scarcely intimidate the Congress, the courts, and other centers of opposition.

Power flows from the energy of symbols. A wall of separation to block the president's power over the nation's symbols is the most important self-defense we must, as we approach this two-hundredth birthday of the nation, now erect.

33

The Necessity
of Dirty Hands

The good political leader must learn, Machiavelli wrote, how *not* to be morally good. As Michael Walzer points out in a recent issue of *Philosophy and Public Affairs* (1973), Machiavelli assumes that his Prince is a good man and that learning how not to be good will be difficult for him. One of the ironies of political leadership, indeed, is that there is no way for a good man to exercise power without implicating himself in many evils; and that, on the other hand, to fail to involve himself in those evils, out of a desire to retain his innocence, is itself a moral evil. John F. Kennedy loved to repeat Lord Morley's maxim: "Politics is one long second-best, where the choice often lies between two blunders." But "second-best" and "blunders" are euphemisms for the hunger of children, for endless inequality, for bitter injustice and, indeed, in games of international intrigue and warfare, for the slaughter of innocents.

The question of morality in politics has for its backdrop contrasting estimations of the human condition. For some, human

life falls under the shadow of "the Father of lies," is inexorably
ensnarled in age-old injustice, ignorance, and malice. No matter
how moral the political leader may wish to be, the exercise of
authority in such a world will always implicate him in evils he
cannot eradicate even if he would.

Such a view is often put to conservative uses. Since life is
hopelessly ambiguous, complex, and flawed, the best one can
do is to preserve, or possibly to extend by a little, the circle of
moral progress. Disorder presses upon us, threatening evils even
greater than those under which we already suffer. Therefore,
the moral course is to hold the thin blue line of order against
the greater darkness, or with modest expectations cautiously to
advance that line.

A second view begins with quite a different estimation. Human
beings are basically good, noble, beautiful. What holds them
back are the inadequate, unenlightened institutions inherited
from the past. Human beings are infinitely perfectible, so that
a "realism" which confines them within the injustices of the
present order is morally regressive. The source of immorality
is the present structure of authority—its traditions, its symbols,
its oppressive institutions—its moral disorder masquerading as
"law and order." What is required of moral persons is that they
band together and create a moral order among themselves, con-
structing a politics whose main characteristic is moral commitment. "For three decades," Francis X. Clines wrote in *The New
York Times*, "the Liberal party has held out the promise that
politics can be a moral experience. Persons who style themselves as highly principled, and who see the two major parties
as given to waffling over issues and craving patronage, have been
invited by Liberal spokesmen over the years to join their party."
(It is ironic, of course, that realists like Reinhold Niebuhr
were among the founders of the party so described.)

These two visions of the world are, of course, too abstractly
drawn to do justice to their many variants in America. The five
Protestant civil religions we distinguished in Chapter 19 are
not exhausted by them. There are also Catholic, Jewish, and secular variants. Nevertheless, even on this level of abstraction, certain issues can perhaps be clarified.

Let us assume the first, pessimistic view in its classic high-church expression. Dean Rusk has remarked about the Watergate conspiracy that men of high principle and hard practicality would never have involved themselves in it; it flies in the face of traditions of public morality; *and* it could never work. The problem reduces itself, then, to one of "leadership." We are best served by those who are trained in the high traditions of public leadership and skilled in the hard practicalities of the real world of politics. But are "high principle" and "hard practicality" proof against the immoral conduct of public affairs? There are those who hold that America's traditional élite, trained in the best schools and favored in the honorable pursuit of their careers, implicated the entire nation in the moral horrors of Vietnam. This élite, indeed, does not escape the nation's hereditary guilt for the destruction of American Indian culture, for the racism of our institutions, and for the arrogance over many generations of the white man in his dealings with Latin America, Asia, and Africa. An education at Williams College was insufficient protection for Jeb Stuart Magruder, as his mentors like James MacGregor Burns and William Sloane Coffin have sadly contemplated.

While it is common for those who hold the first, pessimistic, view of human nature to write of the jungle of corporate life, the ambiguity of the real world, and the necessity of a hard stomach for the exercise of authority, it is not common to hear them indulge in introspection or in breast-beating. They seem to bear their moral burden with equanimity, confident in their moral standing. They speak of one another—they have gone to school together, their careers have intersected frequently—as men of sterling character and high moral aim. If they have "dirty hands," the men of the American establishment (there are, of course, several American power centers, but I speak here of the distinguished boards of directors, cabinet officers, and White House associates of the old American families) show few signs of internal moral turmoil. They think of themselves as the guardians of taste, moral judgment, and cultural excellence for the Republic.

In one sense, this class of men is "liberal." It believes in the basic goodness of the nation's institutions and traditions. It has a sound, prudent faith in science and in progress—it is a little cautious regarding science, for its basic training in the élite preparatory schools and Ivy League colleges was neither scientific nor technical. It believes in civil liberties, in privacy, and —without fanaticism—in the preservation of the environment. (An important part of its education involved respect for nature and athletics, in the mountains, on the beaches, at secluded estates.)

In another sense, this class is conservative. It *is* an élite, and it enjoys its power and the exercise of its responsibilities. It has discovered the secret of indirect control. Through its financial resources, its real estate holdings, its positions of status and power in the government, the churches, the universities, the foundations, and the media, it operates informal systems of reference and recommendation and rejection. Its slow but steady conscription of outsiders into its ranks has been farsighted; instead of provoking direct opposition, it admits persons of talent and ambition into at least the outer of its inner circles. Habit and familiarity rather than ideology tie this class together. "What do you know about Mr. X?" "We checked with Bob and he thinks it's a good idea to go ahead." Few major initiatives in our society have much prospect of large funding and high-level support without the concurrence of some, at least, of those who hold the funds and occupy the high levels. There is not, I believe, anything sinister or conspiratorial or highly organized about this class. Its members laugh gently at the "myth" of an establishment. Habit and familiarity suffice. They are their own large and far-flung "family," with their feuding "godfathers," "capos," and "lieutenants," whose style is civil and nonviolent. Their style has its own hard effectiveness.

"Dirty hands" can scarcely be a problem to those who have been trained to rule and taught that their form of rule is the highest moral achievement of the human race. The members of this class speak occasionally of "the English-speaking race" and its "traditions." In the most civil way imaginable, they take for granted, without need for assertion, its moral superiority. Almost by definition, this class never has "dirty hands." Like Mc-

Kinley tormented by the question of the Philippines, it does what it must, possibly after silent prayer, serene in its essential probity. Regarding Vietnam, the moral posture of many among the nation's élite was rather the same.

If, by contrast, we accept the second, optimistic view of human nature, born, it seems, of secular and "enlightened" traditions, the problem of "dirty hands" is quite different. In part, "dirty hands" are simply avoided. One chooses always to side with minorities, with losers, with those who will never exercise authority. In the words of George P. Elliott, describing the new "liberal ideocracy" [*The American Journal* (1973)]:

> Only Calvinism was as hard on authority as is current anarcho-liberalism. Calvinist authority was a responsibility bestowed on you by God, and He would reward you for acquitting yourself well if He had already elected to do so; but if He hadn't it didn't matter how well you did; the Elect were very few. For a thoroughgoing liberal, any desire for authority is in itself aggressive ambitiousness (power corrupts, etc.); your successes in exercising authority are subject to endless challenge and review; best to refuse it, next best to diffuse it in a committee, and, when you have to exercise it personally as parents do, to do so apologetically and get out from under as soon as you can; errors in the exercise of authority, whether you sought it out or it was thrust upon you are unforgivable and probably fascist. ("Fascist" these days is used to mean any exercise of authority that is not both democratic in form and anarcho-liberal in ideology. "She is a very fascistic mother"—I heard that applied to a young woman whose treatment of her three-year-old son was rightish on the Spock spectrum, but still on it. Non-"fascists" now are as rare as the Elect used to be.)

The dilemma of "dirty hands" makes any liberal political leader who would set out to champion the liberal ideocracy (that is, rule by abstract ideas) subject to inevitable denunciation. So long as he is nondirective, honest, against institutions, in favor of "change," able and willing to speak the language of compassion, commitment, and peace, open, loosely organized, an underdog, and able to pass careful tests for purity of doctrine (is not sexist, racist, imperialist, or hung up on power), he can be a catalytic symbol for the ideocracy. As soon as he begins to become "political," articles ferreting out his true and unredeemed nature, his hidden motives, and his smooth manipulations will appear. "For some of the Liberals," Francis X. Cline wrote, "the worst indictment shaping up appeared to be the accusation that they are just plain politicians." Marvelous irony: that the worst sin of a politician is to be a politician. When a political leader exhibits "dirty hands," the easiest remedy is to wash one's own hands of him. Thus John Lindsay, George McGovern, Bella Abzug, and Herman Badillo, have at various times, at the hands of various connoisseurs, for want of sufficient purity fallen into disesteem.

The relation between morality and politics is not, then, an easy one to grasp—not any easier, surely, then the relation between morality and art. Is the unannotated rendering of sexism sexist? Is pornography always a disguise for sadism and brutality, mostly visited on women? Is the portrayal of uninhibited violence an incitement? Answers do not tumble out in simple slogans.

One offers, tentatively, the following reflections. Against the pessimistic view of human nature described earlier, it seems wise to add two safeguards. First, whatever the actual corruption of human institutions and the moral mediocrity of daily patterns of behavior, the human capacity to question, to dream, and to construct more perfect institutions is not *in principle* obstructed. Social progress is in principle possible; what must be demonstrated is that schemes put forward as "progressive" do *in fact* promise (and ultimately achieve) some measure of social progress. The question is, so to say, empirical. Thus, economic conservatives may argue that their policies in fact do more good for more people than the "hare-brained schemes" of liberals; liberals counter that what conservatives call "progress" is in fact, as measured on the liberal scale, decline.

And yet the question is only in part a question of fact. It is also in part a question of *criteria*. What shall we count as measures of human progress? Liberals, radicals, and conservatives employ different criteria, measure by different values, perceive according to different symbolic forms. (To name but one nest of dilemmas: Shall we favor equality of result or meritocracy? Shall we favor scientific-technical valuès and élites, or less centralized, less highly organized, more amateurish populist values? Shall we favor an activist federal government or local control?)

There are large areas of uncertainty both about the *criteria* for measuring social "progress" and about the enormous mass of *facts* to be measured by those criteria. One wonders, indeed, how people can be so sure of themselves in politics, so certain of the rightness of their visions, so passionately opposed to the views of others. How often does it happen that persons or groups, in the name of their own self-interest, have actually supported policies that injure their self-interest (as later, perhaps, they themselves came to admit)? In politics as in religious faith, we see as in a glass, darkly.

The second safeguard against the pessimistic view of the human situation is an assertion, despite the darkness of political vision, of personal responsibility. Complete understanding and total certainty are never available; still, one cannot on that account evade political responsibility. In a democracy we have far less power than our rhetoric proclaims. The margin within which individuals or organized groups can affect the course of political reality in their lifetime is sometimes significant; but it is usually modest. The actions of each indivdual, especially when organized on a more or less long-lasting basis, can "make a difference." Such differences may be worth the efforts of a lifetime. But they are frequently quite limited. On the *moral* scale, they may be worth a great deal—as examples of courage, integrity, or compassion—while on the political or institutional scale they alter basic patterns of power hardly at all. Basic patterns of power, indeed, are "basic" precisely because they are so difficult to overturn. Even revolutions, more commonly than not, do not alter them.

"Politics," Paul Valéry once wrote, "was at first the art of preventing people from minding their own business. A later age added the art of forcing people to decide what they did not understand. . . . All politics are founded on the indifference of the majority of those involved." Why are majorities indifferent? Because they imagine that the probabilities of any successful bettering of their way of life are not very high. Their experience with politics and politicians, with reformers and revolutionaries, does not convince them that political life is the place in which to lay up the treasures of their heart. "One of the severe totalitarian features of contemporary 'pan-politicalism' is its insistence that politics at all times and in all places, ought to be the concern of everyone," writes Peter Berger in *Movement and Revolution* (1970). "This great lapse of the imagination is one of the most dubious blessings of modern democracy. It has reached a grotesque climax in the 'participatory' ideal of the contemporary left. It is of fundamental importance to reiterate, in the face of these ideological aberrations, that human life is infinitely richer in its possibilities of fulfillment than in its political expressions, and that it is indeed a basic human right to live apolitically—a right that may be denied only for the most urgent reasons."

Nevertheless, "living apolitically" is also a political act. Even those citizens who do not vote contribute to the outcome of elections and affect the drift of policies. Those who do not go to church do not, on that account alone, cease to be religious. And those who do not participate in the rituals of political life do not on that account cease to have political effect or to bear political responsibility.

Against the pessimistic view of morality and politics, therefore, we are obliged to say that social progress lies in principle within human power and is a matter of human responsibility. But the background of these modest claims is that, before each new generation of humans begins to take up its political responsibilities, hereditary evils have already tangled the institutions, patterns of perception, and habits of life they must work with—and corrupted their hearts, too. To become involved in politics is to struggle against structures in which human lies, corruptions, and weaknesses are thickly nested; and also to struggle against oneself. Two kinds of moral sophistication must be acquired.

On the one hand, the *personal* morality of those who enter politics will be severely tested. Accustomed to dealing face-to-face with persons they know and love, those who enter deeply into politics soon discover that they spend most of their hours dealing with strangers, with groups they hardly know of, in twisted patterns of historical relations they may scarcely understand. Even with their loved ones, they have no doubt learned that telling the full truth and maintaining full fidelity are high standards often betrayed. With strangers, in fleeting and partial dealings, in contexts not entirely comprehended, they find their words always and necessarily guarded, less than fully truthful, uncertain in their application. Politics is not a realm of lucid truth but a kind of shadow-world, where meanings shift and contexts wildly oscillate. Money, power, status, loyalty to factions and to persons, fatigue and insecurity, inexperience and false bravado—a host of conflicting pressures swiftly and subtly affect the personal morality each newcomer brings to the political arena.

There is, then, a dimension of social morality which exceeds that of personal morality. In political life one acts not only as a private person but also as a public person. Additional canons of public morality must be followed. New sets of circumstances and obligations must be taken into account. One acts not only as the private person one is, but also for the community one *represents*.

In some respects, the social morality of the community is more demanding than private morality. One is obliged, for example, to treat with amicability many persons whom, in private life, one would avoid or treat with curtness. As a representative of the ideals of the community, one must sometimes be officially generous where, privately, one would explode with exasperation. Social morality is, in such respects, rather like a high liturgical drama in which the official plays a formal role. The intent of this liturgy is to establish social forms conducive, in the long run, to a higher level of civility, reason, and symbolic unity than otherwise might be attained.

In other respects, the social morality of the community is

not as pure, high or demanding as various private moralities. (It is because private moralities vary and because individual agents are subject to various moods and passing interests that stable social canons have been developed.) The forms of social morality hold in focus basic, long-range needs of collectives. They exhibit a certain realism about inevitable conflicts between collectives. They assume a wide range of misunderstandings and incompatible sets of values. Thus, social morality takes for granted a certain grossness in human communication, a certain oversimplification, a certain lack of human virtue. It does not aim at "authenticity" nor at perfect love nor at complete understanding. It aims, rather, at a certain rough equity between communities.

By contrast, the personal morality of a highly sensitive and intelligent humanist may demand that he or she be open, honest, authentic, universal in his or her sympathies, committed to building up total understanding and genuine caring: a society, as Senator McGovern liked to put it, in which people truly care about each other. Such a morality may be realistic for relations between persons, and it has a place within the liturgy of social morality. But it is far from adequate in guiding human behavior in institutional settings.

Parenthood sometimes obliges parents to take actions their own feelings protest against. Lovers discover that the psychic and moral needs of one partner are not identical to those of the other and that rituals of many kinds are creative forces in their love. Thus, already in the complexities of personal morality there are foreshadowed some of the demands of political morality. But the important dividing line between personal and social morality occurs when a person no longer has one-to-one dealings with all those whom his actions affect. Many are unknown to him; or he cannot directly consult with all; or the demands of justice prohibit him from modifying his decision in a different way for each person. If a communal rule is established on a football team, for example, a coach who allows one player to disregard the rule becomes unfair to others. If the Internal Revenue Service gives special personal consideration to the tax problems of a high official—even if in some respects the case is complex and warrants special treatment—it provides, nevertheless, *prima facie* evidence of favoritism.

The intimate, considerate morality of the ideal family does not, then, provide an adequate model for the relatively impersonal and relatively distant morality of the larger collective. A college president, a corporate executive, a mayor, or even the president of the United States may sometimes say fondly, "We are a family." That this is hyperbole everybody recognizes. First of all, most families are full of conflicts, misunderstandings, and quietly murderous passions. However civil and decent the moral relationships within a large collective, they lack the human immediacy, danger, and explosiveness of emotions in the family. Contrariwise, when the family has domesticated passion and operates according to reason, mutual consideration, and civility; when each child is encouraged to develop his or her own "individuality"; when there is intimate trust and deep emotional communication between parents and children, husband and wife —even and especially then, such a home is not a model for the university, the corporation, the newsroom, the chancery office, or the state. Under modern conditions, the family has difficulty fulfilling its own ideals. That many would have the government provide intimate caring, which even families can scarcely manage, is sublime naïveté.

Some Americans persist in certain childlike qualities. They demand authenticity, intimacy, self-fulfillment—one wonders whether they arrived here from some other planet. They hold as *rights* what only the luckiest human beings in history have managed to attain, usually in struggle, suffering, and defeat. They do not realize that such gifts have the form of paradox: when one no longer seeks them, then they are sometimes given.

Worse, still, for the nation, some whose moral expectations are out of tune with reality and whose own lives are publicly unhappy are supposed to rank among our best-informed and most sophisticated citizens. One has only to observe the actual lives of our highly educated citizens to see how morally impoverished and lacking in wisdom many are.

Even apart from the present malaise of our intellectuals, however, there is a long tradition of innocence in American life. American Protestantism, in particular, betrays ambivalence about the exercise of power. Words like "machine" usually mean Catholic forms of politics; "ruthless" can be a code word for Irish Catholic. (Bobby Kennedy in a famous interview in 1968 made Roger Mudd swallow it: "C'mon Roger.") Of Protestant authorities, parallel code words suggest indirect uses of power: "cold," or even "heartless." When Governor Rockefeller allowed armed troopers into Attica, he did not do so in direct involvement or with anger. There is, one feels, in the realm of established Protestant power, a certain want of engagement, a pretense that power does not exist, a mirage of reasonableness and self-control. It is relatively rare to discover a public figure —John Connally is one such—who frankly delights in power and frankly seeks it. About the defendants in the Watergate scandals, it became fashionable to point out that they sought neither money nor self-indulgence. What they did, they did coldly, professionally, for (as it seemed to them) a moral purpose. Why this is supposed to be more human and commendable is difficult to see. A thousand cowboy movies and detective films, Protestant to the core, have portrayed the style.

Power is always present in human relationships, so it is idle to insist that power tends to corrupt. (Doesn't everything corrupt, including intimacy, love, honesty, authenticity?) What is most childlike in America is a pursuit of the institutionless society. Symbolically, the frontier in American life was a rejection of politics. On the frontier, mythically, there were no laws and no political structures, no marriages even, only lonely individuals. The Lone Ranger, moral, masked, and on a pure white horse, in intimate and monosyllabic relation with Tonto (powerful symbol of virility and color), dramatized the nation's fear of politics. It is not sex that was the nation's deepest inhibition, but power politics. When Calvin Coolidge said, "The business of the nation is business," he meant in part that it *wasn't* the despicable field of politics.

What a good American is seldom free to desire openly is authority or power. These must always be disguised. Authoritarian relations must be masked as egalitarian. Demands of power must be made to seem demands of reason. We fancy political leaders who are not, or do not seem to be, political. We dream of cities run by "reform" candidates, presiding over "participant citizens" who rationally achieve "consensus." So vastly out of tune with reality are these pretenses that we impose on politicians the unconscionable task of disguising their main business.

Politics is politics. It is concerned with power, interests, and persuasion. It is not, of itself, concerned with "issues," with personal morality, with intellectual consistency. It starts with the tangled irrationalities of human societies as they are. It begins in situations of conflict, inequality, and injustice. It tries to prevent worse evils from breaking out, to anticipate future evils, and to diminish at least by a little the evils of the present.

It is scarcely in the public interest to try to eliminate all evils either from the human heart or from social arrangements. To do so would require governmental inquisition so vast humankind could not support it. The conviction that human society is malleable and that governments should remake societies according to some moral image of the good society is a tool of political ambition. It does not describe any actual state of affairs, or promise genuine moral progress. If they are not naïve those who hold such a vision seek through it power for their own purposes.

Political morality is not, then, the same as personal morality. It consists, in the United States, in working within the traditions of private liberties and public morality imperfectly but painstakingly established by the generations that have preceded us. It consists, also, in trying to enlarge those traditions, to deepen them, to extend them. It is important to stress modesty in this connection. For public morality is not a matter of laws nor of institutional procedures merely. It is a matter of cultural *traditions,* borne along often unconsciously and tacitly, institutionalized in neglected rituals and observances, accessible to the public memory. When laws prove inadequate or procedures useless, leaders have grounds within the public's sense of history on which to base the case for remedies and new directions. A body of tacit doctrines, principles, and intentions is invoked through which leader and people can collaborate. Thus, Winston

Churchill proposed a form of long-range vision, rooted in a cultural past, as moral protection against an aimless pragmatism: "Those who are possessed of a definite body of doctrine and of deeply rooted convictions on it will be in a much better position to deal with the shifts and surprises of daily affairs than those who are merely taking short views, and indulging their natural impulses as they are evoked by what they read from day to day."

Morality in presidential politics consists, first of all, in a sense of historical direction; in a reading of the long grain of history; in an estimation of the symbolic resources in the bosom of one's people; in a willingness to act and to lead, where new initiatives are called for; in determination and perseverance; in the use of means adequate to one's ends and legitimated by political tradition. Often the political leader, in pursuing ends that are good, will be obliged to employ means that, in his personal life, he would not use. It is not true that the end justifies the means. In employing such means, he may well do moral wrong. But so far-ranging are the individual activities that comprise even a simple social decision that, inevitably, the political leader, in issuing an order, implicates himself in moral evils. Sometimes these evils will be unknown to him (although, if he asked vigorously, he might come to know about them); often, they come unsought to his discomfited attention.

A major candidate, for example, learns of bitter intraparty feuding in a key state like New Jersey; it's costing thousands of votes. He sends up one of his toughest aides to "crack a few heads." What does the aide do? It must not be imagined that he will employ mere personal charm. Heavy money arrangements in the campaign may have to be moved around. Threats to reveal certain embarrassing facts may be necessary. Neither murder nor kidnapping nor burglary may be involved. Whatever is involved, the candidate will not have a press release about it.

The American dread of power makes honesty about the instruments of power difficult. The "moral" politician doesn't mind steering the ship of state, but he doesn't want to know about the grimy engine room. A preposterous situation for mature persons—and mature nations.

The Catholic and Jewish traditions do not labor under these inhibitions. Because both have only marginal power in America, both are cautious about "washing dirty linen in public," and do not always say publicly what they know to be true. So inhibitions, in the end, capture them too. Yet Catholics and Jews, along with blacks, will probably lead the way in giving the uses of power their real political names.

The higher persons advance in any social organization, the greater their complicity in the injustices of which that institution is the inevitable carrier. It is one thing to pretend innocence in one's role in the power structure, however; it is another to discern that in an unjust world dirty hands are the necessary price of the acceptance of moral responsibility. There is no such thing as innocence in high places—or in low places, either. No banker is innocent. No journalist is innocent. No college president is innocent. No truck driver is innocent. The pursuit of innocence is, for adults, both futile and destructive. Our moral responsibility as human beings is not to be innocent, for we are not, but to push outward so far as lies in us the narrow circle of honesty, freedom, courage, and community in human institutions. We will be lucky if we succeed even a little—if matters, when we are finished, are not worse. The outcome of our efforts is not solely in our control. "Man labors, God giveth the increase."

The United States, too, in its public liturgies, must soon declare to the world its dirty hands. For they *are* dirty. They always have been, since blood sprang from the first betrayed Indian, since the first frightened slave was dragged to auction in chains. It is time to grow up.

In this respect, the public may be ahead of the liberal opinion-setters. According to opinion polls in August, 1973, people seem to recognize that President Nixon was wrong in his handling of his staff before Watergate and during the cover-up. Yet they seem to distinguish clearly between moral purity and political competence. In early August only 31 percent approved Nixon's handling of the presidency. Recalling his earlier political successes, however, people overwhelmingly preferred that he not be impeached, that he not resign, but that he get on with the tasks of governing. Thus, the public recognizes some complexities of the relation between morality and politics. They allow for "dirty hands." There are limits to their tolerance; moral revulsion builds slowly to its climax. Public tolerance of political corruption is not apathy; it is a healthy realism—provided that in free speech things are called by their true names, and sanctions are ultimately enforceable.

The presidency is not a sanctuary of priestly, well-laved hands. Pontiffs of old well knew the moral ambiguities of the power they accepted. Complicity in evil is not, as some think, usually the result of deliberate malice and clear intention. All who accept political responsibility (and even those who try to avoid it) contribute to the injustices inseparable from human society. Inherited injustices become *their* injustices. Their efforts to break the coils of injustice require them to put their hands on the writhing snakes, like Laöcoön, and enter the pit of moral responsibility. Attempting to be pure and to show good will, they may subject moral purity to mockery, give good will a bad name, poison the atmosphere, and contribute to greater evils than those they tried to eliminate. Moral intentions do not protect them from evil.

Human society over its long history is regularly, tragically (perhaps fatally) corrupt. Liberty and justice sometimes emerge victorious, in partial, fragile, reversible ways. (It is a miracle how much goodness actually survives. It is remarkable that humans are not always predatory.) Whoever accepts political responsibility may hope to wrest good from evil—but, at best, relative good. Even with the purest of intentions a person may fail politically and thus contribute, sadly, to the sum of evil.

The drama of politics is not a morality play.

34

The Dark Night of Faith

Why do we cherish the American Dream? Did it work for F. Scott Fitzgerald? For Marilyn Monroe? Our literature and cinema show greater wisdom than our politics. In private life, the sources of unhappiness are many; evil, tragedy, failure, and betrayal take their toll. Why does politics remain the last bastion of naïveté?

Should belief in America, after all, be easier than belief in God? It is hard to believe that justice rules the world when one walks along the docks of Oakland, California, where hundreds of white yachts are slapped gently by the evening tide, while two blocks away life is so violent even the muggers go in pairs.

For many Slavs optimism is not bright and springlike; it is rather like a Volga boat song. It is not necessary to believe that the world is getting better. In order to be capable of steady efforts and perhaps also of great deeds, one does not have to believe that one's own life can "make a difference." One can

286

hold a cyclical view of history. By contrast, typically American conceptions hold that "change" is our hope; that a person's life is justified by a contribution to "progress." Suppose, however, that life does *not,* in fact, "get better"; that the world in 1974 is closer to insanity and to destruction than it was in 1954 or 1904 or any other year. That what we are living through is not "progress" but a ceaseless cycle of struggle and morality.

The notion that human goodness is measured by social "progress" is shallow. It allows human beings to be as superficial and trendy as they please in their personal lives. Their salvation comes through living in a scientific-technological (superior) age, and working for the proper social "movements." Grace comes cheap.

When a whole people has known defeat, however, and when its own complicity in evil is undeniable before its eyes, then it may recognize that "decline" is also part of world process. Then there is no extrinsic salvation for individuals. It is not enough either to be "against" or to be "for" the national consensus. The test of moral character does not consist in a checklist of those causes to which one gave support, or against which one labored. It is, instead, intrinsic to one's own person, intentions, and acts. What was the *quality* of one's honesty, freedom, courage, and building of human community? Those men who lied, burglarized, and spied in the campaign of Richard Nixon are not to be judged because they worked for the wrong side, but because of the quality of their actions and their lives. The same is true of those who in the name of peace, resistance, and revolution burglarized draft centers or evaded military service. Some of the latter, it seems, acted for motives and in ways less moral than they imagined. Some, it appears, grew in moral stature. To hold that because their cause was good their acts were good, or that because their cause had peace and justice as its aims it was politically and morally right, is naïve.

In human life there is an almost static or perhaps cyclical pattern underlying the mythology of "progress," and "advance," and "liberation." In this context, morality is not a matter of being on the right side, but of living up to the heroic patterns of human possibility. It is important, in this way, to depoliticize morality. Otherwise, the good guys fall easily on one side, the bad guys on the other, depending solely on one's own political perspective.

Moral quality transcends political affiliation. Moral quality transcends historical trends, movements, or fads. Morality is to be adjudged in another dimension entirely. Morality, in an important sense, lies outside the flow of history, outside time. To be genuinely moral is to fulfill a kind of archetype that is relatively neutral as regards historical settings. Thus, in the midst of Fascist Spain, or Communist China, or right-wing South Vietnam, among the Viet Cong, in the Republican party, or among the flower children—in almost any political-historical context imaginable, one meets morally brilliant and impressive persons. In the ranks of the most praiseworthy liberal causes, one sometimes meets moral ciphers.

Because the public self-understanding of the Anglo-American in the United States is morally complacent, it is important to insist on intrinsic moral standards. Being an Anglo-American does not make one morally superior to Latin Americans or Asians or Southern Europeans. Being part of "advanced" and "sophisticated" groups in the American population, being "forward-looking" and "well informed," does not make one morally superior to natives of Brazil or Nigeria or India—or, for that matter, of Philadelphia's South Side or Tennessee or Wyoming.

But more than this is at stake. The mythology of a special "American Dream" lifted the United States, as it were, outside of history's ambiguities. It protected a new ethnocentricity, based upon our supposed moral superiority. It projected our society as the type of the future. The myth of "the new Israel" led to the image of the United States as a Messiah, the "last, best hope" of humankind. For too long, many persons elsewhere in the world encouraged us in illusions. The romanticism of other peoples conspired to raise up a vision of our life as a secular heaven, where streets were paved with gold and a new society of justice was in birth. Our wealth, our conveniences, our technological miracles—and the mythology or our freedoms, our innocence, our generosity—blinded the eyes of many abroad and at home.

It is true that in the long span of history this nation cut a distinctive figure among world empires. Since 1945, this nation has helped make possible by its generosity the greatest economic and political expansion around the globe in the planet's history. But the United States was never so removed from the hereditary greed, violence, and ruthless force of humankind as our dreamers dreamt or as romanticists wished to believe. Sooner or later, we were bound to be found out in our true nature.

It is unfortunate, in a way, that the Watergate scandals embarrassed the Nixon administration rather than, say, a Democratic administration of the Left. Already, one major effect of the scandals is to have intensified the moralizing tendencies, the self-righteousness, and the smugness of the Left. We are given to understand that a more "moral" sort of leadership, leadership of "a higher type," would have spared us such embarrassment. There is perhaps some truth in this claim; the Nixon administration does seem to have gone farther and in a more repugnant way than other administrations. But the moralism of the Left is as great a danger to the nation as any other—even, in some ways, more so, since the larger part of our social critics and commentators seems less able to see through the illusions of the Left than through those of the Right. Yet the Left is especially prone, far more so than the Right, to imagine that—given sufficient willpower—the future will be more moral, more just, more happy than the present.

It is precisely this myth that it is important for a mature people to disown. We do not know whether there will be a habitable earth fifty years from now. We do not know whether the social dreams of our intellectuals will bring us to greater crises than those their predecessors have brought us to in the present. The assumption that social life on earth is malleable by human will, and susceptible to human understanding, is an exceedingly tendentious one. Thus we must distinguish between adolescent and mature dreams.

There are five ways in which the traditional American dream is merely adolescent or even infantile. Because our politicians hold so often to the adolescent dream, political life in the United States is conducted at a woefully childish level.

First, the adolescent American dream is ethnocentric. That is to say, its primary symbols are white, Anglo-American, Protestant, and male. The central axis of world history, according to this dream, pivots upon the history of the Anglo-American race. London, Boston, New York, and Washington are the world's axial cities. Americans of the outlands are baffling, regressive, superpatriotic, submoral. Contrariwise, for those who hold that the "heartlands" of America—South Carolina, Indiana, Illinois, Georgia, Iowa, Montana—are the true America, the élites of the Northeast and California have fouled their own nests with pollution of every kind. Yet these élites never hesitate to instruct those they take to be their inferiors upon the attitudes proper to assume concerning the latest "crises" supposedly afflicting the Republic. There are two dominant kinds of ethnocentrism, then, that of Middle Americans and that of sophisticated urban Americans. They need each other. Their petty "liberal versus conservative" war neatly freezes out other major cultures of the land.

The American sense of reality ventures only cautiously beyond the United States. Even our use of the word "America" illustrates our habit of mind—we appropriate it for ourselves, without regard to Canada or Mexico or Guatemala or Brazil. Despite vast ourpourings of affection toward opposite groups in Vietnam by our Right and by our Left, it is startling to discover how few Americans have read even a single book by a Vietnamese writer or can recite even a single Vietnamese poem or hum a Vietnamese melody.

In the abstract, Americans are interested in other places on the globe. Mainly, our interest elsewhere seems to lie in noticing and supporting each imitation of ourselves. ("What a large microscope!" the American visitor comments at a university in the hinterlands of Brazil, hardly daring to think about what a university there *ought* to be doing.) So great is our habit of imagining that the rest of the world is imitating *us* that we seldom contemplate the hard, resistant reality of others, asking how we ought to change *ourselves.*

A mature dream, by contrast, would displace the United States from the axial line of history; would discern, and try to overcome, our flagrant ethnocentricity; would seek out others in the world from whom we might learn secrets of life of which we recognize our ignorance. A mature dream would make us question the bias of those values of ours we now announce as "universal." It would make us suspicious that what we call "progress" might be, when the entire planet is taken into view, strangulation of the human spirit. It would make us doubt that our own "modern consciousness" is the hope of mankind. It might make us feel imperfect, ignorant, and inadequate.

Second, as its goal the adolescent American dream pictures not excellence of soul but "success." The history of our first colonies, our pioneer cities, and our local authorities today is a history of plutocratic rule. What we call "democratic" is a series of local fiefdoms. Great effort has been expended in the arts of making money. Confidence games, speculation, swindling, ruthlessness, and the sheer imagination and hard work of empire have absorbed enormous energies. Among us the arts of civilization—genuine conversation, emotional honesty, pleasure in solitude and precise reflection, the nuances and the depths of the spirit—are much less known. By extrinsic measures—in wealth, status, and celebrity—we are successful. By intrinsic measures— in precision of mind and speech, in the complexity and profundity of our interior life—we are underdeveloped. The more "Americanized" a Latin American family becomes, the more it loses its own culture and seems diminished by "the American way of life." The latter is not so much a culture as a system of distractions.

There are excellences in American culture—high discipline among our poets, strong families in some places, an almost religious commitment in politics, creative imagination in voluntary associations—but against the rush of money and celebrity and conglomerated industries, these sources of excellence find survival difficult.

A mature dream for America will expose the quest for superlatives—the first, the biggest, the most—for the shoddy insecurity it is. The pursuit of wisdom, restraint, humility, decency are becoming to a powerful people. It is not morally impressive that the United States is the richest nation in the world with

the highest standard of living; it is important that it be a nation
with a civilized way of life. Now that the United States is at
the height of its military and economic power, will it surpass
all other empires in its ability to learn from others, in its respect
for the integrity of others? For families and individuals, does
the American dream promise excellence of spirit? Let us now
praise not merely those talents prized by a meritocracy of managers, but those talents for gentleness, kindness, consideration,
honesty, irony, and forgiveness vital to the social organism.
Without managers and high I.Q.'s, societies endure. Without
the civic virtues, what good is all the machinery élites produce?

Take, for example, the exchanges we frequently experience
in the United States, in rural towns and in urban centers. You
ask the girl at the counter if she has pipe tobacco. She points.
You choose one and ask how much? She rings it up. Piqued,
you pointedly say, "Thank you." Annoyed, she grunts. Or you
ask at the ticket window how much it costs to go by bus to
Boston. The man pulls out a ticket and shows you. It is too
burdensome for him to speak. What sort of nation is this? What
sort of life has ours become, when human beings experience
one another as burdens too grievous, foreign, and distant to
address? Is this the price of "progress"? This the world's highest form of civilization?

Third, the adolescent American dream pictures idyllic happiness; it is robustly optimistic; it romanticizes the possibilites
of human life; it shuts out brokenness, absurdity, and tragedy.
Thus, millions dream of a private happiness, nuclear, individualistic, separate from others, beyond hunger and poverty and
disease and ignorance. But not beyond evil and tragedy. Dis-
eases of the spirit multiply, not least among the most highly
educated and the affluent. Let us call the plague the "myth of
self-fulfillment." Its victims choke, can scarcely speak, swallow
a rage that steadily corrodes them. Women, some college young,
and even successful, aspiring men—the so-called "oppressors" in
the scheme—rebel. "Whatever happened to the American
dream?" the television shows begin to ask.

They too seldom suggest that it was a childish dream. The
center of human life is suffering, not escape from suffering. The

"pursuit of happiness" is madness. Life has happy moments, and a kind of resignation brings another sort of happiness. But the all-American, shining, successful "happiness" is a fraud that our divorces, drug-taking, speed-driving, and violence render exquisitely obvious. The merchants of happiness make money out of our most powerful religious superstition: that the point of life is self-fulfillment and that self-fulfillment makes one "happy."

Our own educated classes, powerful and affluent, busy and effective, are among the most bitter and patently unhappy people in the world. Their literary parties give one splitting headaches. Seldom will one find in the literatures of the entire world so large a legacy of disillusionment, alienation, and disgust for life. Some of this "alienation" is, of course, a pose. An adversary culture must necessarily prove constantly to itself its discontent with established values, particularly when its own position of power and affluence has become the envy of others.

How can it be that a nation committed in its basic document to "the pursuit of happiness" has so thoroughly misplaced the secrets of happiness? Joy is not our nation's style. From the grim, sternly good housemothers of small Midwestern colleges to our desperately happy-talking disc jockeys, from the cynicism of traveling businessmen to the self-hating pessimism of best-selling novelists—this nation offers up to the world a remarkable confession: We don't know what happiness is.

A mature dream, then, replaces the romantic dream of happiness with an acceptance of evil, the irrational, tragedy, and absurdity. Powerful passions between "beautiful people" end in beatings, feuds, and divorces. Business schemes fail. Marriages go flat. Education is a withering disappointment. High political hopes are dashed by betrayals and failures. There is nothing surprising in all such outcomes except that they surprise so many Americans. Everywhere we witness strange disillusionment, a feeling of having been "cheated," waves of self-pity, remorseful examinations of "what we did wrong." Preachers and presidents note that many today are "weakening" in their "faith" in our institutions, but they fail to go to the heart of the matter: the unworthiness of that faith in the first place. It is not our institutions that first require overhaul, but the absurd, adolescent "faith" we have placed in them. Institutions do not guarantee happiness, self-fulfillment, or unalloyed goodness. Life is not kind to extravagant dreams.

Wisdom begins with insight into the tragic quality of human life. Dreams, faiths, wishes are *necessarily* broken. For the character of human consciousness is such that it envisages total understanding and perfect love, while the fact of human limitation is that these can never be attained. The root of tragedy lies in the ignorance and weakness of will with which we necessarily exercise our freedom of choice. At the time we make our choices, we do not know our own motives, hidden interests, or future needs as lucidly as we must; and we are far from having a masterful comprehension of all the contingent effects and counter-effects that will be set in motion by our actions. Nor are we entitled to perfect confidence in our own goodness and honesty. It is not in the least surprising, therefore, that events seldom turn out as we intended. Our hope that existence will be malleable to our will is so illusory one is boggled by its depth and power. How can so many intelligent people have accepted it as a working assumption? The evidence of its fradulence piles up all around us, strangles even our own inner lives.

A mature version of the American dream, therefore, calls for recognition that our earlier dream was an illusion. A mature dream readies the soul for defeat, tragedy, suffering, endurance. The adolescent dream holds that optimism means that the future will be better than the past; otherwise, why make any effort at all? ("We'll give the system one last chance!" the innocents say, as if "the system"—*any* system—cared about their hopes.) The mature dream holds that even though the future may be more terrible than the past, we can endure. And that, if we do not prevail, if this planet one day wearies of human life and ceases to support it, we can live until that time with some measure of honesty, courage, freedom and community. Hope does not require that we triumph, only that we live with moral beauty.

In the adolescent dream, optimism holds out success as its reward. In the mature dream, optimism holds out excellence of inner life, whether in success or in defeat. For the adolescent, success is everything. For the mature, inner growth is closer to the truth. On the other hand, success need not be feared. The defeat of one's own cause is no sure proof of its moral superiority (as ideologues of Right and Left bittersweetly hold). Success is morally neutral. It is an instrument. The goal is moral growth.

Fourth, the adolescent dream is based upon an illusion of innocence. In the heartlands of America, in "God's country," there is quiet conviction that the heart of the people is good and that bad-mouthing the people is a ploy of the Left's political ambition. In the better universities and among the educated, there is quiet conviction that "social change" is good and that resistance to change is the nub of human evil. In both cases, the myth of innocence is extremely powerful. Evil is to be found in others.

The myth of innocence in the United States has a counterpart: that the forces of evil are powerful and threatening. Thus, George Wallace and George McGovern (alike Scotch-Irish Methodists of fundamentalist background) pictured themselves as captains of embattled minorities, pressed down from all sides, but through adversity and a miracle of grace able to convert the people and to win. In the face of *The New York Times* and the television commentators and the academic "experts" featured in the magazines, working people frequently feel powerless. But liberal, educated people, watching their candidates go down to defeat, also feel powerless. The mythical strength of "the evil other" is a necessary reinforcement to the myth of one's own moral innocence.

Yet, surely, a mature dream teaches one to recognize the evil in oneself. The plague, as Albert Camus put it, is not in others. Its bacilli nest and multiply in every dishonesty, complacence, blindness, and betrayal of our own heart. The adolescent dream holds that individuals are innocent, while evils come from without—from institutions, from outside agitators, from germs thriving out there in the environment, requiring to be cleaned up, sanitized, isolated, outlawed, or reformed. The mature dream holds that evil lurks in the heart of our own goodness and is never more triumphant than when it dons the trappings of morality.

We have no more urgent symbolic need than to revise the dream of American goodness. I do not mean by this an orgy of breast-beating, which is only a disguised method of proclaiming one's innocence. We need simply to take an accurate account of the lashes visited upon the backs of Negro slaves, the death marches of Indian tribes, the violence of our industrial life (maiming even today eighteen hundred persons every week), the destruction of neighborhoods and family life in the name of "modernization," the staggering bombardment of distant nations, and other plain realities of our history.

Upon this innocent nation, this "new world," this "new paradise," this "new order of the ages" descends day by day the necessity to confront the evil within us. Our world is not a "new" world. It is the same world as Europe ever was or is, as Asia ever was or is, as the human world ever was or is— a world not only of loyalty, beauty, compassion, but also a world of bloodshed, violence, and tragedy. Too long we have struggled to blind ourselves to the dark side of our history, the dark side of our daily reality.

Our nation is not a "good" nation. It is a nation like others. We are human like others. Even in the caves of 50,000 years ago, men could love one another—or kill one another.

There is a temptation in American life for each of our major political groups to imagine that its own policies, principles, and partisans are the source of good. Each group notes the violence in the hearts of others and neglects the violence in its own heart.

Thus, liberals sometimes talk as though they themselves are the bulwark of reasonableness, calm, and restraint in our society. They think of science, enlightenment, civil liberties, and urbane discourse as uniquely the product of their own politics. They forget that, along with social justice and democratic creativity, they have also introduced into modern life bureaucracy, rules and roles, abstract and alienating schemes of social order, and all the ambiguities—even horrors—of technology. Enlightened, educated, humanitarian people often believe that "unassimilated" working men and woman are the source of violence and untrustworthy passion in our society, and they fear the "unenlightened." They conveniently forget the violence that the uneducated discern in the ruthless efficiency of the enlightened. From universities and scientific laboratories have come "body counts," antipersonnel bombs of exquisite cruelty, napalm, and the impersonal force of justice disconnected from personal contact. Urbane men, believing in civil rights and social justice, introduce a violence into human life that raises screams of pain from others, though they themselves know not what they do.

Radicals once believed that our best hope lay in the gentleness of our new youth—in their freer sexual lives, their experience with marijuana, their rejection of the uptight discipline of cleanliness, formal dress, ritualized manners. Yet others saw in precisely the same manifestations the very source of unchecked passion, wild violence, and orgiastic fantasy that have brought us, in every generation, such manifestations as political assassinations, Hell's Angels, and the Charles Manson murders.

One group accuses the straight-laced, short-haired, courteous fraternity boys of repressing their personal rage behind the guise of patriotism and Boy Scout pieties. Underneath this repression, they say, seethes the violence of American life not only in Vietnam, but in the KKK, in police brutality, and the rest. One group sees violence in the music of "Up with People." Another group sees violence in rock and roll.

Everybody blames everybody else. Everybody fears everybody else. Each finds his own group gentle, courageous, and good. Each fears the violence latent in other groups. Each sees his own group as a kind of political savior.

Thus, for example, the attempted assassination of George Wallace transcended the categories George Wallace was fond of using to describe our national life. It is not true that America, left to itself, swept clean of "outside agitators" and "troublemakers," or even cleansed of "bureaucrats" is healthy and whole. Ours is a human nation, and "human" means irrational as well as rational, bloody as well as compassionate, savage as well as civil.

The attempted assassination transcended, as well, the categories of George McGovern—trying to lead our nation in the paths of justice, reason, and peace. It transcended the optimism and bouncy joy of Hubert Humphrey. It transcended the self-congratulation that President Nixon visits upon our nation by calling us so frequently "a good people."

For we are an ordinary people, neither good nor evil, bound in a common humanity with all others on this planet, bound in a complex tissue of greed and generosity, trust and hate.

Our hubris has been great. Our humiliation will necessarily be long.

Fifth, the adolescent dream of America exalts the solitary individual, individual achievement, individual self-fulfillment. Such exaltation is out of harmony with human interdependence. Millions of educated persons, jealous of their personal individuality, rights, originality, and independence of mind are, from an anthropological point of view, astonishingly alike. What they share in common is far more significant (in all but rare instances of genius) than how they differ from one another. The ideas they cherish are common creations. The opinions they hold are to an impressive extent predictable from their status, economic position, and educational history. The moral qualities they praise—authenticity, honesty, sincerity, autonomy—are to a remarkable degree born of a social and rather transitory ethos. These values are, moreover, mythical in form rather than descriptive. Authenticity, for example, becomes elusive the more one tests it, and such autonomy as humans attain is so heavily dependent on social learning and continuing social supports that one ought, perhaps, to call it socio-autonomy.

We have come, it seems, to a contextual understanding of individualism. The individual organism exists only as part of a social and cultural network through which language, history, methods, and skills are mediated. The individual organism depends, as well, on a fragile support system arising from the ecology of this planet. Our image of ourselves is undergoing profound shifts. We are not so much the rugged stranger, walking *on* the earth, but rather a organism living *in* the tiny band of the biosphere at the surface of the earth. We swim as in a sea of life-supports, by our behavior feeding the system upon which we draw. We "participate" in it; it "participates" in us. We are not separate from earth. We *are* earth, living in it and it in us.

The same is true of our social belonging. The basic trust by which we act upon our surroundings, accepting them not as hostile but as hospitable to our action, is a gift to us from our parents or parent-surrogates. All through the course of our development we depend for intellectual stimulation and emotional support on the generosity of others. We could not think or talk without drawing on the creation of language down through countless generations. Our inner lives are communal, not solitary. The human community feels and thinks through us; therefore, we are.

Thus the adolescent dream of solitary self-fulfillment, in which an attractive spouse and handsome children are adornments, yields to a communitarian dream. Each of us is a "we." Children, in particular, depend on stable communities of trust. Despite all the brave promethean talk about self-reliance and independence, even adults require stable communities of trust. Traditionally, families have provided a context of conflict and reconciliation, love and hate, understanding and passionate accusation, within which persons have been known and accepted; friendship, by comparison, has been a rarer and more transient support. The isolated nuclear family, its members segregated by age and rendered unhappy by the modern quest for individual "fulfillment," has put enormous stress on women. Thus, one of the first practical requirements of the mature American dream is to find ways to strengthen the networks of communitarian support which the adolescent dream foolishly cast aside. If women's liberation were to seek for women the solitary individual fulfillment falsely promised to men, it would not radically alter the adolescent dream. It would merely extend its range, pouring oil upon the fires that now devour us. Fortunately, there are signs of profound groping toward a more mature dream, which represents human beings as the communal beings we truly are.

Women and men from non-Anglo-American stock may, at long last, be able to lead the way in articulating some of the needed forms of community. The presence of great-grandparents, grandparents, uncles and aunts and cousins at the decisive moments of life, and as often as possible in the normal course of life, is both enormously enriching in its own right, and important for the coherent vitality of society at large. Those who remain close to their families gain two advantages. They remain involved in the concrete irrationalities and vicissitudes of ordinary life (often families span several social worlds, class strata, and levels of educational attainment), and they retain a sense of rootedness and connectedness with the larger society in its harsh variety.

There is a romantic notion abroad that to love humanity one should break with the parochial world of the family. The truth is the reverse. Family life ordinarily involves us with persons very different from ourselves, yet so intimate to us we encounter them on many involuted and entangling levels. If we break away from our family, by contrast, we tend to surround ourselves with persons like ourselves, on less dangerous and intimate levels, in rather more "rational" engagement. As G. K. Chesterton slyly pointed out, it is considerably easier to love humanity than to get along with one's own family. In loving one's own family one meets humanity in concreteness and intimate complexity; in escaping from one's family one best avoids the reality of humankind. It is important to our own moral development to "go home again," and perhaps never thoroughly to leave.

To bring our national symbols into closer harmony with the moral realities of our actual lives, political leaders face a huge symbolic task. It is indispensable that human beings live according to a dream. A morally realistic dream ennobles its participants and offers genuine liberation. An unrealistic dream leads down self-destructive paths toward disillusionment. The original American dream, in its adolescent form, sells short this planet's cultural diversity. It neglects excellence of spirit and the tragic quality of every human life. It knows too little of the ambiguous involvement of the self in evil and of the communal nature of humankind. It is, indeed, an unworthy dream and we are well rid of it. It is not deserving of our faith.

The mature American dream to which we are called promises us a less tractable world; no more than dubious "success"; tragedy; a full share of evil; and the check of the common good and the public interest upon individual fantasies of "fulfillment." It is, in all these respects, a dark faith. For exactly that reason, it has the ring of truth. It promises an obscure joy, that joy which springs from connection to the unfathomable mysteries and terrors of human life.

The persons we choose to be our priests, prophets, warriors, kings will have to forge for us public symbols of such new faith. Otherwise they leave us to our emptiness.

35

The New Dark Civil Religion

There are those who despise the notion of a civil religion, out of fear that symbols of transcendence will be perverted to the uses of the state. Whether we like or dislike the notion, however, every national state generates a civil religion. For a state is not solely a pragmatic, administrative agency. It is also, necessarily, a symbolic agency. The chief officers of the state perform priestly and prophetic roles, conduct huge public liturgies, constantly reinterpret the nation's fundamental documents and traditions, furnish the central terms of public discourse. There is, then, no question *whether* we will have a civil religion. The only important questions are what *kind* of civil religion it will be, and what resources of *criticism* and *opposition* are publicly accessible for reforming and redirecting it.

An additional word is necessary about the pretended neutrality of the state in a "secular" or "pluralistic" society. The disestablishment of the churches, as by the First Amendment, does not guarantee that the state will thereafter be strictly neutral. Quite the contrary. Precisely because a church no longer furnishes the basic symbols of transcendence in the state, a symbolic vacuum is created which the state itself inexorably fills. The disestablishment of the church is a moral gain both for citizens and for the church. But the enormously swollen symbolic power of the state requires checks and balances to which the benign secularism of the Founding Fathers led them to pay too little heed.

Many Americans, for example, are adamantly opposed to granting federal aid, even indirectly, to religious private schools. Yet the same state taxes all citizens to support the secular—supposedly "neutral"—schools. Inevitably, schools tacitly, symbolically, and sometimes even expressly convey to students not merely information or skills but a way of life. The public schools are not a vacuum of neutrality. They are powerful instruments of "the American way of life," often in its most chauvinistic and benighted form. The state, therefore, is not symbolically neutral. It is active and even coercive in enforcing a national, homogeneous "way of life" mediated through the schools. The flag is present in every classroom. The "pledge of allegiance" constitutes a sort of classroom prayer. The world view is shaped by the adolescent form of the American dream. Why should parents be coerced into sending their children for this quite secular sort of religious indoctrination—in the civil religion of the United States?

Political life is unavoidably symbolic life, affecting our inner selves as well as the outer arrangements of the economy and the social order. We must, therefore, be vigilant about the liturgies, the language, and the images through which our political leaders shape the nation.

The civil religion of the United States should be disciplined, for example, so that it meets at least the following four criteria. Political leaders who make these criteria powerful among us will work toward the moral liberation of us all, and toward the realism of our nation's future course.

First, the civil religion must explicitly and publicly in every symbolic expression point beyond itself, and hold itself under moral criticism. For example, the phrase, "under God," is intended to make plain that the state does not stand in command over human conscience. No president and no commanding officer, whether of civilian or of military life, has power to order citizens to disobey their consciences. It is true that the common good, public order, and other considerations sometimes limit expressions of private conscience. But so great has the physical and the symbolic power of the state become that traditional incitements to the faithful accomplishment of professional duty and to simple civic loyalty are now dangerous both to citizens and to the state. Strong national symbols must reinforce the obligation of public officials and private citizens to look first to their consciences, before agreeing to serve the state. Unless this obligation is heeded, the state loses moral sensitivity, and citizens lose moral responsibility.

This criterion entails that the benefit of the doubt in moral matters must no longer be given immediately to the state. The oaths of office which public servants and military men pronounce should now be reworded so that the state itself makes plain its dependence on the free, informed conscience of its officers. Procedures for conscientious dissent should be built into every chain of command. Symbolic emphasis should be tipped more to the side of conscience, away from needs of state, until a more adequate balance is obtained than the nation has enjoyed during the past twenty years. Cabinet officers, the White House staff, officers of government departments, and military men should be given symbolic reinforcement of their *duty* to attend to conscience, to raise moral issues for internal and even for public debate, in the development and execution of policy. Government activities are not merely administrative; they are symbolic and affect the whole of human life—which is to say, they fall under the judgment of personal and communal conscience.

The second criterion for an adequate civil religion for the United States is that it explicitly embrace planetary pluralism, and frankly reject the pretensions inherent in our own ethnocentric "universals." The symbolic values of the nation—justice, liberty, civil rights, and the like—are rooted in our own culture, are finite and imperfect in their concrete expression, are not suitable models for the rest of the planet. No doubt *analogies* of these values are to be found in other cultures. But no doubt, too, there are forms of human polity, justice, liberty and social harmony from which, were we attentive, we still have much to learn. The many cultures of this planet are various, and their variety is vital to the planet's social health. In Chinese thought, Peking is the central city of the human race. Japanese scholars find American scholars ethnocentric, as our scholars find theirs. The parochialism of separate cultures must be broken down. The world ought to be imagined as having many significant centers. Each way of life ought to be regarded as an essential variation on the human theme.

The identity of the United States will be locked away, hidden, obscured until the identity of the Chinese, the Russians, the Latin Americans, the Japanese, the Indians, the Africans, and others are more fully known to us. Only in clearly recognizing others as they are, *other,* do we come to know the outlines of our own concrete humanity. The full significance of the United States in world history, therefore, is not yet apparent. It is our destiny to be one of a family of cultures—to be ourselves, and yet able to respect and to learn from others.

The symbols of power politics, plainly, are not adequate to the realities of cultural difference. Political leaders must, for reality's sake, establish the diversity and the beauty of other cultures firmly in the public consciousness. They can, for example, dramatize not only relations of power but also those of culture: inviting artists of other cultures to perform in our own cities, calling attention often to significant differences in cultural understanding among the peoples with whom the United States is engaged, commenting frequently on the world's diversity. The gap between the reasons that presidents make the foreign policy decisions they do and the reasons they offer to the public is intolerable. The public must incessantly be led to notice the hard realities of diversity, in order to be prepared in advance for decisions that will one day have to be made. President Nixon, by all accounts, acquired over the years a storehouse of fascinating lore which he seldom if ever shared with the people.

The third criterion for a new civil religion is that it reflect *all* the cultural traditions of our own nation, that it draw on *all*

the moral resources available in our own people. The nation
is far richer in moral potential than our public symbols have
yet expressed. In our public rhetoric, for example, we tend to
speak of blacks as "poor," "disadvantaged," and "culturally de-
prived." We do not celebrate the equanimity, family strength,
and even joy that enabled blacks not merely to survive in
America but to find in their hearts tranquillity and charity
and song. Some resources of spirit in black culture, particularly the resources of quiet sensivitity and gentleness, have been
thrust into the background by the media's preoccupation with
militance and anger. Traditions of gentle emotional perception
have been nourished for too many generations in Africa and
here to be much longer overlooked. The nation needs public
symbols that encourage such strengths throughout the population.

The millions of Spanish-speaking Americans, who have come
to be one of the largest cultural groups in our midst, will perhaps furnish us with strengths the philosophy and art of Spanish
culture have long provided: a profoundly personal attitude toward words and speech, a sort of reverence for whole personal
worlds, a tragic sense, a deep skepticism about a society based
on money, a contemplative and even mystical tradition, a passion
for life different from that of other traditions.

From descendants of immigrants from Ireland, from Poland,
from Italy, and from other nations of southern and eastern
Europe, perhaps the nation is already learning new symbols of
morality and realism. An almost hardened, sometimes even cynical response to the cant of political reformers and moralists is
one such symbol. This symbol is dangerous if it merely erects a
formidable defense around an unnecessarily corrupt status quo.
It is an asset if it suggests that one must examine the power and
the interests served by "reform" and "morality," for these are
symbols that often merely reinforce established powers. To a
large extent, the descendants of Catholic and Jewish immigrants
are still "outsiders" with respect to the major civil religions of
the nation. A reinterpretation of all the nation's basic symbols
from the point of view of their experience of America nourishes
both intellectual and political creativity. This nation is morally

and intellectually larger than Anglo-American conceptions allow. Historians and commentators who interpret such basic notions as justice, the individual, community, tradition, freedom, and morality in classical Anglo-American terms are often far more ethnocentric and narrow than they imagine. The writings of James MacGregor Burns, for example, so admirable in other respects, effectively exclude the symbolic life of a majority of Americans; the justice that John Rawls writes of is Anglo-American.

When a trustee of Yale University, to cite another example, speaks of civil rights, it may never have occurred to him to look at himself and the tradition whence he comes from the perspective of the Italian Catholic families of New Haven, who have observed the concrete bearing of such words upon the Italian experience in that city for some four generations. It is not probable that they look upon him as he looks upon himself, or that they accept without skepticism the noble ring he gives his words. Their eyes are likely to be fixed rather more steadily than his on underlying and fundamental disparities of wealth, status, power, and generational succession. Their view of the realities of Connecticut politics is likely to be quite different from his.

Many regions of the United States are underrepresented in national consciousness and national symbolism. The people of Appalachia, the poor whites of Alabama and Georgia, and many others are known through stereotypes rather than through nuanced investigation and illuminating drama.

Women, above all, are underrepresented. When the shouting and tumult of the recent rebirth of feminism have faded a little, as they already have begun to do, ideas will slowly emerge for making more visible to ourselves the actual life of women in our national culture—and perhaps, particularly, the lives of women of working-class families. Understandably, highly educated women will speak for themselves. (The 350,000 subscribers of *Ms.* magazine, for example, have a median age of 29.2 and a household median income of $17,774; 89.8 percent of them have gone to college or beyond.) To recover the history, sufferings, and excellences of the relatively inarticulate will require especially sensitive efforts.

If a nation is a religion, then all citizens need to be nourished by that religion. All need to see reflected in its liturgies and symbols a confirmation of the meaning and worth of their own lives. The most visible civil religion of the United States is remarkably snobbish and limited in the range of its official symbols. It mainly confirms the Northeastern élite in its image of itself.

The fourth criterion of a new civil religion is that it be rooted and concrete. The American civil religion ought to be an *American* civil religion; it ought not to pretend, falsely, to be universal. It grows out of a searing, spirit-forming, finite history. It is linked to a unique land—to recognizable mountains and coasts and plains, to vividly distinctive sights and sounds and colors. There is no contradiction between being both rooted and also planetary in one's vision (between this criterion and the second). It is altogether human both to be oneself, no other, and yet to be open and generous in response to other human cultures and individual persons. It is altogether human to have roots in one place, to love one land above all others, to be grateful for the nourishment (however partial and incomplete) provided by its institutions, to be, in a word, fiercely *patriotic* —without closing one's soul against the rest of the world.

Indeed, the obverse may be a stronger way to make the point. To attempt to be open to all other cultures, without having roots of one's own, is almost certainly to misperceive the otherness of such cultures. It is, perhaps, even to be incapable of culture. For culture is a kind of rootedness. The word itself suggests the patient cultivation of a living, growing plant. To have culture is to be shaped by a social tradition, shaped willingly and joyously so that the shaping is appropriated as one's own, and so that the culture, as it were, becomes alive in oneself under one's own direction. One does not choose the culture into which one is born; but one may choose to go as deeply into it as one can, to realize every human potential it affords. Paradoxically, it is through the route of becoming particular that one finds, at the depths, genuine universality.

A president of the United States presides over the administrative organs of the state. He is also the high priest of the symbols and liturgies of the nation's self-understanding. A president who takes up his symbolic duties with conscious and explicit attention can institutionalize a new self-understanding of this nation's identity among the other nations of this world, this nation's limitations and historic evils, this nation's plain reality. Then a fresh wave of liberated energy will sweep through the entire body politic. What vast relief would flow if our public discourse actually described the nation as it is—if the constraints that stifle us were soon released! Such a president will free the nation's wings.

The symbol maker of a nation holds back the public's energies, or invites them to unfold. His role demands most careful scrutiny, most sober vigilance, most swift and judicious exercise. Let those who nominate the candidates take thought. Let those who wish to be elected king take years to learn their skills and steep themselves in traditions that give life. Let those who choose a king choose wisely.

Were this book to have the shape demanded by the American sense of reality, its ending would be upbeat, lyrical, and practical. In violation of the expected ritual, as a testimony to the new darkness, it closes incomplete.

A Select Bibliography

Ahlstrom, Sydney E., ed. *Theology in America: The Major Protestant Voices from Puritanism to Neo-Orthodoxy.* Indianapolis and New York: Bobbs-Merrill Company, 1967.

Alley, Robert S. *So Help Me God: Religion and the Presidency; Wilson to Nixon.* Richmond, Virginia: John Knox Press, 1972.

Anderson, Charles H. *White Protestant Americans: From National Origins to Religious Group.* Englewood Cliffs, N.J.: Prentice-Hall, Inc., 1970.

Arnold, Thurman. *The Symbols of Government.* New York and Burlingame: Harcourt, Brace & World, Inc., 1935.

Bailey, Thomas A. *Presidential Greatness: The Image and the Man from George Washington to the Present.* New York: Appleton-Century, 1966.

Barber, James David. *The Presidential Character: Predicting Performance in the White House.* Englewood Cliffs, N.J.: Prentice-Hall, Inc., 1972.

Barone, Michael; Ujifusa, Grant; and Matthews, Douglas. *The Almanac of American Politics: The Senators, the Representatives —Their records, states and districts.* New York: Gambit, 1972.

311

Bellah, Robert N. *Beyond Belief: Essays on Religion in a Post-Traditional World.* New York, Evanston, and London: Harper and Row, 1970.
—— "Evil and the American Ethos," from Sanford, Nevitt and Comstock, Craig, eds., *Sanctions for Evil.* San Francisco: Jossey-Bass Inc., 1971.
Berger, Peter L., and Neuhaus, Richard J. *Movement and Revolution: On American Radicalism.* New York: Anchor, 1970.
Binkley, Wilfred E. *President and Congress.* New York: Random House, 1962.
—— *The Man in the White House: His Powers and Duties.* Baltimore: The Johns Hopkins Press, 1958.
Broder, David S. *The Party's Over: The Failure of Politics in America.* New York, Evanston, San Francisco, London: Harper & Row, 1971, 1972.
Buchanan, Patrick J. *The New Majority.* U.S.A.: Girard Bank, 1973.
Burns, James MacGregor. *Presidential Government: The Crucible of Leadership.* New York: Houghton Mifflin, 1965.
—— *Uncommon Sense.* New York, Evanston, San Francisco, London, 1972.
Cherry, Conrad, ed. *God's New Israel: Religious Interpretations of American Destiny.* Englewood Cliffs, N.J.: Prentice-Hall, Inc., 1971.
Corwin, Edward S. *The President: Office and Powers 1787–1957.* New York, New York University Press, Fourth Revised Edition 1957, Third Printing 1962.
Cousins, Norman. *"In God We Trust": The Religious Beliefs and Ideas of the American Founding Fathers.* New York, Harper & Brothers, 1958.
De Vries, Walter, and Tarrance, V. Lance. *The Ticket Splitter: A New Force in American Politics.* Grand Rapids, Mich.: William B. Eerdmans Publishing Co., 1972.
Dewey, John. *Individualism: Old and New.* New York: Capricorn Books, 1929, 1930, 1962.
—— *Liberalism and Social Action.* New York: Capricorn Books, 1935.
Duncan, Hugh D. *Symbols in Society.* New York: Oxford University Press, 1968.
Dutton, Frederick G. *Changing Sources of Power: American Politics in the 1970's.* New York: McGraw-Hill, Inc., 1971.
Edelman, Murry. *The Symbolic Uses of Politics.* Urbana, Ill.: University of Illinois Press, 1967.

Emerson, Ralph Waldo. *English Traits.* New York: Hearst's International Library Co., 1914.

Evans, Rowland, and Novak, Robert. *Lyndon B. Johnson: The Exercise of Power.* New York: The New American Library, Inc., 1966.

————— *Nixon in the White House: The Frustration of Power.* New York: Random House, 1971.

Fackre, Gabriel J. *Liberation in Middle America.* Philadelphia: A Pilgrim Press Book, 1971.

Free, Lloyd A., and Cantril, Hadley. *The Political Beliefs of Americans: A Study of Public Opinon.* New York: Simon and Schuster, 1968.

Gaustad, Edwin S. *A Religious History of America.* New York: Harper & Row, 1966.

Guthman, Edwin. *We Band of Brothers: A Memoir of Robert F. Kennedy.* New York, Evanston, London, San Francisco: Harper & Row, 1971.

Henderson, Charles P., Jr. *The Nixon Theology.* New York, Evanston, San Francisco, London: Harper & Row, 1972.

Herberg, Will. *Protestant-Catholic-Jew: An Essay in American Religious Sociology.* Garden City, N.Y.: Doubleday & Co., 1955.

Hofstadter, Richard. *The American Political Tradition.* New York: Vintage Books, 1959.

Hudson, Winthrop S., ed. *Nationalism and Religion in America: Concepts of American Identity and Mission.* New York, Evanston, London: Harper & Row, 1970.

Lerner, Max. *America as a Civilization: Volume One: The Basic Frame.* New York: Simon and Schuster, 1957.

————— *America as a Civilization: Volume Two: Culture and Personality.* New York: Simon and Schuster, 1957.

Koenig, Louis W. *Bryan: A Political Biography of William Jennings Bryan.* New York: G. P. Putnam & Sons, 1971.

Laski, Harold. *The American Presidency, an Interpretation.* New York: Harper & Brothers, 1940.

Levy, Mark R., and Kramer, Michael S. *The Ethnic Factor: How America's Minorities Decide Elections.* New York: Simon and Schuster, 1972.

Lipset, Seymour Martin, and Raab, Earl. *The Politics of Unreason: Right-Wing Extremism in America 1790–1970* (1970 ADL B'nai B'rith). Harper Torchbooks, Inc., 1973.

Litt, Edgar. *Beyond Pluralism: Ethnic Politics in America.* Glenview, Ill.: Scott, Foresman and Co., 1970.

Mailer, Norman. *St. George and the Godfather.* New York: New American Library, 1972.

Marty, Martin E. *Righteous Empire: The Protestant Experience in America.* New York: The Dial Press, 1970.

Mazlish, Bruce. *In Search of Nixon: A Psycho-historical Inquiry.* New York: Basic Books, Inc., 1972.

McGinniss, Joe. *The Selling of the President 1968.* New York: Pocket Books, 1969.

Mencken, H. L. *Chrestomathy.* New York: Alfred A. Knopf, 1949.

Moynihan, Daniel P. *The Politics of a Guaranteed Income: The Nixon Administration and the Family Assistance Plan.* New York: Random House, 1973.

Myrdal, Gunnar. *An American Dilemma: The Negro Problem and Modern Democracy.* New York: Harper & Brothers, 1944.

Napolitan, Joseph. *The Election Game: And How to Win It.* Garden City, N.Y.: Doubleday & Co., 1972.

Neustadt, Richard E. *Presidential Power.* New York: Mentor Books, 1964.

Niebuhr, Reinhold. *Christianity and Power Politics.* U.S.A.: Archon Books, 1969.

—— *Moral Man and Immoral Society.* New York: Charles Scribner's Sons, 1932, 1960.

—— *The Children of Light and the Children of Darkness.* New York: Charles Scribner's Sons, 1960.

—— *The Irony of American History.* New York: Charles Scribner's Sons, 1952.

—— *The Self and the Dramas of History.* New York: Charles Scribner's Sons, 1955.

Neustadt, Richard E. *Presidential Power: The Politics of Leadership.* New York: John Wiley & Sons, Inc., 1964.

Nixon, Richard M. *A New Road for America, Major Policy Statements, March 1970 to October 1971.* Preface and Commentaries by Richard Wilson. Garden City, N.Y.: Doubleday & Co., Inc., 1972.

—— *Six Crises.* New York: Pyramid Books, 1962, 1968.

Osborne, John. *The Nixon Watch.* New York: Liveright Publishing Corp., 1970.

Peirce, Neal R. *The People's President: The Electoral College in American History and the Direct Vote Alternative.* New York: Simon and Schuster, 1968.

Polsby, Nelson W., and Wildavsky, Aaron B. *Presidential Elections: Strategies of American Electoral Politics.* New York: Charles Scribner's Sons, 1964, 1968, 1971.

Pomper, Gerald M. *Elections in America: Control and Influence in Democratic Politics.* New York, Toronto: Dodd, Mead & Co., 1970.

Reedy, George E. *The Twilight of the Presidency.* New York and Cleveland: The World Publishing Co., 1970.

Rennie, Eric (text), Duffey, Joseph (postscript). *A Campaign Album.* Philadelphia: United Church Press, 1973.

Reston, James. *Sketches in the Sand.* New York: Vintage, 1967.

Robinson, Lloyd. *The Hopefuls: Ten Presidential Campaigns.* Garden City, N.Y.: Doubleday & Co., Inc., 1966.

Rossiter, Clinton. *The American Presidency.* New York and Scarborough, Ontario: New American Library, 1956, 1960.

Sandeen, Ernest R. *The Roots of Fundamentalism: British and American Millenarianism 1800–1930.* Chicago and London: The University of Chicago Press, 1970.

Scammon, Richard M., and Wattenberg, Ben J. *The Real Majority.* New York: Berkley Publishing Corp., 1970.

Schlesinger, Arthur M., Jr. *The Age of Jackson.* New York: New American Library, 1945.

——— *The Coming to Power: Critical Presidential Elections in American History.* New York, Toronto, London, Sydney: Chelsea House Publishers in association with McGraw-Hill Book Co., 1971, 1972.

Sennett, Richard, and Cobb, Jonathan. *The Hidden Injuries of Class.* New York: Alfred A. Knopf, 1972.

Shadegg, Stephen C. *How to Win an Election: The Art of Political Victory.* New York: Taplinger Publishing Co., Inc., 1964.

Smith, Elwyn A., ed. *The Religion of the Republic.* Philadelphia: Fortress Press, 1971.

Stark, Rodney, and Glock, Charles Y. *American Piety: The Nature of Religious Commitment.* Berkeley, Los Angeles, London: University of California Press, 1968.

Stout, Richard T. *People.* New York, Evanston, London: Harper & Row, 1970.

Streiker, Lowell D., and Strober, Gerald S. *Religion and the New Majority: Billy Graham, Middle America, and the Politics of the 70's.* New York: Association Press, 1972.

Warner, W. Floyd. *American Life: Dream and Reality.* Chicago and London: The University of Chicago Press, 1953, 1962.

Whitney, David C. *The American Presidents: Biographies of the Chief Executives from Washington through Nixon.* Garden City, N.Y.: Doubleday & Co. Inc., 1967, 1969.

Wicker, Tom. *J.F.K. and L.B.J.: The Influence of Personality upon Politics.* Baltimore, Md.: Penguin Books, 1968.

Williams, William Appleman. *Some Presidents: From Wilson to Nixon.* New York: New York Review, 1972.

Witcover, Jules. *85 Days: The Last Campaign of Robert F. Kennedy.* New York: Ace Publishing Corp., 1969.

Wilson, Woodrow. *Constitutional Government in the United States.* New York: Columbia University Press, 1908.

Index

319